# PENCE

# PENCE

## THE PATH TO POWER

## ANDREA NEAL

RED ⚡ LIGHTNING BOOKS

*This book is a publication of*

Red Lightning Books
1320 East 10th Street
Bloomington, Indiana 47405 USA

redlightningbooks.com

*Manufactured in the
United States of America*

ISBN 978-1-68435-037-7 (cloth)
ISBN 978-1-68435-040-7 (ebook)

1  2  3  4  5  23    22  21  20  19  18

*For*

GEORGIANNE DAVIS NEAL,

*my mother and editor-in-chief*

# CONTENTS

# PREFACE

THIS BOOK BEGAN DURING A LONG-ANTICIPATED DRIVE
from Indianapolis to Chicago to see the hit musical *Hamilton*. I was
on spring break from St. Richard's Episcopal School, where I have the
privilege of teaching sixth graders the rules of English grammar and
eighth graders the founding ideals of our republic. I answered my cell
phone somewhere north of Lafayette and was greeted by Ashley Runyon, an editor at Indiana University Press. "Would you be interested in
writing a famous Hoosier's biography?" she asked. Yes, I said, imagining the possibilities: Civil War governor Oliver P. Morton; Virginia
Jenckes, the state's first female member of Congress; Miami chief Little
Turtle, known for inflicting one of the worst defeats in US military history; or songwriter Hoagy Carmichael of "Stardust" fame. I had gotten
to know all four of these intriguing figures during my research for the
book *Road Trip: A Pocket History of Indiana* published for the state's
bicentennial in 2016.

As it turned out, Runyon had a more contemporary figure in mind:
the newly elected vice president of the United States, Michael R. Pence.
Her keen editor's eye recognized the historic import of a sixth Hoosier
vice president but also the relevance of his Indiana roots and upbring-
ing. This would be an altogether different challenge. How does one

write a biography of a public figure while news about him is still being made? How could I put into context a member of the unpredictable Trump White House with all of its pitfalls, peccadillos, and chaotic management style? There would be an ever-present risk of daily news superseding my efforts to write a complete biography.

The solution was to tell the story of Mike Pence's path to the vice presidency, with a focus on the events leading up to the day he took the oath of office in January 2017. This book, therefore, follows Pence's life through a decidedly Hoosier lens made possible by forty-five interview subjects—friends, political advisers, and adversaries—who shared with me the stories of their various and varied relationships with the vice president. I am especially indebted to Jeff Cardwell, Jay Steger, Rex Early, and Jim Atterholt, who gave up many hours of their busy lives to meet with me. I am also grateful to have spent time with the Columbus *Republic*'s legendary editor Harry McCawley, who died in September 2017 of cancer. Although Vice President Pence declined my request for an interview, the past thirty years of his life have been spent in the public spotlight, so there was no shortage of public record or primary source material.

Early in the process, I committed to using named sources only, the journalistic practice my bosses insisted on in the 1980s and '90s when I was a reporter for United Press International and the *Indianapolis Star*. As a result, the book omits a few headline stories reported by the Beltway press but never verified. My research confirmed my fear that anonymous accounts, which tend to be unreliable, are the first cousin of fake news. As just one example, a prominent magazine reported that Paul Manafort made up the story of a flat tire on Trump's campaign airplane in July 2016 to keep the candidate in Indianapolis long enough to develop a rapport with Indiana's governor. This assertion, attributed to two anonymous "former Trump aides," was debunked by the motorcade driver I interviewed who spotted the flat tire and reported it to Secret Service. The magazine's mistake brought to mind a long-standing family joke about "true facts," which I hope to be the only kind found here. To that end, all original research has a footnote attached, as do quotations drawn from the hundreds of newspaper articles and other publications that informed my research.

Post-inaugural events and analysis are confined to the epilogue, which concludes, based on a single year's worth of evidence, that Pence is a player with substantial influence in the Trump administration. He is the only one who cannot be fired by virtue of his constitutional office, and that in itself gives him power. A more definitive conclusion must await future historians who will have, as Paul Harvey used to say, the "rest of the story."

# INTRODUCTION

## "AND THEN THERE'S ME"

LIKE THE YELLOW BRICK ROAD IN HIS FAVORITE MOVIE, MIKE Pence's path to power has followed a singular, if sometimes elusive, goal. And it began when he was just a teenager and even then a candidate. Longtime friends and teachers remember with surprising unanimity young Pence's frequent announcements of his political intentions. It is a quest that has never faltered, made stronger by his years at Hanover College, where he studied under the illustrious G. M. Curtis, and his marriage to Karen, who has supported her husband in every run for office. The influence of his Indiana experience is a large part of his public persona, as is the self-deprecating humor that Pence expressed often on the campaign trail, a tactic particularly effective when comparing himself to the flamboyant Donald Trump: "He's bigger than life. Always memorable. Charismatic. And then there's me."[1]

Pence is a paradox to those who admire him and those who don't— "humble" (his all-purpose adjective) yet confident, ultraconservative yet willing when necessary to smooth out the most glaring rough edges. In his own words, he has staked out three positions that have defined his core beliefs: Christian, conservative, and Republican, in that order. It is a combination that has worked so far and weathered an avalanche of criticism, including the contradictory charges that he is either Donald

Trump's puppet or a puppet-master seeking to impose his beliefs on others. Only columnist George Will has dared to make the more scholarly but inevitable comparison to Dickens's obsequious Uriah Heep.[2]

To seasoned political observers, Pence's selection as vice president carried echoes of New Orleans in 1988 when George H. W. Bush startled the Republican faithful by naming Indiana's junior senator Dan Quayle as his running mate. The coincidence was a second surprise from the heartland as the candidates, both Hoosiers with limited name recognition, became household words overnight. The first clue was the Trump entourage convening in Indiana's highly visible governor's mansion, but there were others. Like Quayle, Pence had an already developed voter base, which, though small, was dedicated and supportive throughout his campaigns. Unlike Quayle, who ran in tandem with one of his party's most admired and experienced figures, Pence came loaded with a basket of desirables that Donald Trump badly needed. Pence's appearance was appropriately vice presidential, allegedly prompting an ecstatic Trump to exclaim, "Isn't he just perfect? Straight from central casting."[3] Cartoonists, too, were quick to seize the vice president's pictorial possibilities, developing almost immediately a comic portfolio showing the vice president being sprayed with Teflon or dutifully following behind Trump with a shovel.

On the stump, Pence was articulate, consistently competent, occasionally eloquent. Sometimes referred to in the DC area as "pious Pence," his personal reputation and family life suggested he might be among those most obviously qualified to drain the swamp. From previous congressional terms, he had the necessary capital connections and—best of all—the support and the blessing of the evangelical right. This support, tentative at first, became unconditional by campaign's end.

While critics are prone to ridicule Pence's faith-based orientation, they may be judging him by the wrong audience. After Trump's upset victory, one writer dubbed 2016 the "Can you hear me now?" election. A new voice had emerged from the heartland, as much a frontier of opinion as it is a geographic region. Trump's "forgotten men and women" were ordinary Americans—from farmers to factory workers—who, in the words of Bobby Jindal, "watched both parties, all three branches of government, and the popular culture move from embracing many of their core values to, at best, tolerating them."4

A nation grown weary of secularization and confrontation may welcome Pence's traditional values and cautionary approach. His adherence to the Billy Graham principles of a happy marriage, once mocked, has already spared him the parade of mea culpas seen in Washington DC and Hollywood, whose cultures have long encouraged a cocktail party permissiveness. The key to his future success at the polls depends on his continuing ability to project the image that he is a prudent man prepared by temperament and experience to handle precarious situations—the best man, perhaps—and, yes, as the adjective he has sought so long suggests, presidential.

# PENCE

# 1
★ ★ ★

## GROWING UP HOOSIER

THE HUMORIST GEORGE ADE DESCRIBED A HOOSIER AS "A puzzling combination of shy provincial, unfettered democrat, and Fourth of July orator."[1] *Merriam-Webster* says simply: "a native or resident of Indiana." On all counts, Mike Pence passed the test resoundingly.

Michael Richard Pence was born June 7, 1959, in Columbus, Indiana, and raised with a cornfield view from his kitchen window. As a bona fide Hoosier, Pence inherited a vast body of folklore explaining his state's often-stereotyped nickname, spanning the decades since Indiana statehood and dating at least back to 1832. In that year, a curious sturgeon left Lake Michigan for the pure waters of St. Joseph River and ran afoul of a fisherman's hook. The fish, weighing in at eighty-three pounds, was pictured on the pages of a South Bend newspaper and dubbed a "real Hoosier" because of his size and lack of pulchritude.[2]

Despite the word's various interpretations, both good and bad, Hoosiers have always embraced the term affectionately, much as one appreciates the convenience of an old sweater or the comfort of a well-worn shoe. It is a legacy that has left its mark on sports, tourism, and especially politics, as Pence and his opponent John Gregg would demonstrate in a spirited governor's race to see who could out-Hoosier the other. Campaigns even today mention Hoosier common sense and values and are apt to display candidates standing beside a grain silo or a field of tall corn. This Hoosier identity would form the cornerstone of

Pence's political career and prove helpful along his path from Columbus to the vice presidency.

Pence has spoken frequently of the importance of life's choices. "Dreams can become reality. Your future is the sum total of the moral and educational choices you make," he said.[3] But the most consequential choice was made by his doughty Irish great-grandmother, who in 1923 handed her son a one-way ticket to the United States with a vague promise, "There's a future there for you."[4]

Pence's family followed traditional patterns of early twentieth-century immigration, passing through Ellis Island on the way west in search of work. They eventually put down roots in Columbus.

Grandfather Richard Michael Cawley, born in 1903, grew up in a two-room house just east of a village called Tubbercurry, Ireland, and attended school through the eighth grade. He faced few job prospects in 1920s Ireland, where political upheaval and economic stagnation limited opportunities for the young. At age twenty, he boarded the SS *Andania* with twenty-three dollars in his pocket and the occupation "miner" listed on the ship manifest.[5] After entering the United States at Ellis Island on April 11, 1923, he headed to Chicago, where he found work as a trolley driver, married an Irish American girl, started a family, and became a US citizen in 1941. The young family, joined by Cawley's mother-in-law, lived in a brick two-flat on Honore Street on Chicago's south side. Richard and Mary Maloney Cawley had two daughters: Mary Ellen, born in 1931, followed by Ann Jane one year later. The younger daughter, who went by the name Nancy, would become the mother of the vice president.

Pence's paternal grandparents also hailed from the working-class neighborhoods of Chicago. Edward Joseph Pence Sr. left high school after his freshman year to work at the stockyards, the number-one supplier of livestock for the world's meatpacking industry. Census records show he was a cattle handler at age seventeen and later a hog salesman.[6] Ed Pence married Geraldine Kathleen Kuhn, the daughter of an Irish mother and Prussian father, both immigrants. The young couple lived in a brick apartment on May Street about five miles from the historic

Union Stock Yard Gate and had a daughter and two sons. The eldest was Edward Pence Jr., born in 1929, the father of the future vice president.

It was Ed Pence's dress blue army uniform that caught Nancy Cawley's eye. The two met in a Chicago club, fell in love, and were married on January 7, 1956. Second Lieutenant Ed Pence was a Korean War veteran with the Forty-Fifth Infantry who'd seen combat at the battles of Old Baldy and Pork Chop Hill, earning a Bronze Star in 1953 for meritorious service. "Dad never talked about the war, and that medal stayed in his dresser drawer," Pence said of his father, who died in 1988.[7] Family members who knew Ed from boyhood described him as a happy-go-lucky teenager who became more serious as a result of his military experience. One cousin surmised that Ed experienced survivor guilt, having lost so many comrades in battle. That explanation helped Pence better understand his father's reticence on the subject.[8]

After attending Chicago's Jesuit Loyola University, Ed found work in the oil industry, first in Chicago and then in Indianapolis. Nancy, who had attended secretarial school, stayed home to raise a growing family that would include four boys and two girls. In 1959, an opportunity with Kiel Brothers Oil Company lured them to Columbus in Bartholomew County, a community of 20,778 just forty-five miles south of Indianapolis.

Columbus of the late 1950s was one of the fastest growing areas of Indiana due to the presence of two thriving manufacturers: Arvin Industries, which made automotive parts, and Cummins Engine Company, maker of diesel engines. Both companies dated to the early 1900s, when Indiana played an outsized role in the development of the automobile. Although modern Columbus has earned a reputation for progressive architecture and "enlightened leadership,"[9] 1960s Columbus was still agrarian and homogeneous: 98 percent white and 75 percent native Hoosier. It would be another two decades before Columbus would see the diversity that characterized Indiana's more populous cities such as Indianapolis and Fort Wayne.

The Pence family settled into a three-bedroom brick ranch in a north-side neighborhood called Everroad Park West. "I guess you could describe it as modest at the time, although we never thought in those terms," said Ed Pence, the second of the six children. "It was just our home."[10]

Mike Pence was the first to be born in Columbus, joining Ed and Gregory and soon followed by Thomas and sisters Anne and Mary Therese. With loquacious older brothers, Pence didn't start talking until age three, his mother remembered, and his first words—taught to him by Grandfather Cawley—were "you're welcome" in Gaelic.[11] His next Gaelic lesson was the nursery rhyme "Humpty Dumpty."[12]

Their homes continued to mirror the family's growing prosperity. By the time Pence entered middle school, Ed was rising in the ranks at Kiel Brothers, a wholesale petroleum distributor with a chain of gas stations, and was on his way to becoming partial owner and company vice president. The family had moved to a split-level house in Parkside, a neighborhood where children played in the street and dropped in unannounced on friends. That's how Pence got to know Tom Hodek, who lived across the street. "I'd walk into his house and open the fridge to see what was there. He'd walk in my house and open the fridge to see what was there," Pence said. The two boys played football in a nearby farm field, now the site of a youth soccer complex, and rode bikes to Northside Drugs to buy candy. In the summer, they built model airplanes and, in the winter, snow forts in their yards. "We had a lot of good times," Hodek said.[13]

Another neighbor was Julius Perr, a Cummins executive with a doctorate in mechanical engineering who fled Communist Hungary in 1956. He was recruited by the US Embassy to come to the United States and ultimately to Columbus. During his forty-one-year career, he submitted more than three hundred patents on engine technology improvements, many of them pivotal to Cummins's success. For youngsters on his street, Perr was a role model whose hard work and determination led to national recognition. Years later, on the occasion of Perr's death, Congressman Mike Pence remembered his former next-door neighbor for his contributions to American engineering but more importantly for his "love of culture and allegiance to community."[14]

Raised as Catholics and aware of their Irish roots, Ed and Nancy Pence were among the first parishioners of St. Columba Roman Catho-

lic Church on Twenty-Seventh Street. The parish was founded in 1963
to accommodate Columbus's growing Catholic population and took its
name from one of three patron saints of Ireland. The Pences sent their
children to the parochial school adjacent to the church, a K–8 school
that reinforced the Catholic values of sanctity of life, social action, and
mission.

At St. Columba, Pence earned mostly As and Bs and was known as
a conscientious student. He attended Mass twice a week and served
as an altar boy.[15] Sister Sharon Bierman, a Benedictine nun, taught
young Pence math, science, and religion in seventh and eighth grades.
"He was always very thorough on every assignment," Bierman said. "In
religion he excelled."[16] Pence distinguished himself by memorizing
the principles of his faith: the seven sacraments, the corporal works of
mercy, and the mysteries of the rosary. He was especially motivated
by public speaking. Sister Bierman introduced Pence to the Optimist
International Oratorical Contest, which he entered annually. He won
the local contest as a fifth grader competing against older junior high
students. When his mother watched him perform for the first time, she
felt an unexpected pride. "When it came his turn, his voice just boomed
out over the audience. He just blew everybody away. I had a hard time
associating the boy up there speaking with our son."[17] Years later, Pence
thanked Bierman for nurturing his public-speaking talent.

By the end of middle school, Pence had begun to articulate his political interests, and his peers recognized him as a leader. "When I did
a book for their eighth-grade graduation so many of his classmates
predicted he'd be the president of the United States," Sister Bierman
recalled.[18] Pence spoke openly of wanting to be president one day, a
common childhood ambition that he seemed to take more seriously
than the typical youngster contemplating career choices, observed
classmate Jeff Brown.[19]

Brown, the son of the local newspaper publisher, first noticed Pence
at Northside Junior High, where they attended ninth grade. The two
were in a journalism class that taught news writing basics, which would
come in handy for both—Brown when he took over the family business
and Pence when he enrolled in law school. Pence said his favorite class

was social studies, and it was while at Northside that he began thinking of a career in government and politics.[20]

As Pence and Brown moved on to Columbus North High School, they found themselves assigned to the same homeroom. The boys connected over Pasquale's Pizza and Pence's practical jokes, often socializing on the weekends or double-dating. After the first *Star Wars* film came out, Pence became skilled at imitating Darth Vader, one of many impressions of famous people he would do to entertain friends. His "wicked Irish accent had my mom rolling on the floor," Brown said. Occasionally, Pence would tell Brown's mother that he wanted to be a priest, and she would reply that he should be a stand-up comedian instead and "couldn't be a priest because he liked girls too much."[21]

Although Pence's parents weren't politically active, Brown's were. Pence liked to visit them and tell Mrs. Brown stories from school or discuss politics with Brown's father, Robert N. Brown, who owned the *Republic* newspaper in Columbus. "My dad was a World War II veteran and a conservative Republican," Brown said. One particular conversation involved the New Deal policies of President Franklin Delano Roosevelt. "From my dad's point of view, Roosevelt gave away half of what he fought for in World War II." Although Pence saw himself as a Kennedy Democrat, he did not have firmly held views and devoured the knowledge of elders. "He was forming his political ideology in junior high and high school," Brown said.[22]

At Columbus North, Pence vigorously pursued his newfound passion for public speaking. He continued to compete in the Optimist contest, and he signed up for the school's speech team, called the Bull Tongues, at Coach Debbie Shoultz's suggestion. Shoultz had judged one of the Optimist contests "so I knew he had talent."[23] Shoultz taught Pence that emotion without studious practice did not win meets. Assistant Coach Dennis Lindsey encouraged Pence to listen carefully, probe deeply, and question intelligently. Pence absorbed the lessons from both. "It wasn't just that it came naturally to him. He worked hard at it," Shoultz remembered.[24]

Pence favored the categories of original oratory and extemporaneous speech, both dealing with current affairs. In the extemporaneous division, meet participants randomly drew topics discussed in lead-ing magazines in the three months leading up to the competition and were given forty-five minutes to research and write before performing. In original oratory, students selected a social, economic, or political problem and prepared a speech of no more than ten minutes. Judg-ing was based on delivery, mechanics, poise, use of voice, and bodily expressiveness.

According to Tim Grimm, a member of the award-winning speech team, competition honed Pence's political skills. "At that early age, he learned how to craft an argument and deliver a speech on which there was no other reasonable position. You believe 100 percent in what you're presenting."25 Many of Pence's speeches involved hot-button topics like abortion, which Pence would debate frequently thirty years later as a member of Congress. Steven David, a senior the year Pence joined the team, said the future vice president impressed him immediately with his careful choice of words. "I'd been to a lot of speech tournaments, and then this kid came along and he was even better."26

In his senior year, Pence won first place in the American Legion's Indiana Oratorical Contest. The competition consisted of a ten-minute memorized speech and a five-minute extemporaneous speech based on an excerpt from the US Constitution. One of the books Pence stud-ied to prepare for the competition was *Growth and Development of the American Constitution* by Loren Noblitt, a former Columbus resident. "He read that book over and over, and it obviously had an influence on his life," Shoultz said.27

Three months later, he traveled to Seattle for the National Forensic League tournament to compete against the top six hundred high school orators in the country. Pence advanced through four rounds in extem-poraneous and original oratory and placed third in the impromptu divi-sion.28 That category was especially suited to Pence's skill of repartee. Competitors were given a word or phrase and had thirty seconds to think about it before talking for five minutes.

The speech team ended the 1976–77 school year ranked twenty-first out of 450 member schools. Pence and his next-door neighbor Maria Perr, a fellow senior, both received degrees of distinction from the National Forensic League. It was the team's heyday, and several of Pence's teammates reappeared in headlines a few years later as they applied speaking skills to new careers. Steven David, who competed in impromptu oratory, became a justice of the Indiana Supreme Court. Grimm, who specialized in dramatic and humorous interpretation, became a Hollywood actor, singer, and songwriter. Bob Paris, who competed in dramatic oratory, became an internationally known bodybuilder and the first openly gay man to win Mr. Olympia. That such a motley group could emerge from the same speech team at the same high school amazed Grimm, who attributed their success and diversity to the high-quality liberal arts program offered at Columbus North in the '70s.[29]

Success in speech competitions boosted Pence's self-confidence and encouraged him to get involved in other extracurricular activities. Although he was always physically active, having played football in eighth and ninth grades and softball in a community league, Pence described himself as pudgy. A doctor recommended a strict weight-loss program during the summer between his sophomore and junior years, and Pence followed it religiously. When he returned to school the next fall after losing fifty-five pounds, students asked him, "Are you new?"[30] The regimen he followed predicted the same discipline and work habits that would help him years later on the campaign trail.

As a junior, Pence ran for office for the first time—for class vice president—but lost to Dan Hittle, a friend who lived down the street from him on Hunter Place. "I remember Mike being kind of dejected about it," Brown said.[31] The next year, Pence ran for senior class president and won. From that position, he had a platform to do what he loved: emcee school assemblies and organize events. The student assembly that year held its inaugural Fun Day with Pence serving as chair of the talent show committee and host. He relished any opportunity to speak or crack jokes before a crowd, carefully crafting the candidate he would become. One sunny afternoon, Brown walked into Pence's house and found him watching a cable access channel videotape of himself emceeing a convocation. "He was studying himself. He was trying to hone his speaking skills."[32]

His home life during those formative years emphasized work and service to others. "My father used to say, 'The harder I work the luckier I get,'" Pence remembered.[33] Pence's older brother Gregory recalled their father as a harsh disciplinarian who expected the boys to stand whenever an adult entered the room and would take them upstairs and whack them with a belt if they lied to him.[34] The siblings were instructed to get jobs as soon as they qualified for work permits, and they did. Teenage Pence earned spending money by pumping gas at Ray's Marathon. When he earned enough for a guitar, he walked into Tom Pickett's Music Center, counted out his money, and signed up for lessons. The Epiphone guitar went with him to college, where he entertained friends and accompanied singers in church.

Pence said he was raised to believe "to whom much is given, much will be required."[35] It was a lesson learned early from the Reardon boys, whose special needs rallied the Columbus community. Mike and Mark Reardon were brothers, born one year apart, both diagnosed with muscular dystrophy. Though they were confined to wheelchairs and unable to dress themselves, their parents and siblings did all they could to make their lives as normal as possible. Maynard Noll, a local car dealer and Easter Seals volunteer, organized a corps of high school volunteers to go to the Reardons' home each morning to assist the family in getting the boys ready for school. Gregory Pence volunteered first, and Pence replaced him when Gregory went off to college. Mark Reardon died at age fifteen in 1980, Mike in 1984 at age eighteen. Pence was a pallbearer at both their funerals.[36]

In the fall of 1980, during Pence's last year of college, the Pence family moved again. Their new address was Woodside Drive, a neighborhood of six-figure houses and expansive lots. Grandfather Cawley, newly widowed and suffering from health problems, joined them. To the first-generation American, the two-story, four-thousand-square-foot home seemed like a mansion. One weekend, on a visit home, Pence walked into the family room to find his grandfather sitting alone, his eyes filled with tears. "What's wrong?" Pence asked him. Cawley shook his head. "I just never thought a child of mine would live in a house like this," he replied in his gentle Irish brogue.[37]

Cawley died on Christmas Eve of 1980 at the age of seventy-seven. Pence said his grandfather was "the proudest man I ever knew, and the best man I ever knew."[38] Not long after Cawley's passing, Pence and his cousin Trish Tamler took a trip to Ireland to visit their grandfather's hometown. The pilgrimage connected Pence with his Irish heritage. "We were just all so fascinated with the history," Tamler said.[39] Thirty years later, Pence returned to Ireland with his wife, Karen, and children, Michael, Audrey, and Charlotte. They visited the birth home of Pence's great-grandfather, James Maloney, and met his grandmother's ninety-two-year-old cousin.[40]

By this time, little of the Irish remained in Pence. The onetime Kennedy Democrat had become staunchly Republican; the former Catholic altar boy was now a practicing evangelical Protestant. The Cawley determination to make something of himself held fast, tempered perhaps by a touch of Irish blarney and Hoosier common sense.

# 2

★ ★ ★

## ON THE BANKS OF THE OHIO

MIKE PENCE DISCOVERED HANOVER COLLEGE IN THE SUM-
mer of 1970 while participating in the Hoosier ritual known as basketball camp. The weeklong program featured shooting and dribbling
drills and ball-handling demonstrations by popular Billy Keller of the
Indiana Pacers. The eleven-year-old Pence lived in a dorm, ate meals at
the Campus Center, and walked each day past historic Hendricks Hall,
a memorial to Thomas A. Hendricks, class of 1841, who served as vice
president of the United States in 1885. When it came time for Pence to
apply to college seven years later, he chose the scenic Southern Indiana
campus he so fondly remembered from basketball camp.

His parents dropped him off at Crowe Hall the week before Labor
Day, 1977. Though Pence had been a popular student at Columbus
North High School, he was racked with self-doubt as his parents drove
away. "I was scared. Small-town boy from ninety miles up the road in
Columbus, just one payphone in the lobby. I was homesick by dinner.
And then I met my roommate, attended my first class."[1] In a matter of
months, Pence got to know professors who would nurture his love of
history and fraternity brothers who would become lifelong friends. If
any institution influenced the future vice president's career and character, it was the small liberal arts school just outside Madison, high on
a bluff above the Ohio River.

The Hanover Quad of 1977—like most campus courtyards of that era—was a relatively quiet place. There were no wars to protest or boycotts to join. The last American soldiers had left Vietnam in 1973. Democrat Jimmy Carter occupied the White House after defeating Gerald Ford, who had been elevated to president in 1974 during the Watergate scandal. The biggest news stories of Pence's first year were the return of the Panama Canal to the Panamanians and a massive winter blizzard. Throughout freshman year, Pence's focus was on studying, attending church, developing his social life, and joining a fraternity.

Under Hanover policy, Greek houses conducted member recruitment during the second semester rather than the first, a rule designed with freshmen in mind to ease the demands of college transition. Most of the student body belonged to fraternities and sororities, and social life centered on the themed parties they sponsored. Although the campus was technically dry, the parties nonetheless featured beer kegs and spiked punch. As a result, fraternities played a constant shell game with the administration, trying to keep supplies out of view.

Of the five fraternity houses, Pence preferred Phi Gamma Delta, nicknamed the Fijis, because it had the best reputation and highest GPA at the time: a 3.11 on a 4-point scale. It also had a partnership with sorority Kappa Alpha Theta, which made it easy to enjoy the variety of collegiate activities and even easier to meet girls, said Pence's fraternity brother Daniel Murphy, later to become a Hanover history professor.[2]

Pence's pledge group numbered about thirty and was an eclectic mix of athletes and scholars. "Our fraternity was full of highly competitive brainiacs," Jay Steger recalled.[3] Pence, Steger, and the others did predictable chores for members, the most memorable of which were called wakes, with pledges taking the place of alarm clocks. Pledges were required to rouse members who lived in the chapter house to ensure they made it to class on time. No alarm sounded, however, as pledges were armed only with flashlights.

An informal competition existed among pledge classes to see which had the most school spirit. The Fiji pledges, known as goats, hatched a plan to make a "Goat Power" sign to hang across the front of Parker

Auditorium, the most conspicuous of the college landmarks. Pledges raided the laundry room and borrowed the needed bedsheets. Pence, known for his artistic talent, drew the goat head with blue spray paint. At 4:00 a.m., the pledges, some them bearing ladders and nails, snuck out of their dorm rooms to affix the banner to the columns that lined the building's portico. As they reviewed their handiwork before going to bed, "we felt pretty good about it," Murphy said.[4] College president John E. Horner was not amused. That same morning, he looked out his bathroom window while shaving and caught a glimpse of the sign fluttering in the morning fog. He ordered maintenance staff to tear it down immediately. Although the active members never got to see the pledges' creation, the story of the prank spread across campus, and Pence's artwork became legendary.

In his sophomore year, Pence and his former pledge class members moved into the chapter house. The members dressed and studied in small rooms on the first two floors and slept in a large barracks-like space on the third floor known as the Rack Room, so called because of the metal bed frames stacked like bunk beds. Lunch and dinner were prepared by a cook, but students were on their own to forage for breakfast, typically cereal and bug juice, the nickname for the Kool-Aid stored in vats in the kitchen. "Periodically there were little bugs floating in it," explained Murphy.[5] Community service was expected of all members, as was fund-raising for various charities. The fraternity's fall carnival raised money for the Arthritis Foundation, with Pence playing the part of a fortune-teller and charging customers twenty cents for a reading from his crystal ball. A pancake sale benefited the Heart Fund. At Halloween, members went trick-or-treating for UNICEF. Toga parties were especially popular at the Fiji house after the movie *Animal House* came out in 1978. Although Hanover was not prone to the excesses shown in the movie, fraternity members adopted the film's lexicon. Terms like *double secret probation* became common among the brothers, and Barbara Quilling, vice president of student affairs, was dubbed the Dean Wormer of Hanover.

In an audacious move for an underclassman, Pence ran for chapter president during the second semester of his sophomore year and won.

He soon discovered that heading a college fraternity chapter posed different challenges than being senior class president in high school. The Fiji house was a diverse group, ranging from the so-called God squad, to which Pence belonged, to heavy partiers. In the fraternity house, Pence learned how to coexist with people whose beliefs and backgrounds "were very different," Murphy said. "He was clear about what he stood for but took a 'live and let live' approach to others."[6]

Perhaps the biggest test of his leadership occurred one Saturday night in late winter when word got around campus that the Fijis were hosting a party. Alerted that the dean's office was sending a staff member to investigate, members hastily stashed beer kegs out of sight. Steger, the social chairman, mopped the floor, and other members threw away trash. By the time the emissary from the dean's office arrived, there was no sign of a party. "He toured the whole house to no avail," Steger recalled. Standing at the front door, the inspector hesitated and then summoned the chapter president.

"Did you have a party here tonight?" he asked Pence.

Like George Washington and the apocryphal cherry tree, Pence faced a difficult choice: lie and protect the house or tell the truth and suffer the consequences.

"Yes, sir, we did," Pence answered.[7]

Pence told the truth and suffered the consequences, along with his brothers. The penalty was harsh. The dean's office placed the fraternity on probation and canceled its annual Fiji Islander dance in the spring, the biggest social event of the year, when members would turn the house into a tropical paradise. Years later, some members still blamed Pence for not pleading the Fifth. The episode disillusioned Pence, and he did not run for a second term as president.

By then, Pence's time was consumed by other priorities, his deepening spiritual life foremost among them. Pence had considered his faith dormant when he arrived at Hanover. As a child, he regularly attended Mass with his family, received the sacrament of First Communion, and served his parish as an altar boy. In high school, by his own admission, he had more pressing concerns. "I had no interest in faith."[8] Once on the college campus, he began attending a Christian fellowship group called Vespers that met every Tuesday evening in the Brown Memorial Chapel. By senior year, he was its president. The students prayed and sang, and Pence often played his guitar. "He would have whole flocks of Vesper girls gathered around him," Murphy said.[9]

Vespers sponsored a variety of activities, including trips to the local nursing home on Thursday nights, weekly Bible studies, and twice-a-year retreats at Clifty Falls State Park. Pence explained in an article in the Hanover student newspaper that he initially attended out of curiosity. He saw a cute girl at the first meeting, "so I kept going in hope of seeing her again. I can see now that God used that motivation to bring me back to the fellowship that played a big part in bringing me to Christ."[10]

A senior fraternity brother, John Gable, often spoke with Pence about faith, and those talks left a deep impression as well. Pence has often told the story of the time he admired a gold cross necklace that Gable wore and asked him how he could purchase one just like it. Gable, who later became a prominent Presbyterian minister in Indianapolis, told him, "You know, you've got to wear it in your heart before you wear it around your neck."[11] The comment jolted Pence, whose faith to that point had consisted of regular worship but no deep quest for understanding.

A few weeks later, during the weekend of April 29, Pence attended a contemporary Christian music festival in Wilmore, Kentucky. The annual event was called Ichthus, the Greek word for fish, and featured preaching, singing, and an altar call during which audience members were invited to come forward to make or renew their commitment to Christ. Pence responded. "Saturday night, sitting in a light rain, I walked down . . . and I gave my life and made a personal decision to trust Jesus Christ as my savior," he said.[12] It was not a dramatic, born-again epiphany but rather a next step in his progression from a ritualistic to an evangelical faith.

By the time Pence graduated from Hanover, friends and family described him as "deeply religious."[13] Some years later, in a 1994 newspaper interview, Pence described himself as "a born-again, evangelical Catholic."[14]

If his spiritual transformation was gradual, his political conversion occurred in a matter of months. Pence grew up as a Democrat and cast his first vote for president for Jimmy Carter—not Ronald Reagan—in 1980. As Irish Catholics, Ed and Nancy Pence identified more with the Democratic Party but over time switched their allegiance to the Republicans. Pence remembered admiring President John F. Kennedy from a young age. His maternal grandparents emigrated from the same area in Ireland as the Kennedys, and the Kennedy name appeared down a branch in the Pence family tree. Pence vividly recalled, then four years old, watching the 1963 funeral of the assassinated president on his family's black-and-white television: "I can still hear the clip-clop of the horses as the wagon drawing his casket went by."[15] While in elementary school, Pence made a time capsule that contained photos and newspaper clippings of Kennedy, among other items. In high school, Pence served as youth coordinator for the Bartholomew County Democrats after his father put him in touch with local Democratic leader John Rumple. Pence recruited members, knocked on doors for local candidates, and gave out brochures at the Democrat tent at the Bartholomew County fair.

The conversion to Republicanism began during his senior year at Hanover when Pence enrolled in Professor G. M. Curtis's class on American Constitutional and Legal History. The two-semester course exposed Pence to seminal documents by the Founding Fathers and intellectual arguments in support of limited government and individual responsibility. "Everyone who encountered G. M. Curtis encountered a force of nature," said Lake Lambert, who became Hanover's president in 2015. "He was an incredible force in a lot of folks' memories and has been described as formative for Mike Pence."[16] As is the goal of the standard Hanover classroom, Lambert said, students could not hide from the professor's scrutiny.

Professor Curtis was new to the Hanover campus during Pence's senior year, replacing Professor Robert Bowers, who retired after thirty-one years teaching Russian and American history. Though Hanover's department of history was small, the quality of its faculty rivaled any at the state's top public universities. Curtis, Bowers, Les Eisen, and John Trout were all scholars with expertise unusual on a campus of eight hundred students. Like other history majors, Pence was required to take Great Epochs of History, which exposed him to European, American, and medieval high points, including the rise and fall of the Roman Republic. Bowers, whom Murphy described as brilliant, was a product of the University of Wisconsin in the 1930s, a pacifist who wrote his doctoral dissertation on the peace movement of his era. From Bowers, Pence learned about American foreign policy. From Eisen, he learned European history. Eisen was a conscientious objector who spent World War II working for the government in a logging camp on the northwest coast.

It was Curtis who left the biggest imprint on Pence. George M. Curtis III, called Jim by his friends, went to Hanover at the urging of Stanley Caine, Hanover's vice president for academic affairs, whom he knew from the PhD program at the University of Wisconsin. Curtis later went to the Institute of Early American History in Williamsburg, where he worked as a document editor on *The Papers of John Marshall*, a project whose goal was the editing, annotation, and publication of the papers of the fourth chief justice of the United States. Pence and Murphy served on a committee of history majors that met with Curtis when he came to campus to interview and immediately were among his admirers. "He was dynamic, brilliant, and he looked like Clark Kent," Murphy said.[17]

The time Pence spent with Curtis, in and out of the classroom, was transformative. The course motivated Pence to read, write, and think critically about the founding of the American republic. It also forced him to consider and argue both sides of legal issues, a skill that would later serve him well in law, talk radio, and politics. On his syllabus, Professor Curtis made clear his expectations: "Please read material before we deal with it in class. This is a lecture/discussion course wherein all of us will strive together to enhance our understandings of the past. Working on the straightforward assumption that two heads are better than one, will everyone, including me, please come prepared to share knowledge, insights, and questions about the readings? To do less, it seems to me, makes a mockery of what the study of history is all about, thus diminishing us as people."[18]

On the first day of class, Curtis made students a promise: "If you work your fannies off in here, you are never going to look at the world the same way again."[19] At Pence's urgings, fraternity brother Jay Steger also enrolled in the course, and it consumed them. "We had his class in the morning. We'd come home for lunch, and the entire table would be engaged in the discussion. All we could talk about was G. M.'s classes."[20] Even the textbook, *The American Constitution: Its Origins and Development*, was designed to fuse students' thinking about law and history. The study and application of landmark Supreme Court cases caused Pence to reflect for the first time on federalism, states' rights, and the proper role of government.

As serious as was Curtis, Pence could be a jokester in the classroom. In the midst of probing discussions, the professor had a habit of pausing and staring intently out the third-floor window. One day during an extended pause, Pence got out of his seat to join Curtis. A startled Professor Curtis turned to his student and said, "Mr. Pence, have you lost your faculties?" Pence replied mischievously, "I was wondering whether the book of all truth was hovering just outside your window." The class broke into laughter.[21]

Curtis served as Pence's senior thesis adviser, a mentoring relationship that caused Pence to hone both his writing and reasoning skills. The title of Pence's paper was "The Religious Expressions of Abraham Lincoln." Pence admired Lincoln's presidency but was curious about why the sixteenth president, a man raised in a log cabin in Southern Indiana, was never baptized, never received communion, and never joined a church. Pence's paper traced Lincoln's evolution from a young attorney dismissive of faith to a weary president, molded by civil war, who in his 1864 State of the Union Address proclaimed his "profoundest gratitude to Almighty God."[22] It was a fitting topic for Pence as he explored his own faith and political views.

As graduation approached, Pence was well on his way to finding himself, though he did not yet know what his next steps should be. By vote of his classmates, Pence delivered the senior speech at commencement on May 24, 1981. He was chosen by his peers not for his grades—though he was a Dean's List student with a respectable 3.4 out of 4.0 GPA—but for his eloquence, for which he was well known on campus. The title of his speech was "Getting Even." Rather than the revenge implied in the speech's title, Pence reflected on the many ways his classmates had been supported by their elders and urged generational payback. He used the speech to say thank you to the different constituencies that had helped get the 190 graduates to that moment. Turning to the parents, he said, "You've been there our entire lives, loving, helping, and many times carrying us through when we alone could go no further.... You've given us everything, right down to the gift of our own lives. Against such debt there can be no recompense." In typical Pence fashion, he put emphasis on the last syllable to underscore the pun.[23]

The commencement speaker on that day was Richard V. Allen, assistant for national security affairs to President Reagan, who discussed the role of human rights in the country's foreign policy. It was heavy content for a happy occasion, but Pence found himself listening intently. "The Soviet Union is the grossest, most systematic violator of human rights in the world," Allen said. He cited the cases of Russian Andrei Sakharov, the nuclear-physicist-turned-pacifist living in forced exile, and Anatoly Shcharansky, an Israeli human rights activist imprisoned in a Soviet labor camp.[24]

Few in the audience on that warm spring day could have predicted that six years later President Reagan would stand before the Brandenburg Gate and tell the Soviet leader, "Mr. Gorbachev, tear down this wall." Nor could they have foreseen the subsequent collapse of Communism and the breakup of the Soviet Union. Pence hadn't voted for the movie-star president, but in coming years, he would find himself magnetically attracted to Reagan's charisma, his demeanor, and his message.

# 3

★ ★ ★

# LAW, MARRIAGE, AND MENTORS

MIKE PENCE WALKED INTO PROFESSOR WILLIAM HARVEY'S class with a sense of foreboding. He'd heard stories from upperclassmen about the legendary scholar whose Socratic questioning had sharpened so many Indianapolis lawyers' trial skills. Harvey was "a rock star," according to one former student who took his six-credit civil procedure course at Indiana University (IU) School of Law.[1] He literally wrote the book on the subject—or, more accurately, eleven volumes on Indiana civil procedure and evidence. Known as intimidating but never churlish, Harvey expected his students to stand and recite assigned case law without mistake when called on. Though Pence didn't welcome the pressure, he was impressed by Harvey's teaching style and intellect. Much like Professor Curtis at Hanover, who had introduced Pence to classical liberal thought, Professor Harvey would become a lifelong mentor, modeling not only intellectual gravitas but calm under pressure in the public sphere.

Following his graduation from Hanover in 1981, Pence debated next steps. He applied to IU's law school but was denied on account of a low LSAT score.[2] When Hanover offered him a job in its admissions department, he readily accepted. The next two years found him crossing the state, visiting high schools and extolling the beauty of the woods and the breadth of the majors at his alma mater. On evenings and weekends, he nurtured his interest in politics. Fraternity brother Jay Steger was dating Professor Curtis's daughter Anne (they would eventually marry). Pence often joined Steger at Curtis's home, where they'd stay up late discussing politics and court cases over cold beer. In class, Curtis had kept his political views to himself. In this setting, he felt free to share his libertarian perspective.[3]

"Mike's job at the college came naturally to him, and he was not dating anyone, so that left him with a lot of time on his hands to read, think, and spend some time with G. M.," Steger recalled. "We would spend hours in G. M.'s library."[4]

Years later, Curtis joined the staff of the Liberty Fund in Indianapolis, an organization dedicated to the preservation of human liberty and individual responsibility. At Curtis's invitation, Pence attended and sometimes led the Fund's intense three-day Socratic-form colloquia on topics such as free-market economics, natural law, and politics in literature. Pence's commitment to these sessions, with their heavy reading assignments and expectation of full participation, confirmed one friend's later description of Pence as a "policy wonk" at heart.[5]

Pence retook the LSAT, scored in the eighty-fourth percentile, and was admitted to IU Law at Indianapolis.[6] Like the fictional James Hart in the 1971 novel *The Paper Chase*, Pence began his legal studies with misgivings but quickly learned the ropes and graduated with a B average. Although he would later say, "I cherish my years" in law school, Pence told a reporter in a 1994 interview, "No one I know likes law school. It was a bad experience. I wouldn't wish it on a dog I didn't like."[7]

The statement was part truth, part hyperbole. "We all had frustrations with law school just because it's a grind," explained Bill Stephan, who received his law degree in 1984 and, like Pence, would become active in Republican politics.[8] The two met through mutual friends in the Christian Legal Society, a social group that met once a week during lunch when members could talk freely about current events, faith, and legal issues of a religious nature. Although Stephan graduated two years ahead of Pence, they were at similar stages in their lives and had much in common, including girlfriends who had attended the same Indianapolis high school. The couples socialized, traveled to Chicago to watch the

Cubs play, and hosted each other at backyard barbecues, where Pence was a "dangerous man" with a spatula and a grill. Stephan called Pence "one of the funniest guys I know," someone who liked to make puns and do impressions of presidents, celebrities, and his professors.[9]

Pence's sense of humor surfaced at law school in the form of a comic strip called *Law School Daze* that he drew for the student newspaper *Dictum*. The main character, Mr. Daze, served as Pence's more insecure alter ego. In one strip, a professor promised students that poor performance on their first-semester exam would not affect his perception of them in term two: "You can rest assured that I will continue to treat each of you with the same conscious disregard for your self-esteem as I have all along," the professor quipped. In another, Daze cheerily greeted Professor Tortkinds, who gave him one look and replied, "Drop dead."[10] In most of the pictures, Daze bore an uncanny resemblance to his creator.

Brian Bosma, a law school acquaintance whose path would cross the future vice president's repeatedly through the years, said Harvey's class was among the more stressful experiences but also life-changing for him and Pence. In contrast to Professor Kingsfield in *The Paper Chase*, Harvey worked through the class roster alphabetically, so students had advance notice to prepare their cases. Even so, "when Harvey called on you, you broke out in immediate sweat," Bosma said.[11] Harvey started class five minutes early and expected students to arrive early, having read all assignments, and to take scrupulous notes if they expected to pass.[12] "He wanted everyone to learn how to think and speak on their feet, especially since his specialties were in the area of trial advocacy," his daughter Carolyn Harvey Lundberg said.[13]

The proof of Harvey's success was a long list of former students at the highest levels of government service: two vice presidents, Pence and Dan Quayle; governor Mitch Daniels; US senator Dan Coats; Indiana house speakers Brian Bosma and John Gregg; US attorney Deborah Daniels; Seventh US Circuit Court of Appeals judge Daniel Manion; Indiana Court of Appeals judge Margret Robb; and many other state and federal judges.

Harvey's conduct outside the classroom was equally instructive for Pence as he contemplated a life in the public eye. The former dean of the law school was at the center of two partisan controversies during the Reagan administration, one involving his recess appointment to chair the Legal Services Corporation in 1982 and the other his withdrawn nomination to the Seventh US Circuit Court of Appeals in 1985. In both cases, Democrats attacked Harvey as an ideological extremist, a harbinger of the divisive discourse that would come to mark the judicial nominating process in years to come. "Mike Pence was very aware of all those political battles—at times, firestorms—and how Dad remained steadfast through them," Lundberg recalled.[14]

Despite the rigor of law school, Pence made time for church and his social life. Always frugal, he received free room and board by becoming one of Mrs. Metzger's boys, a suggestion made by friend Jay Steger. Mrs. Metzger was a member of the fabled Lew Wallace clan whose great-grandfather was Indiana governor David Wallace. As was the case of many elderly widows (and widowers) of that era, Mrs. Metzger maintained her independence from friends and relatives by taking in boarders, typically college students who couldn't afford dormitory fees. The exchange was beneficial for both. Pence received his room free of charge, and the crusty widow had her nighttime security.

As fate would have it, Mrs. Metzger lived around the corner from St. Thomas Aquinas Church, where Karen Sue Batten played the guitar during Sunday services. Pence attended Mass one Sunday and was drawn to the brown-haired accompanist. The two chatted just long enough for Pence to learn that her sister attended IU School of Law. After Mass, Pence headed straight to Steger's room at Butler University, where Steger was studying for an MBA and worked as director of a freshman dorm. "He was smitten from the moment he laid eyes on her," Steger said. "He talked for an hour and a half about how he could drown in her chocolate-brown eyes."[15]

Pence had failed to get Batten's phone number, so he visited the school registrar and cajoled from her the sister's contact information. When he called to get Karen's number, Karen herself answered the phone. She was staying at her sister's house for the week, babysitting her niece and nephew. Recognizing the voice, Pence panicked and hung up. A few seconds later, he summoned more nerve. This time, Karen invited him over for taco salad followed by ice skating at Pepsi Coliseum with her niece and nephew. Before Pence went home that evening, the ten-year-old niece bet him one dollar he would marry her aunt.[16]

According to childhood friend Jeff Brown, Pence's approach to dating was much like his approach to politics. "He wanted to date her, and he pursued it. That's the way he did everything."[17]

Karen Batten was seventeen months older than Pence with similar interests, politics not initially among them. Born January 1, 1957, to Lillian Hacker and John Marshall Batten, Karen loved school and the book *Harriet the Spy* and held up her teachers as heroes. In second grade at Park School, Laila Hartman instilled in her "a love of reading and of being read to."[18] In fifth grade, teacher Audrey Peet, a native of England, left such an impression that Karen and Pence named their first daughter after her.

Karen's parents divorced when she was young. In 1967, her mother re-married Bernard Barcio, then a Latin teacher at Park School who made national news when his students built a replica of a Roman catapult. Named Indiana's teacher of the year in 1985, Barcio's conspicuous joy of teaching strengthened his stepdaughter's resolve to become a teacher herself. After finishing sixth grade at Park School, Karen transferred to St. Luke Catholic School for junior high and then Bishop Chatard for high school, where she was speech club president and a member of the French club, cheer block, student council, and National Honor Society. A straight-A student, Karen was named senior class valedictorian of the class of 1975.

Karen stayed close to home for college, attending Butler University, where she received bachelor's and master's degrees in elementary education in preparation for a career as a teacher. Although she minored in art on a whim, she was a talented artist who briefly ran a business painting watercolors of people's houses. At age twenty-one, she married a fellow Butler graduate, Steve Whitaker, on a 1978 trip to Big Bend National Park in Texas, and their wedding was announced in the Living section of the *Indianapolis News*.[19] Whitaker was a medical student at Indiana University and spent long hours at the hospital, and the two grew apart. The marriage was a youthful mistake annulled by the Catholic Church. "We were kids. We probably didn't know necessarily what we were doing," Whitaker said.[20]

With her second husband, Karen found true partnership. As Pence would later say, "She's the best part of my life. Everything we do in public life we do together."[21] From the outset of their relationship, Pence made clear his belief that faith was the cornerstone of a marriage. "When we first started dating, I remember saying something to Mike, something silly, like, 'Oh you're my number one.' And he stopped right there, and he said, 'You know what, I'm probably going to disappoint you if you make me number one in your life.' What he was talking about was you need to have God as number one. Jesus needs to be number one in your life."[22]

Anticipating a proposal, Karen had the word *yes* engraved on a gold cross that she carried in her purse.[23] The moment arrived on August 6, 1984, as the two were feeding ducks along the Indianapolis canal. Pence had hollowed out two loaves of bread, one hiding a small bottle of champagne and the other a ring box for her to find as she tore off bread. Not long after, Pence called Brown and asked if he'd be best man at his wedding. "He was really excited and head over heels," Brown said.[24]

The following June, Reverend Jim Lasher officiated at their wedding at St. Christopher's Roman Catholic Church near the Indianapolis Motor Speedway. The event reunited Pence's large family with friends from childhood and college. Fraternity brother Jay Steger was a groomsman along with Pence's brothers and brothers-in-law.

After a honeymoon to Nassau, the Pences settled into the routine of married life. Karen was teaching second grade at Acton Elementary School. Pence was working as a law clerk at the firm Dutton and Overman with one year of law school left. Following his graduation in 1986, Pence practiced with Stark Doninger Mernitz & Smith of Indianapolis.

Although both Pences were eager for children, the family they wanted was not forthcoming. After several years, they placed their names on an adoption list and began the lengthy process of fertility treatments. With so many of their friends having babies, the young couple kept their struggle to themselves. "I remember my little niece looked up at me one day and said, 'Auntie Karen, why don't you have any babies?' It can be a very heartbreaking experience."[25] Pence was on the road the day Karen learned of her successful pregnancy; he'd stopped at "the dingiest little gas station" to call her from a pay phone, and she answered, "Happy Father's Day."[26] The couple withdrew their name from the adoption list and later welcomed their firstborn, a son named Michael, and two daughters, Audrey and Charlotte, in quick succession. Meanwhile, Pence had made two unsuccessful attempts at Congress and was settled in a comfortable new career.

During these years, Pence maintained his strong connection with Professor Harvey, seeking his professional advice and inviting him to appear on a radio show he hosted in the 1990s. The two spent the millennial New Year's Eve together on December 31, 1999, and were frequent guests on the Greg Garrison radio show in the 2000s. In 2016, with the November election just weeks away, Pence learned Harvey was in declining health and telephoned him from the vice-presidential campaign trail. Pence told Harvey he would not have developed the legal, political, and speaking skills that he did without the professor's teaching and mentoring. Harvey thanked him and replied, "That's very kind, but I think you have a great deal of your own talents that you've developed, and I'm immensely proud of you."[27]

Harvey lived to see his protégé elected to the vice presidency and insisted on voting for the Trump-Pence ticket in person. "Mom drove him to the polling place and offered to help," his daughter recalled, "and he said, 'No, I'm going to do this myself.' He was so happy the night of the election, and they stayed up until 4 a.m. to see the results. They kept saying to each other they should go to bed, but he said, 'I just can't. I have to see this.'"[28] Harvey died on November 17, and Pence issued a statement: "Indiana's loss with the passing of this extraordinary man is my personal loss. I will always remember Professor Harvey as a champion of the Constitution, a mentor, a veteran, and a man of faith."[29]

# 4

★ ★ ★

# THE FIRST CAMPAIGN

MIKE PENCE LAUNCHED HIS POLITICAL CAREER ON A SINGLE-speed bicycle, pedaling across the Second Congressional District twenty miles at a stretch. Two or three times a week during the unseasonably hot summer of 1988, he and Karen hopped on their bikes and traveled the rolling hills and parched cornfields of East Central Indiana. When he spotted someone in a field or front yard, he'd coast to a stop, wave Karen over to join him, and stick out his hand: "Hi, I'm Mike Pence. I'm running for US Congress. This is my wife, Karen."[1]

The smile and resulting conversation were genuine Pence, a natural-born politician who quickly grew to relish the grip-and-grin of the campaign trail. "He was a very friendly young man," recalled John Schorg, the reporter assigned by the Columbus *Republic* to cover Pence's first campaign. "He seemed like the kind of person a lot of people hoped would get into politics."[2]

The bike tour was a gimmick, designed to draw attention to what was supposed to be a yawner of a congressional race. Despite being a Democrat in a historically Republican district, incumbent Phil Sharp was heavily favored for reelection to an eighth term. He had rolled over his last three opponents—Ralph Van Natta, Ken Mackenzie, and Don Lynch—beating Lynch in 1986 with an impressive 62 percent. Insiders gave Pence a one-in-ten chance of winning. They underestimated the novice politician's work ethic, fund-raising abilities, and persistence—and just how close the election would be.

Few had expected Pence to run for office at such a young age—friends, family, and the candidate's wife included. Pence's plan was to get more involved in GOP activities at the precinct level. He had told Karen he might like to run for Congress in his fifties, after he'd made a name for himself. When he went to see Marion County GOP chairman John Sweezy in 1987 to talk about volunteer opportunities, Sweezy had more immediate concerns. No one credible had come forth to run against Sharp, and Sweezy needed a candidate who could raise $200,000 for the effort. "Why don't you run for Congress now?" he asked Pence.[3]

A few days later, Pence and Karen invited a dozen friends to their bungalow in the Broad Ripple neighborhood of Indianapolis to present the idea and get feedback. Karen set out pretzels and Cokes as Pence began laying out a strategy for a House run.

"Wait a minute," interrupted Jay Steger, Pence's good friend and fraternity brother. "Are you talking about running to be a state representative at the statehouse? Because it sounds like you're talking about Washington."

"I am talking about Washington," Pence said.

"Are you out of your mind?" Steger replied.[4]

As the conversation continued, Steger and a few of the others came to see a campaign as a chance to build political résumés, and, if successful, influence positively the future of the state and country. With an MBA from Butler, Steger quickly signed on to serve as campaign treasurer.

"It was a lively evening," remembered Bill Stephan, a friend from law school days. "I was happy to see him throw his hat in the ring, which he literally did." One of those in attendance had brought a straw hat and Hula-Hoop, and everyone laughed as Pence threw the hat into the ring. "I think we were all fairly young, idealistic, and a bit naive about all that would be entailed in a run for political office," said Stephan, who attended rallies and Lincoln Day events with Pence and pedaled along with him on the bike tour from time to time.[5]

It took Pence's father longer to warm to the idea. Ed Pence considered it reckless for his son to run against a veteran lawmaker like Sharp who had high name recognition and a reputation for effective constituent services. Besides, Pence was just twenty-nine, recently married, and had yet to establish himself financially. "Ed was really upset about the decision," Pence's mother, Nancy, recalled in a 2013 interview with their hometown newspaper, the *Republic*. "At first he was dead set against it, and he really grilled Mike about why he would want to do such a thing."[6]

Ed Pence didn't think his son had a prayer of winning. Around Christmas, he summoned Pence's older brother Ed to try to talk him out of the decision. "We both thought it was Don Quixote-ish," Ed recalled. "In the end, Dad came around. In fact he became a big supporter and was really helpful in coaching Mike on raising money for the campaign. He took Mike throughout the district and introduced him to all the acquaintances he had made in his business career. It was invaluable."[7]

Pence announced his candidacy on February 23. The opening line of a newspaper article summed up his reasons for running: "Mike Pence doesn't think Congress works."[8] Before going after Sharp, Pence first had to win the GOP primary. One candidate stood in the way: fifty-six-year-old Greenwood accountant Raymond Schwab. He was no relation to Charles Schwab of the brokerage house, but Pence's team worried his name might seem familiar to voters. (Ironically, Charles Schwab would donate money to the future vice president Pence's political action committee.)[9] Like Pence, Schwab had zero political background. Unlike Pence, he had life experience and tried to capitalize on it, often pointing to Pence's age as a handicap. "I have more experience dealing with issues that come up in Congress than he has time on the planet," he joked with reporters.[10]

With Sweezy's backing, Pence succeeded in getting support from ten of the eleven Republican county chairmen in the district. Generous Republican donors got on board. The nomination looked to be a cinch.

On April 13, however, tragedy struck the Pence family, casting doubt on whether Pence would be able to stick with the aggressive campaigning and fund-raising schedule he had set for himself. It was a Wednesday, and Pence was in the office, on the phone, reaching out to potential donors.[11] Midafternoon, he took an urgent call from a family member. His father, Ed, vice president of Kiel Brothers Oil, had collapsed playing a round of golf at Harrison Lake Country Club, Columbus's premier eighteen-hole course. The fifty-eight-year-old had been rushed to Bartholomew County Hospital. Doctors could not revive him. The cause of death was acute cardiac arrest.

Pence put the campaign on hold for a week as the family made preparations for the calling and funeral. He'd been pushing himself hard and was exhausted. The next day, Pence met Steger for lunch at the Southport Cracker Barrel. Pence appeared downcast, pushing his food around the plate with a fork, hardly talking. "You want me to shut it down?" Steger asked. He figured that Pence needed time to grieve, and the campaign was an uphill shot anyway. Pence slowly looked up at his old friend, his jaw tight with determination. "Dad didn't raise a quitter."[12]

The funeral was on April 16. Mourners packed St. Columba Roman Catholic Church. Reverend Joseph M. McNally eulogized the elder Pence as a dedicated family man and loyal church member, recalling his army service in the Korean War for which he received a Bronze Star. "The next business day, Mike was back at the office and highly charged," Steger observed. "He picked himself up fast. I was surprised."[13] From that moment on, Pence seemed more determined than ever. He sailed through the primary with 71 percent of the vote, trouncing Schwab 36,298 to 14,953. Then he set his sights firmly on Phil Sharp.

Sharp was a Watergate baby, one of forty-seven Democrats elected to Congress after the resignation of President Richard Nixon in 1974. Public disgust with the scandal—an illegal wiretapping at Democratic National Committee headquarters and subsequent cover-up that reached the office of the president—had left many Republicans vulnerable, including Representative David Dennis of Richmond, Indiana.

As a member of the House Judiciary Committee, Dennis had voted against recommending Nixon's impeachment. The former Wayne

County prosecuting attorney argued there was no evidence to show Nixon knew anything about the burglary at the Watergate Hotel. Voters punished Dennis roundly, electing Sharp 85,418 to 71,701. Because the district tilted Republican, Sharp had been in GOP crosshairs ever since.

During the 1986 election season, the *New York Times* highlighted Sharp's tenure as an example of the balancing act required of the Democratic class of '74, many of whom lived in marginal districts and were constantly inventing new techniques to strengthen their base. Sharp survived, the reporter observed, by being intentional about every vote. "It does shape your attitude on the House floor," the congressman said of his district. "If I cast a vote, I might have to answer for it. It may be an issue in the next campaign. Over and over I have to have a response to the question: Why did you do that?" As a result, Sharp had taken positions that were popular with moderate Republican voters in his district. For example, he voted to approve a bill loosening gun control laws. Personally, he opposed the measure but said he wasn't about to commit political suicide.[14]

Further, Sharp had impressive credentials. Raised in Elwood, home of 1940 Republican presidential nominee Wendell Willkie, Sharp studied foreign service at Georgetown University and did his graduate work at Oxford in England before going home to Indiana. He served as aide to Senator Vance Hartke in the mid-1960s and as professor of political science at Ball State University in Muncie from 1969 to 1974. As seven previous Republican candidates had learned, Sharp was a formidable opponent. Voters appreciated his intellect, his good looks, and his political pedigree.

None of this fazed the young Mike Pence. After easily winning the primary, Pence sunk his teeth into the issues. He painted himself as a free-enterprise capitalist and Sharp as a "regulation-type guy" who sought unnecessary government oversight of oil and gas industries. "In very broad strokes I am against it (regulation)," Pence said. "Monitoring is necessary, of course. And environmental concerns must be recognized. But regulations have hampered the economy."[15]

Pence assailed runaway spending and the use of continuing resolutions in the budget process, a practice that keeps the government operating when Congress can't agree on appropriations bills. He aggressively went after earmarks, a position that would become a hallmark of future campaigns, criticizing the "ridiculous boondoggles" that benefited individual members of Congress at taxpayers' expense.[16] One in particular that bothered him was a $25 million appropriation to help build Alliance Airport in Fort Worth, Texas, which he said was a useless city-owned facility going up in House speaker Jim Wright's district. Pence's positions reflected his strict adherence to principles of limited government and fiscal responsibility. But none of them drew voters' attention quite like the bicycle tour—or his risky political calculation not to accept political action committee (PAC) money to fund his campaign.

Newspaper stories highlighted Pence as the bicycling candidate, and his tour across the district demonstrated something for which both parties were notorious: gerrymandering, the designing of legislative boundaries to favor one party or another. After the 1980 US Census, Republicans in the state legislature drew the Second District in a way they hoped would maximize Republican votes. It meandered famously from Muncie on the north to Columbus on the south, weaving its way through Richmond, New Castle, and Greenwood but mostly bypassing Democratic Indianapolis except the south side, where Pence and Karen had moved to live within the district. The district encompassed three TV markets—Fort Wayne, Indianapolis, and Cincinnati—which made advertising expensive and increased the importance of earned media from events like the bike tour.

From June 11 to July 16, the Pences biked 261 miles, a remarkable distance considering the inhospitable Hoosier roads and back-to-back hundred-degree temperatures. It was the summer of the North American drought, one of the worst in US history, and Indiana farmland was not exempted. "I think people respond well to someone who comes riding along down the street straddling a bicycle," Pence explained to a reporter. "It's nothing more than one person relating to another, and I don't think you can get any more effective in campaigning than that." To ensure maximum exposure, campaign worker Melinda Fowler drove the route first, telling residents that a congressional candidate was on his way. Ryan Streeter followed in a van carrying "Pence for Congress" signs that he hoped to plant in voters' yards.[17]

Reporter Schorg, a biker himself, joined the Pence entourage on his Huffy as they rode from Winchester to Richmond, a trip of twenty-five miles. Pence seemed unperturbed as semis at full throttle kicked up dust and frustrated motorists shot the group obscene gestures. "Get the hell outta the way!" one of them roared.[18] "It was not an easy trip," Schorg said. "We were riding on state roads, and he would stop and say hi if he saw people along the side of the road. He would jump off the bike if he saw somebody working in a yard."[19]

Formal stops that day included a bait-and-tackle shop in New White-land, a grain elevator in Manilla, a grocery store in Fountain City, and an auto dealer in Winchester—all places where Pence could gather a half dozen or more voters in one shot and list the reasons he believed Congress was broken and needed new blood.

One of those reasons—the one that resonated most with voters—was the excessive influence wielded by lobbyists and special interest groups in Washington. To underscore his position, Pence refused to accept donations from PACs. Formed for the express purpose of raising money to elect and defeat candidates, PACs typically represent business, labor, and ideological positions.

PACs could give up to $5,000 to a candidate in each primary or general election cycle in contrast to the $1,000 limit placed on individual contributors at that time. Because PACs accounted for about one-fourth of all political spending, some saw Pence's decision as foolish, if not fatal. Steger said it was a political calculation designed to generate positive publicity for Pence, who probably wouldn't have raised much PAC money anyway.

On this issue, the contrast between Sharp and Pence could not have been clearer. In July, Pence's campaign purchased a plaque to recognize Sharp as the first Hoosier congressman in history to raise $1 million from special interest groups and lobbyists. "This is certainly an event we do not want to see pass by without some form of recognition," Pence quipped while holding up the plaque for a journalist to photograph.[20]

By September, the Pence campaign had enough money on hand to buy ads on five Indianapolis-area TV stations targeting the incumbent's

PAC record, which made Sharp's people visibly nervous. They attacked Pence's TV ads on the subject as "half truths, distortions, and outright lies." The ads left the impression with TV viewers that Sharp had raised the $1 million in the 1988 election cycle when, in fact, the amount had been collected over eighteen years, they noted.[21]

As the PAC issue gained traction, Pence's fund-raising was going gangbusters, thanks to two things: Pence's willingness to ask for money from people he'd never met and advice brought to the campaign by Mike Laudick, a professional fund-raiser. Pence had heard Laudick's name mentioned favorably by colleagues and wanted to bring him on board in a volunteer role. Laudick, at the time, was working for Franklin College in development, but he had built his reputation in political fund-raising. He had no idea who Pence was when the candidate phoned him and asked to meet.

"I said I hadn't been involved in politics for several years and wasn't interested in getting involved again," Laudick remembered. "He said it would only take an hour and that he'd buy me breakfast. So I grudgingly said yes. When I got there, I opened the breakfast by saying, 'I think you've got one chance in ten of winning,' hoping to make the conversation shorter. But he really sold me on himself." Laudick agreed to help the upstart candidate, donating about ten to fifteen hours a week.[22]

The best pitchman for Pence was the candidate himself. He didn't hesitate to call total strangers on the phone or drop in unannounced and ask for money. That's how he met businessman Chuck Quilhot, an ideological soul mate who would become a regular donor to Pence's political efforts and later recruit Pence to help organize a conservative think tank devoted to free-market ideas. In August 1988, Quilhot was working as a junior account representative at Marsh & McLennan in Indianapolis when Pence showed up at his office without an appointment and asked the receptionist if he could speak with "Mr. Quilhot."

When Quilhot came out to greet Pence, he noticed immediately that the candidate was hot and sweaty, and his shoes and shirt were covered with dust. Although his appearance was untidy, the visitor was about Quilhot's age with common interests, and the two "immediately meshed" on issues ranging from school choice to economic freedom. "I went back to my desk and wrote him a check for the maximum amount."

Quilhot wasn't sure how Pence got his name; he wondered if Pence had him confused with his more prominent father, who was active in Allen County Republican politics.

Soon after, Quilhot hosted a fund-raiser for Pence in his home, where the candidate met more young professionals. More important to Pence's future career goals, Quilhot introduced him to his parents and relatives in Fort Wayne, headquarters of the family's pioneering—and profitable—medical malpractice insurance company called Medical Protective. "The family became a big supporter," Quilhot said.[23]

A cold call also paid off with Jeff Cardwell, a real estate developer and co-owner of a hardware and home improvement store on Madison Avenue. Cardwell would become one of Pence's most trusted advisers and later, in his role as Republican state chairman, cast the Indiana delegation's vote for the Trump-Pence team at the 2016 GOP National Convention.

Pence called Cardwell out of the blue one day and invited him to lunch at the Dutch Oven, a popular pie shop and café next to Southern Plaza. Cardwell figured that Pence had done his research before phoning him. "Congressman Dan Burton was a friend of mine. My real estate signs were everywhere." Cardwell was a Reagan Republican who liked Pence's Reagan-esque message, especially regarding national security and economic growth. After dining, the two went back to Cardwell's office, where he wrote the Pence campaign a $1,000 check. The best news for Pence was yet to come. "I want to introduce you to some friends," Cardwell told Pence. "I want to help you."[24]

The connection opened doors to influential south-siders, including Charlie Laughner of Laughner's Cafeteria, Judge Jay Haggerty, and George Bixler, the developer of Southern Plaza, the first major shopping center built in that part of town. Next, Cardwell went to see John Hammond Jr., a well-known lawyer and school board member in Perry Township. "I'd like to organize a fundraiser for Mike," Cardwell told him. The two planned a $25-a-head event to be held in the Hammonds' two-story Cape Cod home on Banta Road. Charlie Laughner catered the pie. Mrs. Hammond served Folgers coffee in china teacups. Candidate Pence stood in the parlor and shared his vision. "It was very successful. The main purpose was just to introduce Mike."[25]

In fact, so much money was coming in that the campaign's volunteer staff, typing on IBM Selectrics, was struggling to keep up with Federal Election Commission (FEC) rules and due dates. The Pence campaign missed three finance report deadlines and misreported some gifts so that it appeared they had accepted donations in excess of the $1,000 federal limit. Democrats seized on the errors to attack Pence for campaign finance violations.

Indiana Democratic state chairman John Livengood charged Pence with accepting at least twelve contributions above the individual cap, including one from well-known restaurateur Jonathan Byrd. "In the case of Mike Pence we have a candidate who has willfully and flagrantly ignored and violated the law," he declared.[26]

Colin Chapman, Pence's campaign manager, fired back. The errors had involved donations from couples that were not properly listed as coming from separate individuals. "Mike's best friend and his mother are the ones filing the reports," he explained. "They are volunteers, and they are doing the best they can." Pence called the allegations sleaze and expressed personal offense at Livengood's insult to his mother. But the campaign acted quickly to clean up the errors and returned one donation that had exceeded the limit. With the PAC issue still front and center, Lou Bayard, Sharp's press secretary, accused Pence of hypocrisy. "The fact is that Mike Pence has made campaign financing an issue in this race, and he's unable to keep his own house in order."[27]

As Pence was pedaling through the Second District, Republicans on the national level were preparing for the presidential nominating convention to be held in New Orleans at the Louisiana Superdome. The GOP had high hopes of keeping the White House after eight prosperous years under President Ronald Reagan. Unemployment stood at 5.5 percent, the best since Reagan took office. Gas was a dollar a gallon, the lowest in eight years. Although economic storm clouds were looming, Reagan himself remained immensely popular, ranking at the top of Gallup's annual list of the world's most admired men.

The question was whether Vice President George H. W. Bush, who had outlasted Bob Dole, Jack Kemp, and others to claim the party's presidential nomination, could keep the momentum going. Leading up to the convention, Bush had been tight-lipped as to whom his vice-presidential running mate would be, at one point saying he would not make the decision public until the last day of the convention. He was banking that a last-minute surprise would give the ticket a convention bounce coming out of New Orleans. On August 16, the convention's second day, he abandoned his plan to keep the choice secret and surprised almost everyone with his announcement: Indiana's junior senator Dan Quayle, whom he described as "a young man born in the middle of this century and from the middle of this country."[28]

Although Indiana was a sure Republican vote in the fall, Bush hoped that Quayle would attract support in other key Midwestern states where industrial decline and the farm drought had become Bush liabilities. Whether or not Quayle was the cause, Bush did get a thirteen-point bump in the polls following the convention and stayed ahead of Democratic nominee Michael Dukakis for the duration of the campaign season.

Back home in Indiana, Pence was exuberant at the unexpected development, which he felt gave his campaign a shot of adrenaline. "I find this news to be so doggone exciting," he gushed. "I can't believe it. This is an opportunity to vote for a person from this state who is only a heartbeat away from the presidency."[29] Little could he imagine that twenty-eight years later he'd be the one balancing a presidential ticket and for many of the same reasons.

By September, political analysts were beginning to think Pence had a shot. A September 30 editorial in the *Daily Journal* of Franklin noted, "Pence has been working extremely hard in his first effort for public office, and the results are beginning to show. He is gaining more name recognition and is apparently turning the race into a close one." The editorial went on to chastise Sharp for avoiding debates with the upstart candidate. Pence had challenged Sharp to a debate in each of the district's eleven counties, and Sharp agreed to two. The newspaper and Franklin College had jointly offered to sponsor one of the debates in Johnson County; Sharp said he was too busy with business in Washington.[30]

When November 8 finally arrived, things looked promising to the Pence team, which gathered on election night at Jonathan Byrd's Cafeteria in Greenwood to monitor the results. Cardwell, Steger, and Byrd were there, as well as Gene Hood, a Nazarene pastor, and campaign staffer Mark Walker. For much of the evening, Pence led in the early polls, and at one point, an Indianapolis TV station called him the apparent winner. What Pence's team knew but the TV station didn't yet realize was that Richmond and Muncie, Sharp strongholds, had yet to report. Pence ended up winning Bartholomew, Johnson, and Marion Counties, but Sharp captured the other eight and hung on for a 53 percent victory, 116,915 to 102,846. Still, it was Sharp's closest race since his 1974 election. Schorg interviewed Pence and Karen after the race was called. Pence was his typical upbeat self, while Karen appeared visibly disappointed.

Sharp press secretary Lou Bayard attributed Pence's good showing to a strong national ticket that brought out a lot of Republican voters. In the presidential election, Bush carried all but ten states and won 54 percent of the vote to Dukakis's 46 percent. Sharp, in part, blamed himself for not campaigning enough due to his wife being ill for much of the year. "My opponent ran a tough campaign, some of it that I thought was terribly negative," he added.[31]

Even in defeat, Pence was viewed as a winner, having raised $350,000 and achieving 47 percent of the vote in a district that had not gone Republican since Watergate. "We really thought we had a chance," Cardwell said of that first election. "But it was not a devastating loss. This was a trial run. We'd go at it again. We all regrouped quickly."[32]

The day after the election, Pence traveled across the Second District—this time by car—thanking the voters who had voted for, financed, and encouraged him. Some of them urged him to run again. "I've got to tell you, today I really found myself fighting off a lot of pressure to make an announcement," Pence told reporters.[33] Unbeknownst to the media, Pence was already plotting a rematch. Six months later, his campaign committee filed its incorporation papers with the Indiana secretary of state, and Pence was back on the campaign trail.

# 5

★ ★ ★

# THE AGONY OF DEFEAT

FROM THE OUTSET, THE 1990 ELECTION SEEMED DIFFERENT. For starters, the inaugural meeting of the campaign committee took place not in the Pences' living room but in the Tea Room at the prestigious Columbia Club on Monument Circle in Downtown Indianapolis. Consultants from Washington attended. The National Republican Congressional Committee (NRCC) promised money. Pence's mother no longer handled FEC filings. And somewhere along the campaign trail, the candidate lost his way.

There had been no question that Pence would run again, having come unexpectedly close in the '88 race against incumbent Phil Sharp. Although George Bush pounded Michael Dukakis in the presidential race that year, Bush's victory did not translate into GOP success at the congressional level. Democrats retained control of both chambers of Congress. In the House of Representatives, where Democrats held a majority of 255 seats to 177, all but two incumbents—one from each party—were reelected. As it turned out, Pence had conducted one of the most successful, and therefore studied, races in the country, prompting even House minority whip Newt Gingrich to inquire about his campaign strategy.

As early as spring of 1989, Pence was mapping out his 1990 platform. He told friends his campaign would revolve around five Fs: free enterprise, family, faith, freedom, and fair elections. In June, he traveled to Washington DC to meet with Republican National Committee chairman Lee Atwater and Ed Rollins, co-chair of the NRCC. Rollins's job was to make Republicans competitive again in the House, where they'd been in the minority since 1955. If Republicans could gain thirty seats in 1990 and continue to make progress, Rollins figured they might be able to reclaim the majority by the mid-1990s. Perhaps Pence could play a part in their comeback.

Despite Pence's single-minded focus on Sharp, the party machine back home faced a quandary. Marion County Republican chairman John Sweezy, who talked Pence into running in 1988, had to manage the Goldsmith problem in 1990. Indianapolis prosecutor Stephen Goldsmith was eager to get his name back on the ballot after an unsuccessful run for lieutenant governor and an abortive campaign for the US Senate seat left vacant by the election of Vice President Dan Quayle. According to *Indianapolis Star* political writer Pat Traub, Goldsmith had created "a solid core of party leaders who would like to find some way to get him out of their hair."[1]

One possible solution had Goldsmith taking on Sharp in the Second District and Pence running for secretary of state against Democratic up-and-comer Joe Hogsett. Sweezy lined up considerable Marion County support for the idea and offered to pay for a public opinion poll to show how popular Goldsmith would be in the Second District.

The idea annoyed Pence, who'd made his intentions clear to all interested parties by Thanksgiving of 1989, a full year prior to the election. "I insisted then that I wasn't interested in running for anything else, and I was committed to this," he told a Muncie reporter.[2] In the end, Pence got his way. He ran unopposed in the Second District primary, and four-term Indianapolis mayor William Hudnut, barred from seeking a fifth term as mayor, ran for secretary of state. Goldsmith cooled his heels until he could pursue Hudnut's job one year later. (Hudnut would lose to Hogsett in one of the biggest surprises in modern Indiana political history. Goldsmith would go on to serve two terms as mayor.)

Because Pence came so close to Sharp in the previous election, the contest drew the national party's attention. Pence welcomed the support of Rollins and others at the NRCC and eagerly accepted advice from professional fund-raisers and pollsters. Even at that first meeting Pence deferred to their judgment, observed Hanover classmate Steger, who remembered the session clearly because he was first to arrive at the Columbia Club. No one else was there, not even Pence. Eventually Steger made a few calls to determine if he had written down the wrong meeting time or date. When he finally got ahold of Pence, the candidate explained that the consultants were running late because their plane had been delayed out of Washington.

It was obvious to Steger that the consultants didn't understand Pence's effectiveness as a one-on-one campaigner. They insisted that the key to victory was raising money for the airwaves, not direct voter contact. "I said to him, 'These guys are not playing to your strengths. You just need to be you, and people will like you.'" Steger was so adamant about it that he met up with Pence at his south-side gym early one morning and followed him around as he rotated through the weight machines. Whether Pence agreed with his old Hanover classmate or just wanted to placate him, Steger left reassured that he would be allowed to organize a ground game.[3]

By the next campaign meeting an hour later, things had changed. The consultants showed no interest in using Steger to head up a voter engagement program. At first, Steger sat quietly as advisers discussed fund-raising, marketing, and media strategy, but inside he fumed, "I can't spend this kind of time to sit on the bench." He closed his binder and walked out of the meeting.[4] From that point on, Steger's role was that of observer on the sidelines and occasional confidant.

Pence made his formal announcement on February 19, appearing in all eleven counties on the same day. By that point, he'd collected $150,000, a promising start in what would become a million-dollar race. "I am told by my friends in Washington that I have raised the most of any Republican congressional challenger in the country," he touted.[5] The next day, he held a rally at Muncie's Horizon Center, telling supporters, "This is a people's campaign, and I won't accept any money from any Washington lobbyist or special interest group. I will be nobody's congressman but yours, I promise you that."[6]

The PAC issue resonated with voters two years earlier, so Pence stuck with it, a decision that required him to devote much of his time to individual donor cultivation. As he demonstrated in 1988, Pence had a gift for raising money, and he and Sharp ran neck and neck. Pence explained his success with a familiar biblical quote: "Ask and ye shall receive, seek and ye shall find." Refusing PAC donations "has helped us in a strange way," he added. "Some people have contributed solely on the basis that I don't accept PAC money."[7] Final reports showed Pence raised $465,000 during calendar year 1990 compared to $529,000 for Sharp, a remarkable achievement considering Sharp's advantage as an incumbent and his extensive PAC connections.

Fund-raising was the only thing going right for the Pence team. In contrast to the previous campaign, with its naive optimism and unexpected successes, the 1990 effort displayed an aggressiveness bordering on desperation. At virtually every turn, Pence and his campaign staff attracted controversy. The first flare-up involved the campaign committee itself. The People for Mike Pence had been set up as a for-profit business under state law instead of as a nonprofit campaign committee. This gave the committee the ability to make contracts, borrow funds, and acquire stock, among other things, none of which were standard campaign practices. Dennis Lee, director of the Corporations Division at the Indiana secretary of state's office, said the arrangement was highly unusual if not unique. Campaign manager Sherman Johnson said the structure protected the candidate from legal liability in the event of a lawsuit and avoided the bureaucratic hassle of filing as a nonprofit. His explanation perplexed folks familiar with the relatively straightforward process of organizing candidate committees.

More likely, Pence thought the committee's for-profit status would be more appropriate for his plan to reimburse himself for living expenses while he ran for Congress, a decision that would come back to haunt him. Quarterly FEC reports showed that the campaign covered the Pences' $922 monthly mortgage, a $222 monthly payment on Karen's car, and about $1,500 in credit card bills, as well as sundry grocery bills, parking tickets, and golf greens fees. In an article in the *Daily Journal* of Johnson County, an FEC spokesman indicated the practice was legal as long as the expenditures were reported. Pence went a step further, saying, "It's the morally right thing to do for me because I believe a man ought to provide for his family."[8] Democrats immediately seized the issue. Billy Linville, Sharp's campaign manager, said, "The more that is known about Mike Pence, the stranger things get."[9]

In August, the Democratic Congressional Campaign Committee (DCCC) filed a formal complaint with the FEC against Pence and three other congressional candidates around the country who were claiming living expenses, all of them Republicans. One was Pence's friend Rick Hawks, a Baptist minister from Fort Wayne who was running for Congress against Jill Long in the Fourth District. Pence justified the practice as essential if nonincumbents were to wage competitive races. He had stopped working in January 1990 to run full time. Karen earned $35,753 as a teacher, and the couple had $50,000 in savings, but it was hardly enough to cover their costs.

The partisan wrangling overshadowed what could have been a legitimate issue for Pence and other challengers: the advantage enjoyed by incumbents in congressional elections. It is an insurmountable advantage 95 percent of the time, in large part because incumbents have staff, both in Washington and at home, working daily on behalf of the citizens they serve. Members receive full-time pay while running for reelection and travel back and forth to the capital on the taxpayers' dime. Challengers, in contrast, have to figure out how to pay their bills while running. Some go into personal debt in the process. As Pence noted, he wasn't a rich man. "Without being able to legally appeal to my campaign committee for basic living expenses my wife and I would have been forced to spend our entire life savings and take out a second mortgage on our house just to keep the bills paid."[10]

Although the incumbent advantage is well known, neither party has incentive to change things, and Democrats had no intention of giving Pence a pass. Their complaint accused him and the other three of violating the terms of the Federal Election Campaign Act (FECA) of 1971. The use of campaign funds for personal expenses "works a fraud on the campaign contributors," they charged, adding, "The commission must not allow this mockery of the campaign laws to continue."[11] The issue received intense publicity in the press, and the national party distanced itself from the campaign.[12] After some Republican voters expressed discomfort with the practice, Pence announced he would live off his savings. In news articles reporting Pence's decision, Sharp spokesman Bob McCarson noted the fact that Pence took a poll before doing so, which he said "shows that Mike Pence is a pure political animal: that before deciding that it's wrong and that it shouldn't be done, he has to take a poll."[13] The FEC didn't act on the complaint until a few weeks after the election, when the partisan commissioners deadlocked 3–3 on whether to proceed with an investigation. The case was closed on November 27.

More FEC complaints were in the pipeline. One alleged that Pence had illegally used a corporation to raise money. Campaign law prohibited businesses and labor unions from giving money directly to federal candidates. Two Indianapolis auto dealers were unaware of that restriction when they mailed a letter to about thirty of their peers urging donations "to this fine candidate who has a real chance to win." Ray Skillman and Gary Pedigo signed the letter written on stationery of Auto Auction, which Pedigo owned, thus creating a potential violation of the FECA. When contacted about it, Pedigo said, "What can I say? I didn't know any better."[14] Pence pledged to accept no donations that might have resulted from the letter.

A similar complaint was filed when Harcourt Outlines, a school supply company, urged its workers to give money to the Pence campaign. The company was co-owned by Jean Ann Harcourt, Second District GOP vice chairwoman, who admitted she failed to consult campaign finance laws when she sent a flier to employees inviting them to a weekend fund-raiser. "Hope you and your family can enjoy July 7 with Mike and his wife, Karen, while they are in Milroy. P.S. You are not limited to a $10 contribution. If you would like, you could give more money to Mike." The flier was distributed in the same envelope as the June 28 payroll. A few employees grumbled. When Rush County's Democratic prosecutor Ronald Wilson got wind of the invitation, he went straight to Sharp. With the campaign's encouragement, Wilson filed an FEC complaint that accused Pence of "resorting to political intimidation to illegally raise campaign money!" Pence was incensed that Wilson would use such language to call out a beginner's mistake and responded in kind: "The intimidation allegations are damnable slander."[15] Harcourt posted a note of apology on the company bulletin board, and the FEC threw out Wilson's complaint because of a filing error.

By this point, the two campaigns were locked in all-out war. The NRCC retaliated for the Harcourt complaint by filing a case against the Democrats. This one alleged that Wilson's legal work on the Harcourt case constituted an illegal in-kind contribution from his law firm, which had prepared the press release accusing Harcourt of illegally seeking money. The FEC eventually rejected both matters.

By far the biggest flap of the campaign involved a television ad that attacked Sharp's record on foreign oil. The ad depicted an Arab sheik standing against a sandy backdrop, wearing a black robe, white headdress, and sunglasses, and speaking in a feigned Middle Eastern accent. "My people would like to thank you Americans for buying so much of our oil," the speaker said.[16] "Luckily for me and my camels Sharp spent more time raising money from energy companies than he did on oil policy."[17] A long-standing rumor had Pence playing the sheik's role, which campaign manager Sherm Johnson categorically denied.[18] The spot closed with the Arab clasping his hands, adorned with gold rings, and blaming Sharp for increasing US oil dependence on Arab nations.

Complaints poured in. "It's a cheap shot," said George Irani, an Arab American instructor at Franklin College. The Washington-based Arab American Institute called on Pence to pull the ad off the air, calling it "offensive, demeaning, and inflammatory."[19] He refused. More than two hundred members of the Arab American community in Indianapolis gathered on October 13 at St. George Orthodox Church to protest. Jamal Najjab, field organizer for the Arab American Institute in Washington, addressed the rally and declared the ad an insult to 2.5 million Americans of Arabian descent.

Pence defended the ad's message, noting that imports of foreign oil had risen significantly over the past five years. While Pence did not consider the ad mean-spirited or callous, journalists took him to task for ethnic stereotyping. One of the harshest critiques came from liberal *In-*

*dianapolis Star* opinion columnist Dan Carpenter, who said it showed a cluelessness to the diversity of the electorate. "The depth of our society's ignorance of other peoples is dangerous indeed when even eager, young aspiring leaders are snared by stereotypes, the basis of propaganda, that essential weapon of war," Carpenter wrote.[20]

With so much time devoted to negative campaigning, there was little opportunity to discuss free enterprise, freedom, or any of the other issues Pence intended to make the focal point of his campaign. By the time Election Day arrived, only one debate had taken place, and it was almost called off when Pence objected to the political leanings of some of the questioners. Sponsored by the League of Women Voters on September 28 in Sharp's hometown of Muncie, the discussion demonstrated clear differences between the candidates on issues ranging from the Strategic Defense Initiative to energy policy to campaign finance reform. A second debate scheduled for October 5 at Columbus East High School—in Pence territory—was canceled when Sharp had to stay in Washington to deal with budget matters. The House had rejected a $500 billion deficit reduction package to keep the government operating, and members were told to stay on Capitol Hill should leadership reach an agreement.

At rallies and other campaign events, Pence stuck to popular conservative positions, including a strong national defense and balanced budgeting. He often appeared with a life-size fiberglass elephant, the symbol of the GOP, which was carried around on a flatbed trailer that a campaign volunteer had purchased at an auction. But it was a tough time to be a Republican.

President Bush, who campaigned in 1988 on a promise of "no new taxes," had made the fateful decision in 1990 to support a tax hike to lower the deficit, which became an issue in the off-year election. "I think George Bush is dead wrong if he thinks people will put up with more taxes," Pence said on the campaign trail. A journalist joked with Pence that Bush's slogan might as well have been, "Read my lips. No new Republicans," because it would likely doom GOP challengers on November 6. "We have been running a campaign on independence from the Washington establishment," Pence insisted.[21] He repeatedly tried to paint himself as an outsider who would go to Congress and do things differently. But his words belied his actions. County GOP officials griped that the Pence people were out of touch with local moods and attitudes, a complaint that campaign manager Johnson seemed to substantiate when he told a reporter, "The reason why we don't deal with the local people is because we have a national campaign. The local people don't understand what it takes."[22]

As the election got nearer, the tactics got uglier. On October 9, Pence accused Sharp of being an environmental hypocrite, a potentially damning charge considering Sharp's position as chairman of the House Energy and Power Subcommittee. The claim involved the proposed sale of the 130-acre Sharp family farm near Martinsville, Illinois, to the state of Illinois for use as a low-level nuclear waste facility. Sharp, his stepmother, and his two brothers were in line to split the $900,000 sales price and had already made $26,000 by selling the state an option on the land. Neighbors organized to fight the project, which they feared would pollute three aquifers under the land, including one that fed the public drinking well. Pence suggested that Sharp had used his leadership role to influence the site selection to benefit his family. The Illinois Department of Nuclear Safety, which oversaw the project, said Sharp had never contacted its office about the matter.

Thinking they had found Sharp's Achilles' heel, Pence's DC consultants crossed what should have been a clear ethical line. In the final days of the campaign, telemarketers claiming to represent local advocacy groups called thousands of potential voters in an effort to dissuade them from voting for Sharp. The callers said their organizations—Martinsville Environmental League and Family Services—had withdrawn support for Sharp and endorsed Pence. The groups were phony, and the callers were paid by a Utah telemarketing company called Matrixx Marketing. The ploy was what is known as a push poll, a form of negative campaigning that aims to affect election outcomes rather than survey voters on their opinions.

The callers asked voters if they supported Pence or Sharp. If the voter said Sharp, the caller read from a script attacking Sharp on either the environment or his support of abortion rights. The environmental script focused on the controversy surrounding the family farm in Illinois. It said: "We wanted you to know that for the first time the Martinsville Environmental League has withdrawn its support of Congressman Phil Sharp in the election Tuesday. We believe that because he's selling his family farm for a nuclear waste dump near here, he shouldn't get our vote on Tuesday. The Sharp farm nuclear dump could pollute the ground water supply and contaminate the agricultural crops near here. Also, Phil Sharp has taken campaign contributions from the big companies profiting from the nuclear waste dump."[23]

Details of the phony push poll emerged on the eve of the election. The *Daily Journal* of Johnson County broke the story about the "controversial phone blitz" on Election Day and quoted Pence spokesman Ed Sagebiel saying, "We don't know anything about it."[24] In a follow-up article a day later, a Matrixx Marketing official implicated members of Senator Dan Coats's campaign, in particular Mike Connell, his part-time director of voter programs, who had provided the scripts to Matrixx.[25] Within hours of that revelation, Michael Laudick, Coats's campaign manager, resigned and Connell was fired. Laudick had been volunteering his time and talents to Pence since 1988, when Pence tapped him to assist in fund-raising. Pence denied knowledge of the scheme. He said he had not read the scripts in advance and assumed the phone poll was a typical get-out-the-vote effort, an explanation many in the media doubted. "In the heat of the battle there are poor judgments made. The buck stops here, and I take full responsibility," Pence said.[26]

Unlike the earlier campaign blunders, this one could not be written off as bad judgment or a beginner's mistake. The Indiana Republican State Central Committee ordered audits to determine if any of its money had been used to underwrite the project. Coats, stunned to read of the involvement of his campaign staff, hired Indianapolis lawyer Daniel F. Evans Jr. to investigate. After a seven-week probe, Evans concluded that the push poll bordered on wire fraud, and he urged all future campaigns to refrain from doing them. He also found that the phone poll was Laudick's idea; Tony Payton, a consultant to the NRCC, wrote the script; and both Pence and his campaign manager, Sherm Johnson, knew of the telemarketing effort.

Although polling showed Sharp firmly in the lead, Pence continued to predict victory right up to the election, a claim based either on wishful thinking or youthful bravado. His defeat was worse than expected, 59 to 41 percent. Pence lost Johnson County, where he lived, and Bartholomew County, where he grew up, both of which supported him in '88.

Election night was a somber affair. Pence gave a polite concession speech at Jonathan Byrd's Cafeteria but afterward declined interviews with reporters. Jay Steger, at home watching the results on TV, jumped into his truck and headed to Greenwood when it became obvious Pence was going to lose badly. "At that point, I'm just being his friend. I'm going there to say, 'You got creamed. I love you, pal.'"[27] By the time Steger arrived, almost everyone else was gone. The Pences were ready to go home, and Steger gave them a lift in his black Chevrolet Suburban. Pence, quietly seething, said little during the ride home.

Sharp called the election results "a real rejection of trash politics."[28] In large measure, he was right. Sharp campaign polling right before the election found an electorate sick and tired of negativity, and Pence's TV ads in particular. Jeff Owen, editor of the *Daily Journal* in Franklin, put it succinctly: "The Mike Pence for Congress effort was a perfect example of how not to run a political campaign and should be included as such in every Political Science 101 college course textbook."[29]

Immediately after the election, Pence lashed out, blaming his defeat on Republican dissatisfaction with President Bush. "It wouldn't take a Rhodes Scholar to figure out that 1990 will be remembered as a darn near Democratic landslide."[30] For a midterm election, which typically favors the opposition party to the president, it could have been much worse. Republicans lost only eight seats in the House and one in the Senate. In comparison, four years later under President Clinton, Democrats lost fifty-two House and eight Senate seats. In the eyes of most Republicans, Pence's defeat was of his own making. He had been too negative, too reliant on the advice of outside consultants, and too focused on winning at any cost.

On November 21, the Columbus *Republic* published a letter to the editor from Pence that struck an almost remorseful tone. He promised in the days ahead to engage in self-reflection about negative campaigning in general and his role in particular. "In the give and take of a competitive congressional race both sides do the best they can to make their own case and dismantle their opponent's, but it still seems to me that we can do better. Not that our campaign didn't 'give as good as we got.' I honestly regret much of the tone of our content on both sides and believe that there must be a better way."[31] The letter went on to congratulate Sharp for a hard-fought win. It wasn't exactly an apology, but one was coming.

# 6

★ ★ ★

# FROM REPENTANCE
# TO REDEMPTION

IN LEWIS CARROLL'S *ALICE'S ADVENTURES IN WONDERLAND*, after falling down a rabbit hole in curious pursuit of adventure, Alice meets a caterpillar who asks, "Who are you?" She replies, "I—I hardly know, sir, just at present—at least I know who I was when I got up this morning, but I think I must have changed several times since then." For Mike Pence, whose life had been a model of integrity for the better part of three decades, the 1990 election had been a free fall down a rabbit hole, and the outcome was jarring. He had raised more money, worked harder, and drawn more attention than in the 1988 campaign, yet he had lost by a much wider margin, and his reputation as a good guy had suffered. The affable candidate of '88 now was credited with running the most negative campaign in Indiana history. As Pence reflected on the events of the previous year, he barely recognized the person described in media accounts of his race.

Senator Coats, meanwhile, attended to damage control. Although the Evans report identified no specific violations of law, the poison poll conducted on Pence's behalf under his staffers' supervision troubled him. As Coats and his press secretary, Curt Smith, flew back to Washington after the election, they discussed how things could have spun so wildly out of control. When Congress returned to session, Coats walked to the House floor and personally apologized to Representative Sharp. Some in his party urged Sharp to pursue legal action with the FEC, but the Muncie Democrat let the matter drop with Coats, his friend and a former House colleague.

Pence entered a period of contemplation and soul-searching. It wasn't the loss that upset him; it was the self-inflicted damage to his reputation. "Mike told me it was his seminal political moment," Curt Smith recalled. "He said, 'You call people and they don't call you back, not because you lost but because they don't think you're a good guy.' He knew he had somehow crossed the line in political ambition."[1]

Karen Pence allowed her husband to wallow briefly in self-reflection before telling him to "get off the couch and get a job."[2] But the thought of returning to legal practice held no appeal for Pence, whose passions were politics, policy, and communication. The ideal position would combine all three of those interests while allowing him to remain in the public eye and repair his reputation.

As it happened, the ideal job was about to materialize. Pence's friend Chuck Quilhot was ramping up a project designed to highlight the best in Indiana conservative thought. The Indiana Policy Review Foundation (IPR), incorporated a year earlier, had hired an editor to produce a journal featuring articles by free-market researchers and academics. In Quilhot's view, it was time to expand to become a full-fledged think tank. Pence's political views, which had been molded by G. M. Curtis at Hanover and William Harvey at IU Law, suited the foundation perfectly. Quilhot offered Pence a $50,000 salary plus expenses to become the first president of the IPR.

Pence had been involved with the think tank from the beginning in an advisory role. On December 7, 1988, an informal group of seven had gathered for breakfast at Acapulco Joe's in Indianapolis to explore the possibility of creating a magazine along the lines of *National Review*, the prestigious policy magazine founded by conservative icon William F. Buckley in 1955. Those present included Pence, Quilhot, Toby Mc-Clamroch, Jeff Terp, John Ruckelshaus, Steve Williams, and Sherm Johnson, who had been Pence's campaign manager in 1990. Over coffee and huevos rancheros, the men decided on next steps each would take to put the idea into action. Johnson and Quilhot agreed to draft a purpose statement, McClamroch and Ruckelshaus to make a list of policy issues to tackle. Williams, a lawyer, would investigate incorporation. All agreed that their creation should be independent from the Republican Party. "Our perspective is to create a quality conservative journal that we can get into the hands of Indiana's power brokers," Quilhot recorded in his daily planner.[3]

The Quilhot family was eager to underwrite the initiative because of a personal experience that had demonstrated to them the necessity of a robust conservative press. In 1988, Chuck's younger brother John was suspended from Dartmouth College while working as photo editor for the *Dartmouth Review*. The independent student-run newspaper accused a professor of inferior teaching, and staff members approached him in his classroom seeking a response. The professor claimed harassment. A disciplinary board sided with the instructor and sanctioned Quilhot and two other students. After serving his suspension, Quilhot returned to Dartmouth and became president of the *Review*. The episode reinforced Russ and Jeanette Quilhot's commitment to the First Amendment, which they felt was under attack at liberal institutions such as Dartmouth. In their view, their son John had been unfairly punished for his ideas and not his conduct.

With his family's financial backing, Chuck Quilhot moved ahead with his plan, assembling a high-profile advisory board that would add gravitas to the organization. Among its members were Russell Kirk, author of *The Conservative Mind*, which Pence would later cite as the second most influential book in his life after the Bible; syndicated columnist Cal Thomas; and Dinesh D'Souza of the American Enterprise Institute. D'Souza was a kindred soul whose credentials included editor of the *Dartmouth Review* and managing editor of *Policy Review*, the quarterly policy review of the conservative Heritage Foundation.

The IPR filed its articles of incorporation on January 19, 1989, with Quilhot as chairman. The founding members included six of the seven who had met at Acapulco Joe's (Ruckelshaus decided his interests lay more in elective politics) plus Craig Ladwig, the combative associate editor at the Fort Wayne *News-Sentinel*, and Byron Lamm, Quilhot's first cousin. The foundation declared as its mission the marshaling of "the best research on governmental, economic, and educational issues at the state and municipal level."[4]

In February, Quilhot, Ladwig, Johnson, and Williams traveled to Washington DC to network with other conservative organizations and thought leaders. D'Souza, who planned much of the itinerary, polled his colleagues at American Enterprise Institute about the best possible strategy for a start-up think tank. They recommended a model that the foundation uses to this day: commissioning research on local issues, translating the research into high-journalism essays for placement on op-ed pages, and hosting seminars to discuss the findings and policy implications.[5] The group's agenda in Washington included lunch at the White House with Juanita Duggan, special assistant to President George H. W. Bush, and meetings with the Catholic scholar/journalist Michael Novak, diplomat Alan Keyes, and Judge Robert Bork, President Reagan's unsuccessful 1987 nominee for the Supreme Court.

While there, the Hoosiers ran into Georgia congressman Newt Gingrich, who was just starting to move up in Republican leadership circles. Quilhot recognized him from across the street and shouted his name. During a brief sidewalk conversation, the Hoosiers asked what the first priority of a state think tank should be. Gingrich answered, "Education reform."[6] The conversations in Washington convinced the IPR founders that their plans were not only viable but also sound and that national figures would be receptive to speaking invitations in Indiana.

A few months later, Quilhot hired Ladwig to serve as editor in chief of the journal. Ladwig was a former Kansas City *Star* reporter who had twice experienced corporate takeovers of locally owned newspapers and was ready for a career change that would liberate him from what he felt was the groupthink of newspaper chains. The foundation set up its first office on the second floor of the Kendallville *News-Sun* in renovated space owned by newspaper publisher George Witwer Sr., a prominent Noble County Republican and kin to the South Bend Studebaker family. The foundation's first major study challenged the Indiana law allowing public sector collective bargaining. Following Gingrich's advice to focus on education, Ladwig hired D'Souza to do the second study on parental choice in the Fort Wayne public school system. After a year in donated space, the foundation was able to pay rent, and it moved to Fort Wayne, where Ladwig and Lamm lived.

While Ladwig was commissioning a first round of research papers, Pence was campaigning for Sharp's congressional seat. About a month before the election, Quilhot called Pence and asked him, "What are you going to do if you lose?" The question startled Pence, who, up to that point, had not entertained the idea of defeat. Quilhot pressed on: "If you do lose, would you be interested in joining Craig at the Policy Review?"[7] The conversation became a lifeline for Pence, who contacted Quilhot after the election to see if he had been serious about the offer. Quilhot was dead serious, and Pence began the new job on January 1, 1991.

With Ladwig overseeing the publishing and academic side and Pence the fund-raising and marketing, the IPR quickly became a formidable player in Indiana policy discussions. The foundation's public profile rose further when prominent scholars—including University of Notre Dame law professor Douglas Kmiec and Indiana University's William Harvey—signed on as senior fellows. By July of 1991, six months into Pence's term as president, the foundation had three thousand names on its mailing list, a $375,000 budget, and offices in Indianapolis and Fort Wayne. In 1991, the foundation hosted visits from William F. Buckley, Newt Gingrich, Cal Thomas, and P. J. O'Rourke.

Ladwig, who crisscrossed the state visiting newspapers, functioned almost like a wire service for opinion pages, distributing for statewide exposure well-researched articles on Indiana topics. There was high demand for the material because newspapers were beginning a wave of staff cuts that resulted in less local coverage of state and local government, especially on opinion pages. Ladwig's stable of writers included professors from Ball State University's department of economics, which was known for its expertise in public choice, the theory that political behavior can be explained using economic concepts such as supply and demand and cost and benefit. The most prolific of the group was Professor Cecil Bohanon, who brought to the IPR not only libertarian sentiments but deep knowledge of the economic ideas of Adam Smith and Frédéric Bastiat. The foundation prided itself on reporting "what nobody else is telling you"[8]—for example, that less than half the money spent in Indiana's largest school systems made it to the classroom for instructional purposes.

No article attracted as much attention as one Pence himself wrote in August of 1991 titled "Confessions of a Negative Campaigner." It was Pence's grand mea culpa for his disastrous 1990 campaign, especially the ad hominem attacks he leveled against Sharp over the potential sale of the family farm in Illinois for a nuclear waste site. Pence's commentary began with a Bible verse, 1 Timothy 1:15: "It is a trustworthy statement, deserving of full acceptance, that Christ Jesus came to save sinners, among whom I am foremost of all." Pence apologized for his tactics, not because negative campaigning isn't effective but because it distracts the candidate from a higher purpose—discussing issues and solutions that matter to the citizenry. He wrote:

> Negative campaigning is wrong. That is not to say that a negative campaign is an ineffective option in a tough political race. Pollsters will attest—with great conviction—that it is the negatives that move voters. The mantra of a modern political campaign is "drive up the negatives." That is the advice political pros give to Republican and Democratic candidates alike, even though negative ads sell better for Democrats. (My admittedly biased explanation is that Republican voters disregard a Democrat's negative ads as "predictable" while expecting a Republican to be "above that sort of thing.") But none of that explains my conversion. It would be ludicrous to argue that negative campaigning is wrong merely because it is "unfair," or because it works better for one side than the other, or because it breaks some tactical rule. The wrongness is not of rule violated but of opportunity lost. It is wrong, quite simply, to squander a candidate's priceless moment in history, a moment in which he or she could have brought critical issues before the citizenry, on partisan bickering.[9]

The essay drew intense speculation about Pence's future career plans. The *Indianapolis Star* editorial page called the confession refreshing in an "atmosphere of expensive 30-second sound bites where any discussion of serious issues is overwhelmed by the pursuit of trivia."[10] The *Daily Journal* of Franklin welcomed Pence's words but lamented the fact that none of the campaign workers responsible for the phony push poll were held responsible.[11] When the Muncie *Star*'s Brian Francisco asked Pence if he had personally apologized to Sharp, Pence said he had no intention to do so. "My opponent is really irrelevant to this equation. I'm talking about me."[12] Pence's answer led Francisco to wonder if the confession were the opening shot in a campaign to resurrect a political career. "By denouncing his past campaign style, is Mike Pence positioning himself for another run at elected office?" Pence's answer to that question was an equally definitive no. The 1990 campaign memories were too fresh, he was enjoying his work at the policy review, and—most important—after several years trying to conceive, Karen was "heavy with child," as he put it. The Pences were excited to start a family and put politics aside "for the foreseeable future."[13]

Not everyone saw Pence's confession as a positive first step in re-inventing himself. The *Indianapolis Star's* award-winning columnist Dan Carpenter, who had harshly criticized Pence's Arab sheik ad in the 1990 campaign, took another shot at him in a December 1, 1991, column about "right-wing think tanks." The column criticized both the nascent IPR and the globally minded Hudson Institute, which moved to Indianapolis in 1984 from Croton-on-Hudson, New York. After declaring right-wing think tanks "a contradiction in terms," Carpenter went on to suggest that Pence's days in politics were done: "Besides slapping our intelligence around with pro-pollution papers and 'free market' advice to countries ripe for exploitation, the think tanks function as retirement homes for washed-up Republicans such as failed congressional candidate Mike 'Ahab the Ay-rab' Pence."[14]

Carpenter opined that think tank scholars were not intellectuals but "political hustlers with lots of connections and reliable ideology." He further claimed that the organizations were funded largely by government and corporate grant money, which was far from reality for the IPR. The column drew a sharp response from Quilhot, who complained to *Star* managing editor Frank Caperton that Carpenter's column was biased and wrong. For one, the IPR received zero grant money from the government and less than 5 percent from corporations. Further, the labeling of the IPR as right-wing proved to Quilhot that Carpenter was more interested in stereotyping the organization than honestly evaluating its role as a nonprofit education foundation. The *Star* did not correct Carpenter's column but did run a handful of letters to the editor accusing Carpenter of "self-righteous criticism" and "monumental cynicism."[15]

To Carpenter's dismay, Pence proved to be anything but washed-up. With Pence at the helm, the think tank continued to grow—and make headlines. In 1992, the foundation lured Harvard-trained economist William Styring III from his position as vice president at the Indiana Chamber of Commerce to become research director. That same year, the foundation published *Indiana Mandate: An Agenda for the 1990s*,[16] designed to influence debates at the state legislative level. The book was a compilation of policy positions, essays, and public opinion surveys on issues of concern to Hoosiers, ranging from educational choice to tax code reform to sanctity of life.

One of the essays authored by Pence renounced partisan redistricting and gerrymandering and called for term limits for Indiana legislators, an idea supported by 69 percent of Hoosiers surveyed. Pence argued that gerrymandering, the drawing of district lines to favor the party in power, had essentially robbed Hoosier voters of meaningful choices at election time. The only way to overcome the incumbent advantage was to limit an incumbent's term, he argued. "By adopting term limits, Indiana would enhance not diminish the meaningful choices of democracy," he said.[17] Other policy positions in *Indiana Mandate* foreshadowed positions Pence would champion in his later political career. It urged a ban on abortion except in cases of rape, incest, or to save the life of the mother. It called for a balanced budget amendment to the state constitution, which Pence would advocate as governor. It recommended a statewide voucher system to bring competition to public schools, a program expanded during Pence's time in the statehouse. "That document represents Mike as well as anything," Ladwig observed.[18]

Another momentous event in 1992 affirmed for conservatives the wisdom of the state think tank movement: President George H. W. Bush's loss to Bill Clinton in the November election. During the 1980s, more than thirty-five such organizations had been created as President Reagan worked to dismantle federal programs and send money and policy decisions back to the states. Reagan himself had encouraged the idea and tasked his adviser Thomas Roe with setting up an um-brella group that could serve as clearinghouse and coordinator. With Clinton in the White House and Democrats in control of both houses of Congress, Republicans focused their attention on the newly created State Policy Network (SPN). Lamm and Pence were deeply involved in the coalition from the beginning. Noted Ladwig, "The rise of state think tanks has played a historic role in American politics, and Mike both recognized that early and played a huge part in developing it."[19] Lamm became the first executive director of the network, which was initially headquartered in Fort Wayne. Pence made dozens of friends through SPN at the state and national levels, many who would support his subsequent attempts at elective office and Republican leadership.

Even as Pence postured for a possible return to politics, he saw no reason to kowtow to party brass. Pence joked that the foundation alien-ated Democrats and Republicans equally. On issues of good govern-ment, the think tank called out deal making and crony capitalism on both sides of the aisle. The best example of this occurred in February 1993 when Pence individually and on behalf of the foundation filed a lawsuit against the Indiana General Assembly and all 150 of its mem-bers, challenging the notorious practice of logrolling—the merging of unrelated bills into a single piece of legislation to obtain enough votes for both. The lawsuit involved a controversial increase in lawmakers' pensions tucked into a bill that placed Indiana in compliance with the Americans with Disabilities Act (ADA). The measure passed at the eleventh hour of the 1992 General Assembly and took effect without the signature of Governor Evan Bayh, who objected to the pension hike but didn't feel he could veto the ADA language.

Notre Dame law professor Charles E. Rice, a member of the founda-tion's advisory board, wrote the legal briefs on Pence's behalf. He ar-gued that the law violated two sections of the Indiana Constitution con-cerning the legislative branch. The first, Article IV, Section 19, requires legislation "be confined to one subject and matters properly connected therewith," yet Senate Bill 29 quite obviously dealt with two unrelated subjects. The second, Article IV, Section 29, states that lawmakers may not increase their pay "during the session at which such increase may be made." The pension measure took effect the same year. Legal scholars felt the suit had merit; the Indiana Civil Liberties Union joined in as a friend of the court challenging the legislation. But Marion superior court judge James S. Kirsch showed no interest in second-guessing the legislative branch. Kirsch dismissed the suit, claiming—unconvincingly, in Pence's view—that the legislative pension hike and ADA measure were not completely unrelated because both addressed pensions in some fashion. Kirsch also rejected the pay raise challenge because lawmakers wouldn't actually receive higher benefits until they were eligible to draw their pensions after leaving the legislature.[20]

The IPR's appeal went directly to the state supreme court, where it fared no better. The court ruled 4–1 on June 20, 1995, that Pence, despite being a citizen of Indiana and a taxpayer, lacked standing or legal capacity to challenge the law in the first place. The court took a dim view of the role of citizens as watchdogs of government processes. "While the availability of taxpayer or citizen standing may not be foreclosed in extreme circumstances, it is clear that such status will rarely be sufficient," Justice Roger DeBruler wrote for the majority. "For a private individual to invoke the exercise of judicial power, such person must ordinarily show that some direct injury has or will immediately be sustained." Pence had made no such showing, the court found.[21]

In his dissent, Justice Brent Dickson lambasted his colleagues for setting an impossibly high bar for citizens objecting to legislative actions. He wrote, "I believe that plaintiff Pence has standing as an Indiana taxpayer to challenge the constitutionality of the expenditure of public funds by state officials under the statute in question." Dickson went on to comment about the underlying issue in the IPR lawsuit—the constitutionality of logrolling. It was clear to the justice that the authors of the state constitution considered the one-subject requirement necessary to safeguard the integrity of the legislative process. They did not want lawmakers making deals with each other behind closed doors. Unfortunately, Dickson said, the court had "often permitted the legislature's combination of questionably related subjects into a single act."[22] It would take a compelling case and a great deal of judicial will-power to change things, he said, and Pence's case apparently was not compelling enough.

The lawsuit, although unsuccessful, put a spotlight on the IPR and proved it was no mere facade for the Indiana Republican Party as some had predicted it would become. The lawsuit had infuriated lawmakers in both parties. By February 1993, the foundation had seven paid staff members and a half-million-dollar budget. Its mailing list had grown to five thousand, and its journal boasted a new glossy, professionally designed cover. That year, the foundation hosted talks and receptions with conservative celebrities Russell Kirk, Mona Charen, and Robert Woodson.

With rapid growth, however, came a host of new challenges. Bigger staff meant more demands on Pence to raise money. Yet it became harder for Pence to raise money from establishment and chamber of commerce Republicans. The former distanced themselves from the IPR when Quilhot and Pence objected publicly to Senator Richard Lugar's vote to confirm Dr. Joycelyn Elders as surgeon general in September 1993. Elders's selection by President Clinton was controversial because of her strong pro-abortion views and statements favoring condom distribution in public schools. In the December issue of the journal, Quilhot publicly called on Lugar to retire, saying he had "used up the trust of that group of Hoosiers on whose backs you built your career."[23] The attack on a beloved senator made moderate Republicans cringe.

The pro-business establishment was equally frustrated with the foundation's opposition to tax incentives for economic development—so-called corporate welfare—including handouts to professional sports teams like the Indianapolis Colts. At one point, Pence asked Quilhot if he could hire an additional fund-raiser and a consultant to work on direct mail solicitations to boost membership. The idea did not go over well with Quilhot, whose family had given generously to the foundation in hopes it would become self-supporting. By the last quarter of 1993, the relationship between Pence and the foundation's four-member board had soured, and Pence was exploring new opportunities in print and broadcast media.

It was clear to all parties that Pence's future no longer lay with the IPR. For three years, it had been a welcome port in a storm, rescuing Pence from the self-doubt and melancholy that followed his 1990 electoral loss. In return, Pence had helped build the IPR into a credible voice on Indiana policy and governance. Both sides had leveraged all they could from the relationship.

A December memo from Quilhot to Pence stated, "As much as I want you on board I am convinced the immense skills and desires you have do not match the current needs of the Indiana Policy Review."[24] Pence resigned as president of the foundation on January 31, 1994, telling acquaintances that "differences of opinion" with the board caused his departure.[25] In an interview with Muncie reporter Francisco, the soon-to-be syndicated talk show host said his interests lay more with public policy debate while the board wanted to focus on research and analysis. He also hinted that Quilhot's call for Lugar to retire had rubbed Republicans the wrong way and put Pence in a tough spot.[26] Considering Pence's own criticism of Lugar a few months earlier, his comment made clear he was starting to place his own political future over the foundation's. Regardless, it was an amicable parting. His colleagues at the IPR had every reason to believe that Pence would continue to battle for the same conservative principles they advocated, wherever his next job might take him.

# 7

★ ★ ★

## "GREETINGS ACROSS THE AMBER WAVES OF GRAIN"

A COLD WINTRY NIGHT CONFRONTED IOWA REPUBLICANS AS they assembled in schools, churches, and fire stations for the first round of the 1996 presidential campaign season. The Iowa caucuses, newsworthy because they occur first, give the Hawkeye State excessive influence in choosing a president, often forecasting the eventual nominees. Senator Bob Dole claimed the win as expected, while conservative columnist Pat Buchanan, according to the *Des Moines Register*, enjoyed "the biggest bounce."[1] Indiana senator Richard Lugar, admired as he was in his home state, placed a distant seventh in a field of nine. Democrats conducted no caucuses because President Clinton was unopposed for reelection.

The next morning, Mike Pence was on the air, broadcasting live from WKBV-AM in Richmond, Indiana. "Welcome to the only talk radio show *in* Indiana that goes *to* Indiana on a regular basis. This is *The Mike Pence Show*." In his recognizable Rush Limbaugh cadence, studiously modeled after the new conservative talk show sensation from Sacramento, Pence analyzed caucus results while inviting feedback from his two hundred thousand daily listeners. "We have *got* to talk about Iowa yesterday—absolutely extraordinary results from the Iowa caucus."[2] As host of *The Mike Pence Show*, broadcast daily across Indiana from 9:00 a.m. to noon, Pence had developed a reputation as a knowledgeable pundit. And no topic engaged his passion quite like presidential politics.

Pence was broadcasting this particular show on the road. The occasion was IU Radio Day, an annual affair that raised money for scholarships for deserving Wayne County students attending Indiana University's Richmond or Bloomington campus. The program followed a standard formula: discuss the day's news, take calls, interview guests, promote a good cause, make political points without being angry about it, offer a bit of sports commentary, and do an impersonation or two (Bill Clinton and Limbaugh were favorite targets). The February 13 show also featured a live auction to benefit the scholarship fund, selling to the highest bidder such auction favorites as Caribbean trips, sports tickets, and signed basketballs from IU coach Bob Knight and Purdue's Gene Keady.

Back in his law school days, Pence could not have foreseen earning a living as a full-time radio host. He had considered law the best preparation for government service, and, indeed, it had sharpened his ability to argue competing sides of an issue. But his interactions with news media during his first congressional race opened his eyes to the power of the press to promote not just politicians but also their ideas.

Louis and Sharon Disinger, who ran WRCR-FM in Rushville, met Pence during his first campaign in 1988 and suggested he'd make a good talk show host. "I reminded him that Ronald Reagan had also lost a bid for office and done a radio show to keep his name out there," Sharon Disinger recalled.[3] The Disingers offered Pence a thirty-minute weekly show called *Washington Update with Mike Pence*. On Saturday mornings, Pence drove from his home in Indianapolis to Rushville and filled the time slot with discussion and analysis of national issues. The Disingers sat with Pence after each show to replay it and offer tips for improvement.[4] About the same time, the ABC Radio Network offered Missouri-born Limbaugh a nationally syndicated program, which quickly became the highest-rated show on the air. Pence immediately sought to emulate Limbaugh, Louis Disinger said. "When he started off he had the gift of gab, but he was mimicking Rush. It took a while before his true personality came out."[5]

In late 1992, while working at the IPR, Pence again ventured into talk radio, hosting an hour-long public affairs show on Friday afternoons that aired on a small Christian station in Plainfield, Indiana. Program officials from nearby WNDE-AM happened to hear the show and invited Pence to bring the program to their station to run on Saturday mornings, a move that ensured a much wider audience. Featuring conservative commentary and interviews with local politicians, this was the precursor to what would be syndicated as *The Mike Pence Show*.

In 1994, after Pence stepped down from his position at the think tank, he approached Network Indiana with the idea of going statewide. Founded in 1972, Network Indiana was a news service that fed audio material to radio stations that belonged to the Indiana Broadcasters Association. Pence, who had already received commitments from two stations to carry the show, proposed a live, three-hour talk format that would air from 9:00 a.m. to noon and lead directly into the noon to 3:00 p.m. slot filled by Limbaugh on many stations across the state. Pence wanted to be like Limbaugh but without the combativeness. He would later refer to himself as "Rush Limbaugh on decaf."

Scott Uecker, creator of the Network Indiana broadcast news agency, coincidentally was looking for ways to grow the network and had started to explore options for long-form programming, such as talk shows that lasted an hour or more. After listening to a cassette tape of Pence sent by Pam Ferrin, WNDE program director, Uecker agreed to give Pence a chance. "I've always said about talk shows, when you're putting them together: People have to welcome you into their lives. You have to provide something that gives them a reason to spend time with you," Uecker said. "Mike was very good at that."[6]

Uecker had another idea that he hoped would complement *The Mike Pence Show* and further Network Indiana's statewide profile. He called up his old friend Bob Lovell, former basketball coach at IUPUI, and suggested he host a three-hour sports talk show that would air on Friday and Saturday nights from 9:00 p.m. to midnight. "We've already spent the money to do a statewide political show," Uecker told Lovell. "Yours will be a call-in show, and the number is going to be 1-800-603-MIKE."[7] Lovell's show would quickly surpass Pence's in the number of stations served statewide, but the two would continue to share the same call-in number.

Pence launched the syndicated radio show on April 11, 1994, with eight stations signed on as partners. Lovell's show went live in August. At the time, the network was owned by Wabash Valley Broadcasting Corporation, the media enterprise of the Hulman family of Indianapolis Motor Speedway fame. Pence divided his seventy-hour workweek between his home on the south side of Indianapolis, the Network Indiana studio on the north side, and his car, often taking Lovell with him to visit potential affiliates. The two were on a constant quest to sign up new stations and had particular success in the district where Pence had run for Congress. At its peak, *The Mike Pence Show* aired on eighteen affiliates from WPCO in Evansville in the south to WAKE in Valparaiso just south of Chicago.

Steve Hall, *Indianapolis Star* radio and TV critic, called the show "hokey,"[8] and in some ways, it was. Pence would open segments with his trademark phrases, including "Welcome back to the never-a-dull-moment radio network" and "Greetings across the amber waves of grain." The latter slogan, featured on motorists' license plates in the mid-1990s, would resurface a few years later in Pence campaign ads.

A typical day found Pence up by 5:30 reading the newspapers and Associated Press wires to prepare. Guests covered the gamut and routinely featured people with whom he disagreed, such as Stan Jones, a former Democratic legislator and higher education commissioner; former Democratic Party chairwoman Ann Delaney; and Harrison Ullmann, editor of the progressive weekly newspaper *NUVO*. Ullmann never hesitated to join Pence, whom he considered "respectful of facts, unlike some of his colleagues at that end of the spectrum."[9] Pence's reliance on Ullmann, whose opinions were always liberal, upset one conservative radio affiliate so much that it gave Pence an ultimatum: stop inviting Ullmann to be a guest, or we won't run your show. "I refused, because

I want my show to be fair, civil, and open to all sides of an issue," Pence said.[10] WXLW-AM followed through with its threat and canceled the program in November 1995.

In contrast to Limbaugh, whose listening style has been described by one communications scholar as rhetorical "dismissiveness,"[11] Pence was deliberate in trying to understand the perspective of callers and guests on the other side. "My obligation first as a Christian is to try to respect that person," Pence explained. "There's a great misunderstanding out there about that. If you can't disagree and maintain some civility, then forget democracy."[12]

Producer Todd Meyer, who worked with Pence from 1998 to 1999, said it was never difficult to book guests on the political left, even though Pence himself billed the program as "Indiana's only conservative talk radio broadcast."[13] "His was a statewide political show, and people wanted to be on it."[14] Open-phone Fridays coincided with casual dress day at the station, which for Pence meant tailored slacks not jeans. Pence invited listeners to call in their opinions and let folks have their say before chiming in. "As opposed to Rush Limbaugh, Mike could have a completely different view of an issue and still have an intelligent conversation about it," said Emily Mantel, sales manager during the first years of *The Mike Pence Show*. "Even when he had to interrupt guests, he was always polite."[15]

After his disastrous 1990 campaign and subsequent "Confessions of a Negative Campaigner," Pence established for himself a bright line policy to govern his commentary: no ad hominem attacks. He applied the rule religiously to his talk show. "Conservative media, including Rush, have a tremendous blind spot when it comes to making a distinction between differences in public policy and personal differences," Pence said.[16] His policy did not deter pointed commentary on political, economic, and even moral behavior.

In May of 1997, Pence devoted a segment to the case of First Lieutenant Kelly Flinn, who'd resigned the previous day from the US Air Force rather than face a court-martial for having an affair with a married civilian, "a disgrace of the armed forces," according to the charge filed against her.[17] Public opinion, including that of a few leading members of Congress, mocked her superiors for applying old-fashioned values to oust a highly qualified service member, the first female B-52 pilot in the air force. Republican senator Trent Lott called on the air force to "get real." But Pence presented a different view. "Is adultery no longer a big deal in Indiana and in America?" he asked his listeners. "Would just love to know your thoughts. I, for one, believe that the seventh commandment contained in the Ten Commandments is still a big deal."[18]

Humor lightened the mood when political discussions became heavy. In late 1995, Pence warned Democratic governor Evan Bayh to prepare for harder questions than the usual. Because Bayh and his wife, Susan, were expecting twins at the time, Pence surprised him with a pop quiz to see how much he knew about parenthood. Bayh flunked the test, to Pence's delight, after failing to define Pence-family words *binky* (pacifier) and *woobie* (blanket).[19] A favorite Pence schtick was a top-five list similar to the top-ten list made famous by Hoosier comedian David Letterman. Pence once warned his audience that some of the "top five signs your child is about to become a Republican" were when he "begins wearing double-breasted pinstripes to school" and "asks what his allowance will be after taxes."[20]

Pence discussed sports with as much fervor as politics, whether baseball, football, or his favorite topic, the Indianapolis 500. On September 6, 1995, Baltimore Orioles shortstop Cal Ripken Jr. played in his 2,131st consecutive game, breaking Lou Gehrig's record for most consecutive games played. The next day, Pence took on all the hoopla. "Somebody *puh-leeeease* call me and explain what the big deal is about a guy who shows up for work three or four days a week, maybe three hours at a time, six months out of the year and gets paid $5.9 million to do it," he implored his listeners.[21] During the month of May, Pence regularly commented on the qualification sessions for the Indy 500, which he had attended almost yearly since childhood. On this subject, unlike most others, Pence abandoned all hint of objectivity to promote the race, the drivers, and the crowds.

Although Pence was a salaried employee, he took special interest in advertisers, understanding that his show's future was tied directly to their willingness to buy blocks of time on Network Indiana. Pence would go on sales calls with Network employees and often invited sponsors to visit the studios. Mantel said many of the advertisers she represented were nonprofit organizations that benefited from the relationship because Pence would talk about their good works between program segments.[22]

For Pence, sales calls required the same skills that he had developed during his two failed political campaigns and his tenure at the think tank. First, he would promote himself and then the benefits of sponsorship. "Mike would set it up. We'd go have lunch," said Russ Dodge, who succeeded Mantel as sales manager in 1995. More often than not, it worked. After Pence and Dodge shared a meal with Howard Hubler, the Hubler Automotive Group signed up for a year's worth of thirty-second spots. Hubler, Hofmeister Personal Jewelers, and Golden Rule Insurance were frequent advertisers, and the owners of all three would later become Pence campaign contributors.

Pence loved taking the show on the road in collaboration with his program sponsors. During the summer of 1995, he joined Indiana's Operation Pullover at stops in Anderson and Bedford to make sure Hoosiers buckled up. Bob Evans Restaurants sponsored a "Breakfast with Mike" series at restaurants in Richmond and Huntington, during which he'd chat with local citizens. By far his favorite road show occurred each year at the Indiana State Fair. He would ride the shuttle, hopping off at various stops to talk to visitors and vendors. First priority was the American Dairy Association's Dairy Bar. Pence never missed ordering a chocolate milkshake.

By 1996, *The Mike Pence Show* aired on seventeen stations and had become a popular forum for politicians in pursuit of voters. Indiana had an open seat for governor that year, and candidates turned to Network Indiana for both earned media and paid advertisement time. Democrat Frank O'Bannon, hoping to replace the popular Bayh, who was barred from seeking a third term, accepted every invitation from Pence to go on the air. After his decisive election over Republican Steve Goldsmith, he told an acquaintance that he credited his popularity, in part, to the middle-of-the-road voters he reached on Pence's program.[23] In the six weeks leading up to the election, the network's ad inventory completely sold out, with some $250,000 in revenue coming from political ads. During that period, Network Indiana's profits were directly tied to Pence's success.

The year 1997 was a turning point for *The Mike Pence Show* and *Indiana Sports Talk*. In August, Emmis Communications, the nation's ninth-largest radio group, purchased Network Indiana. Pence and Lovell moved to Emmis's new world headquarters on Monument Circle, a seven-story building with soaring atrium and state-of-the-art digital technology, a far cry from the modest Wabash Valley studio that used the Pence family kitchen table as a microphone stand. Emmis owned the 50,000-watt WIBC-AM (1070), the number-one news station in Indianapolis, on which Pence desperately wanted to air his show. It did but on tape delay from midnight to 3:00 a.m., not live as Pence had envisioned. "There was no other place to put it," said Jon Quick, WIBC / Network Indiana director of operations from 1995 to 2009. At the time, WIBC aired the nationally syndicated *Dr. Laura Program* during morning drive time. "It was getting incredibly high ratings for us," Quick said. "We didn't want to change that."[24]

Pence's office was right next to that of Dave "The King" Wilson, one of WIBC's best-known personalities. Pence came off the air each day just as Wilson arrived, so the two would lunch together at a nearby pasta place to talk business and family. The friendship endured after Pence left radio for politics. Congressman Pence would return to Indianapolis in August during the state fair and join Wilson's afternoon talk show for an hour or two. "We'd stop at the pig barn and talk to the pig farmers," Wilson said. Later, when Pence decided to run for governor, Wilson emceed his announcement rally in Columbus.[25]

As Pence became increasingly comfortable on radio, he took over a Saturday morning call-in show on WIBC and expanded to television. The TV version of *The Mike Pence Show* debuted on September 23, 1995, on WNDY-TV (Channel 23) in Indianapolis, owned by Wabash Valley. The program, whose purpose was "to entertain and inform, in that order," aired in Indianapolis at 7:00 p.m. on Saturdays and was carried on cable systems in Fort Wayne, Terre Haute, Evansville, and Northwest Indiana.[26]

Wabash Valley CEO Chris Duffy hatched the idea for the show and loosely modeled it after *This Week with David Brinkley*, which featured correspondents interviewing guest newsmakers followed by opinionated roundtable discussions. Pence wanted to add humor to the highbrow talk and did so by throwing in an occasional joke or glib comment, beginning with his own introduction as "the man who would have been the next James Bond, if his mom would have let him."[27] After the first airing, critic Steve Hall gave "central Indiana's nice-guy conservative" a solid review: "The TV show's a slick affair with splashy, computer-generated opening credits, a studio audience, and an ultramodern set dominated by a blue glass wall," Hall said. "Pence took his ideas and values seriously, but not himself."[28]

The format served Pence well, forcing him to dig deeply into thorny issues that would repeat themselves throughout his political career. During the summer and fall of 1998, the independent counsel investigation of President Bill Clinton was a popular topic though Pence rarely injected personal opinion into the discussion, leaving more subjective analysis to his guests. His standard practice was to invite two commentators from different ends of the political spectrum and one who could offer historical context, often his old Hanover mentor, G. M. Curtis.

Pence also hosted a few episodes of *Indy-TV After Dinner*, an entertaining cross between Dick Cavett interviews and Robin Leach's *Lifestyles of the Rich and Famous*. The program grew out of a hallway exchange between Pence and Chris Duffy, who thought it would be educational for viewers to probe business and civic leaders about the habits that led to their success. The quarterly special premiered at 10:30 p.m. on October 27, 1996, taped in the private dining room of Tomisue and Stephen Hilbert after guests had dined on an elegant dinner of fried ravioli salad, pan-seared salmon, and a medley of desserts.

The inaugural show featured an A-list of Indianapolis business leaders. In addition to Hilbert, the chairman and CEO of Conseco, the group included banker/publisher Mickey Maurer; PSI Energy president John Mutz; Eli Lilly and Company's Mitch Daniels; Fred S. Klipsch of the consumer electronic manufacturer; CEO Charlotte Fischer of Paul

Harris Stores; and Chris Duffy of Wabash Valley Broadcasting. Pence asked the guests to talk about what they valued most in life, and then they went around the table describing their company profiles. Pence said he hoped the show had given a human face to the people who make Indiana's economy thrive. From that group, Pence made lasting connections; Klipsch, Mutz, and Hilbert each played significant roles in future Pence political endeavors.

During the radio and TV years, Pence also produced a monthly newsletter, the *Pence Report*, under the copyright Hoosier Conservative. A subscription cost $19.95 a year, and Pence had 250 subscribers. The newsletter summarized past shows, previewed future ones, and featured Pence commentary about issues in the news. In the August 15, 1995, edition, Pence reported on his attendance at the annual Republican State Dinner at the RCA Dome with keynote speaker Newt Gingrich. Pence described his company as memorable—he and Karen sat with Jim and Corinne Quayle, the parents of former vice president Dan Quayle—but he found Gingrich's remarks lacking. Gone was the firebrand who came to power during the Reagan revolution of the '80s, Pence said, replaced by "Santa Newt, waving to the crowd of adoring Republicans who knew little of the gut 'em and leave 'em politicians of days gone by." Pence's article was headlined, "I want the old Newt back."[29]

By this time, Limbaugh had succeeded Gingrich as Pence's inspiration. From the comfort of the studio, Pence watched with alarm as Republicans searched for their identity in the age of Clinton. His radio and TV shows and his newsletter gave Pence a statewide platform from which to analyze the Clintons and Congress. On the night of the Republican State Dinner in 1995, Pence was not yet contemplating another run for Congress. *The Mike Pence Show* was flourishing. It had a record number of advertisers, and he was thoroughly enjoying both his family and career.

Over time, the political ambition would resurface. Four years later, Pence and Lovell were on a road trip seeking new affiliates in Northern Indiana when Pence confided he was considering a return to politics.

He had invested so much time, money, and effort into the radio show that he was reluctant to give it up. But an opportunity had arisen, and he was giving it serious thought.

"What do you think, Bob? I really value your opinion," Pence asked him.

Lovell, known for straight talk bordering on abruptness, looked Pence in the eyes and said, "If you're going to be a dumb ass like you were the last time, you probably shouldn't do it. But if you learned your lesson like you say you have, I think you can win."[30]

UNITED STATES OF AMERICA
PETITION FOR NATURALIZATION        No.
No.30,040

# UNITED STATES OF AMERICA

### DECLARATION OF INTENTION
(Invalid for all purposes seven years after the date hereof)

UNITED STATES OF AMERICA, | In the ........ DISTRICT ........ Court

NORTHERN DISTRICT OF ILLINOIS | THE UNITED STATES of CHICAGO.

I, ...... RICHARD MICHAEL CAWLEY,

now residing at ...... 5521 So. Honore Street, Chicago, Illinois, ......
occupation ...... motorman ......, aged ...33... years, do declare on oath that my personal description is:
Sex ...... male ......, color ...... white ......, complexion ...... fair ......, color of eyes ...l. blue ......
color of hair ...d. brown ......, height ...5... feet ...9... inches; weight ...160... pounds; visible distinctive marks
...... none.

race ...... Irish ......; nationality ...... British ......
I was born in ...... Sligo, Ireland, ...... on ...... February 13, 1903,
I am ...... married. The name of my wife or husband is ...... Mary ......
we were married on ...... August ...1930..., at ...... Chicago, Illinois, ......; she or he was
born at ...... Chicago, Illinois ......, on ...... March 22, 1907, ......, entered the United States
at ...... with me. ......, on ......, for permanent residence therein, and now
resides at ...... with me. ...... I have ...two... children, and the name, date and place of birth,
and place of residence of each of said children are as follows:
...... Mary Ellen born Oct. 30, 1931;
Anne Jane born Nov. 28, 1932; both born at and now residing
at Chicago, Illinois.
I have ...... heretofore made a declaration of intention: Number ......, on ...October, 1923,
at ...... Chicago, Illinois, ......
my last foreign residence was ...... Ashton in Makerfield, England,
I emigrated to the United States of America from ...... Liverpool, England.
my lawful entry for permanent residence in the United States was at ...... New York, New York,
under the name of ...... Richard Cawley ......, on ...April 11, 1923,
on the vessel ...... Andania

I will, before being admitted to citizenship, renounce forever all allegiance and fidelity to any foreign prince, potentate, state, or sovereignty, and particularly, by name, to the prince, potentate, state, or sovereignty of which I may be at the time of admission a citizen or subject; I am not an anarchist; I am not a polygamist nor a believer in the practice of polygamy; and it is my intention in good faith to become a citizen of the United States of America and to reside permanently therein; and I certify that the photograph affixed to the duplicate and triplicate hereof is a likeness of me: So HELP ME GOD.

Richard Cawley

(The seal of the court will be impressed so as to cover a portion of the photograph)

Richard Michael Cawley

Subscribed and sworn to before me in the office of the Clerk of said Court,
at Chicago, Illinois this 28th day of July
anno Domini 19..36. Certification No.11 150508 from the Commissioner of Immigration and Naturalization showing the lawful entry of the declarant for permanent residence on the date stated above, has been received by me. The photograph affixed to the duplicate and triplicate hereof is a likeness of the declarant.

[SEAL]

HENRY W. FREEMAN, Clerk of the ...... DISTRICT ...... Court.
......, Deputy Clerk.

Form 2202—L-A
U. S. DEPARTMENT OF LABOR
IMMIGRATION AND NATURALIZATION SERVICE

No. 44025

Richard Michael Cawley, Pence's grandfather, immigrated to the United States in 1923 and filed this "Declaration of Intention" to become a citizen in 1936. He became a naturalized American citizen on March 19, 1941. (*National Archives and Records Administration.*)

The Pence boyhood homes in Columbus reflected the family's growing prosperity as Ed Pence moved up the ranks at Kiel Brothers Oil Company. (*Photos by Andrea Neal.*)

Columbus North High School speech coach Debbie Shoultz gave
Mike Pence the "Speaker of the Year" award at the 1977 end-of-
year banquet. Photo from 1977 yearbook, *The Log. (Courtesy of
Bartholomew Consolidated School Corp. Additional use is not
allowed without written permission of BCSC.)*

*Facing top,* Pence, pictured with Mike Stevens, dated his
acceptance of Christ as his personal savior to 1977 when he
answered an altar call at a Christian music festival in Kentucky.
*(Photo courtesy of Jay Steger.)*

*Facing bottom,* Pence helped raise money for the Arthritis
Foundation by reading fortunes at a Greek fundraiser at
Hanover College. *(Photo from Revonah yearbook,
courtesy of Hanover College.)*

The student Christian fellowship group Vespers met weekly on Tuesday evenings and often featured Pence at the guitar. *(Photos from Revonah yearbook, courtesy of Hanover College.)*

Mike Pence's Hanover senior photograph. *(Courtesy of Hanover College.)*

Michael R. Pence

*Below,* Chosen by his peers, Mike Pence gave the senior commencement speech at his May 1981 graduation from Hanover College. *(Courtesy of Hanover College.)*

# Mike Pence.
## Congress '88

- Born and raised in Columbus, Indiana
- Bachelor of Arts Degree in History, Hanover College, Hanover, Indiana
- Doctor of Jurisprudence, Indiana University School of Law
- Successful Attorney
- Nationally recognized public speaker
- Republican Precinct Committeeman, Roundtable Member, G.O.P. Club
- Married—Wife, Karen is an elementary school teacher

Mike and Karen Pence greeted William Harris of Winchester on the candidate's 1988 bicycle tour through the 2nd Congressional District. *(Darron Cummings/*The Republic, *Columbus.)*

*Facing top*, Flier from Pence's first campaign for Congress in 1988. *(Courtesy of Jay Steger.)*

*Facing bottom*, Phi Gamma Delta chapter president J. Alex Smallwood, class of 2018, takes visitors past the room occupied by Mike Pence when he was a Fiji brother at Hanover. *(Photo by Andrea Neal.)*

William F. Buckley posed with early leaders of the Indiana Policy Review Foundation. Left to right: Rick Hawks, Chuck Quilhot, Craig Ladwig, Byron Lamm, Buckley, Brian Pointer, Mike Pence. *(Photo courtesy of Craig Ladwig.)*

*Facing*, A fiberglass elephant accompanied Mike Pence to events and rallies during the 1990 campaign for Congress. *(John Sheckler/*The Republic, *Columbus.)*

Mike Pence liked to lighten the mood on his daily radio show with jokes, impersonations, and Looney Tunes ties. (*With permission from Art Vuolo, Jr.*)

*Facing top*, Congressman Pence delivered the commencement address and received an honorary doctorate of laws from Hanover in 2008, reuniting with Phi Gamma Delta brother Dan Murphy, a Hanover history professor. (*Photo courtesy of Dan Murphy.*)

*Facing bottom*, Pence spoke on the House floor for the last time as a congressman on December 20, 2012: "As a boy I dreamed of some day representing my hometown in our nation's capital, and twelve years ago the people of the Sixth Congressional District made that dream a reality," he said. (*C-SPAN.*)

Mike Pence brought 100 supporters and 13,000 signatures to a February 9, 2012, news conference prior to filing his candidacy papers for the office of Indiana governor. *(Photo courtesy of Jeff Cardwell.)*

Mike Pence became Indiana's 50th governor on the steps of the statehouse on January 14, 2013. *(Photo courtesy of Ed Simcox.)*

Governor Pence assisted with an August 2015 Habitat for Humanity home build in Gary, Indiana, with aide Jeff Cardwell and Gary Mayor Karen Freeman-Wilson. *(Photo courtesy of Jeff Cardwell.)*

*Facing,* Every Halloween, Mike and Karen Pence sponsored the Governor's Great Pumpkin Patch to raise money for the Midwest Food Bank. Pence put his caricature drawing skills to use on a pumpkin purchased by Bill McCleery at the October 2015 event. *(Photos courtesy of Bill McCleery.)*

*Above,* The Rev. David Mary Engo, a Franciscan priest from Fort Wayne, greeted Governor Pence at a 2015 rally sponsored by supporters of the controversial Religious Freedom Restoration Act. *(Photo courtesy of Curt Smith.)*

*Right,* After signing the Religious Freedom Restoration Act into law on March 26, 2015, Governor Pence autographed some bill copies and gave the pen to Indiana Family Institute president Curt Smith. *(Photo courtesy of Curt Smith.)*

Religious freedom
supporters wore green
buttons at Statehouse
rallies and while lobbying
lawmakers during the 2015
Indiana General Assembly.
*(Photo courtesy of
Curt Smith.)*

Governor Pence, speaking
at a 2015 rally, said the
legislation known as RFRA
would strengthen Indiana's
constitutional religious
liberty protections. *(Photo
courtesy of Curt Smith.)*

Mike and Karen Pence, Supreme Court Justice Mark Massa, and former lieutenant governor Becky Skillman joined Eric and Janet Holcomb in prayer before Holcomb's installation as lieutenant governor, March 3, 2016. (*Governor Mike Pence Facebook Page.*)

Debates over gay marriage and the Religious Freedom Restoration Act prompted Indianapolis real estate agent Kevin Warren to sell yard signs opposing Pence from his front stoop. *(Photo by Andrea Neal.)*

# 8

★ ★ ★

## MR. PENCE GOES TO WASHINGTON

MIKE PENCE WANTED TO BE IN CONGRESS FOR AS LONG AS HE could remember. Like so many good things that happen in a person's life, opportunity came when he least expected it.

Few had expected David McIntosh, a fellow Republican, to walk away from a safe seat in the US House of Representatives in 2000 to run against an incumbent Democratic governor, leaving vacant the very position Pence sought unsuccessfully in 1988 and 1990. But after six years on Capitol Hill, McIntosh welcomed a change. He had promised voters he would not serve more than six terms, and the time seemed right to pursue statewide office. "I was ready to go back home, having grown up in Indiana," McIntosh recalled. "Governor Frank O'Bannon was a good man and was beloved in Indiana, but things weren't running well in the state."[1] Urged to enter the race by state Republican leaders, McIntosh returned to Muncie, hoping to apply his free-market, antiregulatory philosophy to the state's economy. His decision paved the way for Pence to achieve a lifelong dream.

Pence was in no position to pursue Sharp's seat when the ten-term congressman decided to retire in 1994, just four years after Pence waged what pundits called the most negative campaign in Indiana history. *The Mike Pence Show* was newly syndicated and heard daily on more than a dozen stations across Indiana, with more stations signing on almost monthly. A TV show was in the works. Karen was pregnant with their third child and busy at home with toddlers. Most important, memories were still fresh from the 1990 race. Although "Confessions of a Negative Campaigner" had been well received by leaders in both political parties, Pence needed more time to rehabilitate his image.

Sharp surprised folks in both parties when he announced in February of 1994 that he would not seek reelection. Republicans jumped on the chance to win back what should have been a solid GOP district, with Pence content to opine from the sidelines. Although McIntosh had made political allies working for Vice President Dan Quayle, State Auditor Ann DeVore emerged as the favored candidate. She had name recognition and gender on her side as Republicans looked to show off the diversity that had developed within their leadership ranks. To DeVore's chagrin, in one of the biggest blunders in Indiana political history, her staff failed to file her candidacy papers with the secretary of state's office by the February 18 deadline, and she had to abandon her campaign just as it started.

The error benefited McIntosh, who faced three opponents in the May 3 primary: Eddie Traylor, a retired air force officer from Pendleton; Robert Marsh, a retired General Motors engineer from Anderson; and businessman Bill Frazier, a former state representative and perennial candidate from Muncie whose name identification was high after five previous campaigns for Congress. McIntosh squeaked past Frazier by 472 votes in the primary and proceeded to beat Democrat Joe Hogsett with a 54 percent margin in the general election.

McIntosh arrived in Washington as part of the Republican class of '94, elected on Newt Gingrich's *Contract with America*, a revolutionary document that set forth ten conservative policy goals that candidates pledged to support if elected. On his first day in Congress, McIntosh was tapped by Gingrich—the first Republican speaker in forty years—to chair the Subcommittee on Regulatory Relief, which had oversight of environmental, labor, and Food and Drug Administration regulations. It was a plum assignment and the envy of colleagues decades his senior. Over the next two electoral cycles, McIntosh's victory margins grew. In 1998, he defeated Democrat Sherman A. Boles with an impressive 61 percent of the vote. The Second District seat seemed his for as long as he wanted it. Pence, meanwhile, had come to terms with the likelihood he would not get another shot at Congress. He told Columbus *Republic* reporter Brian Blair in 1995, "I'm done dreaming. All my dreams today have to do with my faith and wife and kids. I take all the rest a day at a time. I say that from my heart because my lifelong dream was always to serve in Congress."[2]

By early 1999, McIntosh was reassessing the political landscape. As head of a group of lawmakers called the Conservative Action Team, he led an effort to oust Gingrich as speaker and was taking some of the blame for stalling the conservative agenda on Capitol Hill. "The first two terms were a very heady experience," McIntosh remembered. "The momentum had used itself up, and things started to become business as usual. I told myself I'm not making that big of a difference here anymore."[3] The timing could not have been better for Pence.

McIntosh had gotten to know Pence in 1994 when he sought the two-time candidate's advice about challenging Sharp. In the spring of 1999, Pence was one of the first people McIntosh consulted about the governor's race. The two met for lunch at Acapulco Joe's in Indianapolis, the same Mexican restaurant where Pence had strategized earlier political decisions. "I am thinking about running for governor," McIntosh told him. "Would you think about running for my seat?" Pence did not immediately jump at the chance. "We're finally in the black on this radio operation, and we love doing it," Pence replied. "I think we're probably done with politics." McIntosh encouraged Pence to go home and pray over the matter with Karen, and Pence agreed. The next time the two saw each other was in August at the Brickyard 400 at the Indianapolis Motor Speedway. McIntosh pulled Pence aside and asked if he had given the election any more thought. Pence said he had and that he and Karen were "open to it."[4]

In fact, Pence had been methodically thinking through what it would take to run a successful campaign. After his lunch meeting with McIntosh, Pence paid an exploratory visit to his good friend Bill Smith, a veteran of Capitol Hill. The two had met at political functions during Pence's unsuccessful congressional campaigns when Smith worked as chief of staff for US representative Dan Burton, a conservative Republican who represented the north side of Indianapolis. Their paths crossed again in 1991 when they found themselves in similar jobs with offices just around the corner from each other in Downtown Indianapolis. Pence was heading the IPR think tank, Smith the Indiana Family Institute (IFI), a nonprofit education association focused on the health and well-being of Hoosier families. The two occasionally met for lunch and discussed policy issues of mutual concern to their organizations.

After Pence left the foundation for full-time radio, they kept in close touch. Like Pence, Smith hosted a radio talk show, and the two would fill in for each other when one was out of town. Smith's daily show, called *Indiana Family Forum*, dealt mostly with strong families and character building. In 1996, Smith asked Pence and Karen to serve on the IFI Board of Directors, which they readily agreed to do. The two families interacted socially, so it was only natural that Pence would turn to Smith for counsel about his next job move. But Pence wanted more than advice from Smith. "You know, Bill, I pretty much thought my career in politics was over," he told him. "Karen and I have been praying about this. I just want your thoughts. Would you leave IFI and be my campaign manager?"[5]

As much as Smith wanted to help his friend, he could not picture giving up his work at the IFI, which had developed an influential voice on public policy matters before the Indiana legislature. Pence reflected a moment and made another offer: "Can you just take a leave of absence and help me get through the primary?"[6] Smith agreed, and thus began a political relationship that would carry on to the vice presidency.

Interest was high in an open seat in a majority GOP district, and Pence knew he needed a professional operation to win the primary. Six Republicans were fighting over the nomination: Pence; state representative Jeff Linder of Shelbyville; Luke Messer, a former staffer to Representative McIntosh; Brad Steele, a former assistant to Dan Quayle; substitute teacher David M. Campbell; and Cliff Federle, who ran as a Libertarian for the same post in 1998. With name identification better than 50 percent thanks to seven years on talk radio, Pence appeared to have an advantage over his competitors. He publicly declared his candidacy at the Horizon Convention Center in Muncie on February 16, 2000.

Even before his formal announcement, Pence came under fire from Linder, who was looking for a way to stand out in the crowded field. Pence had filed a statement of candidacy with the FEC on November 9 and gave up the radio show on December 31 to campaign full time. Under FEC guidelines, broadcasters had to treat all candidates running for the same office equally. If one received free publicity, an opposing candidate got equal time. In early January, Linder claimed that Pence had been a declared candidate during the final weeks of *The Mike Pence Show* so opponents deserved the same amount of airtime from Emmis Communications, parent company of Network Indiana. By Linder's count, Emmis owed the candidates ninety hours of coverage each, an impossible demand that Emmis immediately rejected. Attorneys for the media company said Pence was still in the exploratory stage at the time of his FEC filing and not subject to the equal-time rule.

The primary was an otherwise amiable affair with Republicans sticking mostly to economic issues, such as tax reform, Social Security, and the fate of the family farmer. More than the others, Pence mentioned faith-based social issues such as abortion, and he referred to himself publicly as "a Christian, conservative, and Republican in that order"—a line he would recite in every campaign thereafter. In an interview with *Indianapolis Star* reporter Michele McNeil Solida, Pence acknowledged that his policy views were about as far right as they could get.[7]

From the outset, Pence led in name identification and fund-raising, and the field never gained on him. "This is supposed to be a Linder-Pence race, but I just don't get any sense of momentum from him (Linder)," political analyst Amy Walter told the *Indianapolis Star* in April with the primary still a month away.[8] Walter worked for the *Cook Political Report*, an independent nonpartisan newsletter that tracked the thirty-one open congressional races across the country that year. Democrats were hoping to win enough of them to regain the majority in the House, but the Second District was not on their priority list. The GOP primary was the real election, the district having been labeled "safe Republican" by pollsters.

Pence easily won the primary with 44 percent of the vote to 24 percent for Linder, his closest competitor. As planned, Bill Smith returned to the IFI, and Lani Czarniecki took over as Pence's campaign manager for the fall election. Staying true to the promises made in his '91 "Confessions," Pence challenged Democrat Robert Rock Jr. to an issues-oriented campaign that would avoid personal attacks. "We are interested in bringing renewed civility and respect to Indiana politics," Pence said.[9] Rock, the son of a former Anderson mayor, obliged. His message focused on jobs, strengthening national defense, and securing the future of Social Security and Medicare.

One unknown variable in the election was the entry of third-party candidate Bill Frazier, the perennial GOP congressional hopeful who qualified for the ballot as an Independent after gathering eight thousand signatures. Frazier campaigned on a fair-trade platform, blaming Pence and other free traders for costing jobs and closing factories in East Central Indiana.

On environmental issues, Pence's critics found what they hoped would be his weak spot. Pence had written an article that challenged the claim that greenhouse gases were contributing to the warming of the planet. "Just like the 'new ice age' scare of the 1970s," Pence wrote, "the environmental movement has found a new chant for their latest 'chicken little' attempt to raise taxes and grow centralized government power. The chant is, 'the sky is warming, the sky is warming.'"[10] Pence's article cited various studies to suggest that greenhouse gases were real but mostly the result of volcanoes, hurricanes, and underwater geologic displacements rather than the burning of fossil fuels, a claim the experts largely debunked. His reference to a "new ice age scare" stemmed from a 1971 paper in the magazine *Science* that blamed industrial emissions of aerosol particles for falling global temperatures from 1940 to 1975 and predicted further global cooling. The paper prompted a smattering of popular media articles about a coming ice age but was largely discounted by the time Pence ran for Congress.

When the *Star Press* newspaper in Muncie found Pence's global warming piece posted on his campaign website, they sent it to three climate change experts to review. All three concluded that Pence's position was antiscientific. "The ignorance that this article shows is astounding in its scope," Peter Gleick, president of the Pacific Institute, told the newspaper. "This is like believing the earth is flat."[11]

Although Rock tried to capitalize on the issue, it did not resonate with Hoosiers, whose electricity came almost entirely from the burning of high-sulfur Indiana coal. The 1997 Kyoto Protocol—one of the first international agreements governing greenhouse gas emissions—would have cost Indiana one hundred thousand jobs and increased electricity bills 50 percent, Pence argued. That message concerned East Central Indiana voters more than environmental concerns.

Because Republicans held a slim majority in the US House, the race caught the attention of the national party. The RNCC sent big names in to campaign for Pence, among them Arizona senator John McCain, Senate majority leader Dick Armey of Texas, and House majority whip Tom DeLay of Texas. Speaker of the House Dennis Hastert visited on September 25 and appeared at two private luncheons with donors paying $150 or $250 a plate.

The lessons from previous defeats stuck with Pence, who ran a much different campaign than that of ten years earlier. One newspaper account noted, "Pence is a considerably grayer and more measured candidate than the brash lawyer who ran for Congress in 1990."[12] His prematurely silver hair was the most visible change but not the most substantive. Pence continued to raise money effectively from individual donors, but in 2000 accepted the PAC money he had rejected on principle during his campaigns against Sharp, spending $1.1 million in all. "We made the decision in this campaign not to turn away any friends," Pence explained.[13] He followed a disciplined campaign game plan, avoiding the creative risks that got him in trouble in 1990, such as the Arab oil ad that had been denounced as ethnic stereotyping. His standard stump speech boiled down to three points that clearly defined his priorities: reduce taxes for working families and businesses, strengthen the military, and "restore respect for the sanctity of human life," a reference to the Supreme Court's *Roe v. Wade* ruling that he strongly condemned.[14]

Throughout the summer, Republican polls looked promising, and by fall, Pence felt comfortable planning a move to Washington. Once again, he turned to Bill Smith, whose political expertise he considered essential to a successful DC office operation. "When it got closer to October, he asked if I would be his chief of staff if he were elected," Smith recalled. His time with Dan Burton had convinced Smith he did not want to uproot his young family to move to the nation's capital. "He kept asking and gave me enough ability to design the office and stay in Indiana and commute as necessary." Smith gave Pence a one-year commitment, which quickly became an inside joke. Toward the end of Pence's congressional service, he would introduce Smith by saying, "Here's Bill Smith, my chief of staff. He's in the twelfth year of a one-year commitment."[15]

Election night found Pence in a celebratory mood as family and supporters gathered at the Anderson Fine Arts Center. Pence won 51 percent of the vote compared to 39 percent for Rock and 9 percent for Frazier. In his victory speech, Pence spoke openly of his "faith in Jesus Christ, the God of second chances, who granted us not so much victory as the grace to run a campaign of integrity."[16] At the same time Pence was delivering his acceptance speech, McIntosh was in Indianapolis congratulating Frank O'Bannon on his reelection. News media declared O'Bannon the victor moments after the polls closed at 6:00 p.m. His 57 percent margin guaranteed sixteen consecutive years of Democrats in the governor's office, confirming that Hoosiers, while conservative, were too independent-minded to vote straight party ticket. Pence telephoned McIntosh that evening to compliment his concession speech, a move McIntosh described as "quintessential Pence."[17]

The Mike Pence who attended congressional orientation activities the week of November 18 was excited yet circumspect about the task before him. As Pence posed on the Capitol steps for a group picture, he reflected on the unexpected twists his life had taken over the past decade. "I don't find myself as enamored of the external (trappings of power) as when I was a young man, a young candidate," he told a reporter. "My attitude is more workmanlike. It's a job with a lot of responsibility."[18]

The Pences' first big decision after the election was whether Pence should commute from their home in Edinburgh in Bartholomew County or move the family to the Washington area. During orientation, sitting members and their spouses shared experiences about lifestyle options, and the Pences were encouraged by some of the strong marriages they observed. Nine out of ten members of Congress reported dissatisfaction with the amount of time they had for family, friends, and personal life, but Pence and Karen were intent on beating the odds. Their oldest child, Michael, was nine and in third grade, and Pence thought it critical to be home with him in the evenings unless Congress had pressing business. The couple also consulted with Dan and Marilyn Quayle, who had faced the same choices. If Karen and the children stayed in Indiana, every time Pence returned home for the children's sporting events or other activities he would be swamped by constituents wanting to talk, they warned them. In the end, the family moved to Northern Virginia and enrolled the children in a private Christian school where Karen found a job as an art teacher. "I just know my kids need quality time to be with their dad," Pence said of the decision.[19] The family took with them a dog, a cat, a rabbit, two gerbils, a fish, and a lizard.

The next decision was how to decorate Pence's Washington office to make it seem like home to visitors from the Second District. On arrival at 1605 Longworth House Office Building, Karen and Pence got to work covering the freshly painted walls with Hoosier memorabilia. First to go up was a framed picture of a farm and country church in Shelby County that the Pences often drove past on their way home after long days on the campaign trail. Shortly after the election, Pence had told Karen he'd like a picture of the scene for his office, thinking she would paint for him a watercolor landscape. Preoccupied with the move to Washington, Karen instead took a photograph that she had framed and inscribed with the words: "Remember the heartland." Other homey touches in the lobby included comfortable stuffed chairs and a popcorn machine serving—naturally—Weaver Gold popcorn made in Whitestown, Indiana.

The Pences made some lifestyle decisions, too. To create a "wall of protection" for their marriage, Pence decided he would not dine alone with women and would make sure Karen accompanied him to social events where alcohol was served. The so-called Billy Graham rule was their answer to the question "How do you best protect your family and your reputation against the mere appearance of impropriety?" Bill Smith explained.[20] Pence also decided at that time to switch from drinking an occasional can of cold beer to nonalcoholic O'Doul's based on his understanding of a verse in the New Testament that leaders should at all times be self-controlled and sober-minded.[21]

The 107th Congress convened on January 3, 2001. New House members took an oath to uphold the Constitution during a group ceremony on the House floor. With family members looking on, Pence joined the other freshmen in stating, "I do solemnly swear that I will support and defend the Constitution of the United States against all enemies, foreign and domestic; that I will bear true faith and allegiance to the same." John Clark of the Columbus *Republic* reported that Pence was overwhelmed by emotions "as he was sworn in for the seat he has hoped to hold since he was a child."[22]

Three weeks later, on January 20, Pence attended the inauguration of President George W. Bush. Hostile protesters met the crowd of three hundred thousand that gathered to see Bush take the oath of office from Chief Justice William H. Rehnquist. From his seat eight rows above the dais, Pence placed a cell phone call to his mother, Nancy, to share with her the inaugural sights and sounds. Moments before, she had spotted her son on national television as he walked onto the platform and was reveling in her son's achievement. Pence too was struck with the enormity of the moment. "It was really quite a thrill for a small-town boy," he said.[23]

Pence was moved by President Bush's inaugural address. The president dedicated himself to unifying the nation following his disputed win over Vice President Al Gore, an election tainted by ballot counting errors in Florida that went all the way to the Supreme Court for resolution. "Today we affirm a new commitment to live out our nation's promise through civility, courage, compassion, and character," Bush declared. "A civil society demands from each of us good will and respect, fair dealing, and forgiveness."[24] Pence liked what he heard. He told reporters that it was clear, after eight years of the Clinton administration, that character mattered again. The novice congressman was eager to do his part advancing the president's agenda. Pence had no idea how difficult that would be.

# 9

★ ★ ★

# THE UNFORGETTABLE
# 107th CONGRESS

NEWLY ELECTED CONGRESSMAN MIKE PENCE HAD HIGH hopes for his first term representing Indiana's Second District. As a fiscal conservative, Pence shared President Bush's agenda of cutting taxes, paying down the debt, and strengthening the future of Social Security and Medicare. As a social conservative, Pence brought a pro-life agenda to Washington. He quickly demonstrated to GOP leadership both his ideology and his ambition. After a few weeks on the job, Pence was named assistant to House Majority Whip Tom Delay of Texas. Next, he was tapped to chair a key subcommittee. "There seems to be no stopping U.S. Rep. Mike Pence as he rises to the top of the freshman class of the U.S. House of Representatives," observed the *Star Press* of Muncie on February 11, 2001.[1]

September 11 changed priorities overnight. In the aftermath of the attacks by al-Qaeda terrorists, Congress turned its attention to strengthening the border, increasing airport security, and launching a war on terror. Efforts to shrink government were set aside for more urgent matters. Pence's first session of Congress became known by congressional historians as "the unforgettable 107th."[2] For the Indiana freshman, whose Capitol Hill office would be quarantined in an anthrax attack, the title could not have been more fitting.

When Pence took office, Republicans held a slim majority of House seats, while for the first time ever, the Senate was divided evenly between Democrats and Republicans. As president of the Senate, Vice President Dick Cheney could break tie votes, which meant technically Republicans controlled both the executive and legislative branches. The narrow margins, however, suggested nothing would come easy to the 107th Congress. And nothing did. By 2001, the Reagan revolution had faded, and "big government Republicans" were back at the helm.[3] On many issues, conservative and moderate wings clashed, and President George W. Bush typically sided with the moderate members.

Pence aligned himself immediately with the conservative bloc and sought to apply the media skills he had honed over seven years of *The Mike Pence Show*. One of his first actions after taking office was to install a mini radio studio in his Capitol Hill office. He spent $3,000 from his congressional budget on a microphone and digital telephone system to guarantee clear connections to constituents. In a newspaper profile of Pence early in the term, *Indianapolis Star* Washington Bureau reporter Maureen Groppe joked, "You can take the congressman out of the radio talk show, but you apparently can't take the radio show out of the congressman."[4]

Every Monday morning, Pence spoke live with Greg Garrison, who had taken over Pence's old show on Network Indiana. He visited with listeners of WHBU in Anderson on Wednesdays and was a regular on stations in New Castle and Columbus. As the only congressman with a studio, he frequently advised Republican colleagues on how to take advantage of talk show opportunities. Rule number one, he told them, was to compliment the host by name. Rule number two: keep answers short. The Republican Conference was so impressed with his setup that it ordered three similar telephone sets for its caucus members.

From the outset of his congressional career, Pence sought to influence those with power and to challenge the establishment when it veered off the conservative course. George Bush had campaigned on a $1.3 trillion, ten-year tax-cut plan that became the first order of business for the 107th Congress. During a Republican retreat at Williamsburg in early February, Pence teamed up with fellow freshman Representative Jeff Flake of Arizona—like Pence, a conservative with think tank credentials—to push for deeper cuts. They directly lobbied Vice President Cheney to no avail. "We played tag-team through much of the conference on the subject," Flake recalled.[5] The two pushed, again unsuccessfully, for an amendment to make the proposed cuts retroactive to January 1 rather than phased in over five years. The idea won the endorsement of the *Wall Street Journal* editorial board but not the House Rules Committee. "It would seem that it would be easy for Republicans to do this," Flake lamented. "After all, Republicans were born to cut taxes. But it is not."[6] Pence and Flake nonetheless remained enthusiastic about the tax bill and joined 239 representatives and 58 senators to approve the president's plan, which resulted in rebate checks for taxpayers ranging from $300 to $600.

The next time Pence and Flake joined forces was in March during the debate on the $1.96 trillion budget bill. The two could not understand why President Bush wanted to increase spending by almost 6 percent when the rate of inflation was 3.16. Although their amendment attempts failed, they took advantage of the floor debate to lay out their thinking on what it meant to be a conservative. Pence and Flake became known as Butch Cassidy and the Sundance Kid for their eagerness to take on GOP leaders. On nights when Congress met late, they'd be on alert for bills they opposed, and one or the other would run to the House floor to speak. "You'd see the looks of the leadership staff because they knew we were there to object," Flake said.[7]

Following in David McIntosh's footsteps, Pence became chair of the regulatory reform and oversight subcommittee of the House Small Business Committee. The only freshman named to a subcommittee chairmanship, Pence sought to accomplish what his predecessors had failed to do: reduce the burdensome government regulations that he believed hindered job creation. Despite the Reagan administration's commitment to reform, the Code of Federal Regulations had increased by 28 percent from 1991 to 2000 and showed no signs of stopping in 2000 when 4,699 new rules were enacted. As Pence frequently pointed out, the code—a complete record of executive agency rules—consisted of an unwieldy seventy-four thousand pages.

A modest but early victory came with the passage of House Bill 327, the Small Business Paperwork Relief Act, authored by Indiana representative Dan Burton. The law required federal agencies to streamline paperwork for businesses with fewer than twenty-five workers. Pence made one of his earliest speeches on the House floor in support of the measure and expressed dismay that citizens spent so much time filling out government forms—enough to occupy "an army of 3.5 million workers working 40 hours a week, 52 weeks of the year."[8] Yet Pence was no more successful than McIntosh in reducing the size of the regulatory state. By the end of Bush's second term, the code had ballooned to 157,974 pages.

One reason for the increase was House Bill 1, a massive education bill known as the No Child Left Behind Act, passed by the 107th Congress. The bill mandated annual testing of all public school children from third through eighth grades and sanctions on schools that could not raise standardized test scores. Pence was seated next to his conservative colleague Flake as Bush unveiled the details of the bill in his State of the Union Address on February 27. When the members stood and applauded, Pence felt compelled by common courtesy to join them. "Just because I'm a clappin' for it doesn't mean I'm a votin' for it," Pence told Flake.[9]

Championed by Bush and Democratic senator Ted Kennedy, the bill was hailed as an example of bipartisan cooperation that would boost the accountability of failing schools. Pence considered the bill's nine hundred pages a gross example of federal micromanagement of states that would increase paperwork but not improve the quality of education. Though Pence was not averse to reform, his preferred approach was school choice. He had hoped that House Bill 1 would give states flexibility to spend federal dollars on vouchers or tax credits that would help parents move their children from failing school systems to private or faith-based schools, a position he would later champion as Indiana governor. Pence was one of only thirty-four House Republicans to vote against No Child Left Behind, all of them claiming vindication fifteen years later when a bipartisan review of the law by the National Conference of State Legislators deemed it unsuccessful.

On one policy matter, Pence almost singlehandedly succeeded in bringing President Bush to his point of view. From his first days in Congress, Pence lobbied Bush to restore a ban on federal funding of human embryo research. The debate was a classic confrontation between scientific progress and religious conviction. Researchers hoped to use embryos discarded from infertility treatments to search for cures to genetic disorders such as Parkinson's and muscular dystrophy. Pence believed it was "morally wrong to create human life to destroy it for research" or to force pro-life Americans to subsidize that research with their tax dollars.[10] Other conservatives, including Senators Orrin Hatch and Connie Mack and Health Secretary Tommy Thompson, disagreed with Pence and argued that the issue was about saving lives and should not be compared to abortion.

Although Pence found himself in a distinct minority, his arguments proved to be "a defining factor" in Bush's decision to oppose the practice.[11] In August 2001, the president issued an executive order limiting the research to stem cell lines created prior to his order. Twice more during his tenure, Bush faced the issue, and both times, he sided with Pence. In the first veto of his presidency, Bush blocked an expansion of federally supported embryonic stem cell research that had passed Congress with large bipartisan majorities. "Leading up to that moment, Mike was ridiculed," reflected friend Jeff Cardwell. "He really was standing alone at that time, and in the end, the president sided with Mike."[12] Cardwell attended the veto signing with Pence in the East Room of the White House. The crowd included patients treated for diseases with adult stem cells and children born from frozen embryos adopted from fertility clinics.[13]

In eight short months, Pence had demonstrated the valuable political skill of getting along. He worked amicably with House and Senate leaders and the president, whether he was in stark opposition or full agreement with their positions. Though he complained incessantly that Republican budgets were too large and tax cuts too small, he was welcomed into the upper echelon of GOP decision makers. A vocal opponent of President Bush's signature No Child Left Behind program,

Pence eagerly sought Bush's support on pro-life issues and, more often than not, secured it. "Through it all," Cardwell observed, "he stood on principle."[14]

Then came September 11. On the morning that changed the direction of the 107th Congress, Pence was headed to the Capitol for a meeting of the House Agriculture Committee. The farm bill was on the agenda, a measure of clear importance to Pence's constituents in Indiana, ranked fifth nationally in corn and soybean production. Pence had met a staff member for breakfast and was preparing for the meeting when tragedy struck. At 8:45 a.m., American Airlines Flight 11 crashed into the north tower of the World Trade Center in New York City, the first strike in what was quickly determined to be a terrorist attack against the United States. Within the hour, American Airlines Flight 77 crashed into the Pentagon, sending up dark plumes of smoke that could be seen four miles away on Capitol Hill. The Capitol and West Wing of the White House were evacuated at 9:48 a.m. Sirens filled the air.

Pence made his way with other congressmen to the top floor of the headquarters of the Capitol police chief, directly across the street from the Capitol. Although details were scant, House and Senate leaders huddled while the Capitol police chief conveyed intelligence information received by phone. "Shortly after I arrived, the chief of police set the phone back down and informed the leaders gathered there that there was a plane inbound to the Capitol, and he said it was twelve minutes out," Pence remembered. The room became silent, and Pence found himself looking out the window toward the Statue of Freedom on the top of the Capitol dome. He prayed silently as he waited for news. "It was the longest twelve minutes of my life, but it turned to thirteen minutes, then fourteen, and then we were informed that the plane had gone down in a field in Pennsylvania."[15] United Airlines Flight 93, believed to be headed for the Capitol or the White House, had crashed around 10:00 a.m. southeast of Pittsburgh. In an extraordinary act of self-sacrifice, passengers, made aware of the other hijackings in cell phone calls to 911 and family members, rose up to thwart the terrorists.

By this time, Washington's cellular carriers were overwhelmed with the surge in traffic, and many in the city were unable to call out. Pence still relied on a handheld BlackBerry, which was able to receive and transmit data. From the Congressional Command Center, Pence issued a statement: "The American people should pray. They should be confident in the strength of our national leadership. . . . We will prevail, and we will respond."[16]

The attack consumed Congress's attention for the remainder of the year and much of 2002 as lawmakers put ideology aside to respond to the greatest threat to the country since Pearl Harbor. One of its first votes, on September 14, was to grant $40 billion in emergency aid to victims and for military support related to the attack and $15 billion to help bail out the airlines industry, which shut down for three days before slowly resuming operations. On October 1, Pence joined one hundred congressmen to tour the remains of the World Trade Center and to meet with fire and rescue workers. "It is almost too difficult to describe," Pence observed. "There is literally 15 stories of twisted steel, still burning with fires that we were told were 1,500 to 1,600 degrees underground. This is a war zone."[17]

Next on Congress's agenda was beefing up intelligence. President Bush proposed a package of measures, which came to be known as the Patriot Act, that attempted to walk a fine line between enhancing security and safeguarding civil liberties. On October 2, Speaker of the House Dennis Hastert named Pence to fill a vacancy on the Judiciary Committee to strengthen support for the president's proposal, which sought expanded police powers and enhanced electronic surveillance of noncitizens. The very next day, Pence took part in the vote to move the bill to the House floor. The restrictions on liberty were in many ways antithetical to Pence's core beliefs but necessary, he said. "Because of the attacks of September 11, we must change some aspects of criminal law," Pence said in a news release. "Compromises will have to be made."[18]

As Congress attempted to manage the threat of terror in the skies, another form of terrorism was unfolding in the mail. Within a week of 9/11, anonymous letters laced with anthrax began arriving at media companies and government offices in Florida, New York City, and Washington DC. Over the next few months, five people died from inhaling anthrax, a rare bacterium undetectable to the naked eye. On October 15, an intern for Senator Tom Daschle of South Dakota, opened a letter that said, "We have this anthrax. You die now. Are you afraid? Death to America. Death to Israel. Allah is great."[19] The incident triggered a massive FBI investigation and testing of all congressional offices.

On October 26, Speaker Hastert telephoned Pence to tell him that trace amounts of anthrax had been found in three offices in the Longworth House Office Building, and Pence's was one of them. Pence's heart raced as he imagined the danger to his staff and family. Hastert quickly assured him the number of spores was too small to be life-threatening—fewer than one hundred compared to the billions found in Daschle's office. More than likely, a letter to Pence had brushed up against a contaminated envelope in the congressional mailroom and transferred spores to Pence's desk and computer screen. Despite the minimal risk, Pence's office was quarantined, and cell phones, pagers, and guest books abandoned. "It looked like a scene out of the movie E.T.," remembered Pence's chief of staff, Bill Smith. "They shut down the hallway. Workers in hazmat suits ripped out carpets and woodwork."[20] Time-sensitive files, including pending applications to the military academies, were sealed until further notice.

Pence, his wife, Smith, and nine other staff members were told to report immediately to the Rayburn Office Building for treatment and given a sixty-day prescription for Cipro, a powerful antibacterial drug. The next day was Saturday, and Pence and Karen sat the children down to gently deliver the news. "Poison powder was found in Daddy's office," Karen told them. The family prayed, read from the Bible, and then talked about what was going to happen next. "We wanted to assure them that Mommy and Daddy were okay, and that all the staff people they know are well," Pence recalled.[21] Although there was almost no risk that the children had been exposed to anthrax, House physicians prescribed a weeklong antibiotic regimen as a precaution.

Pence's office was closed until well after Christmas, and he and key staff members worked out of a Government Accounting Office building six blocks from the Capitol. In the meantime, Pence complained about the FBI's inability to track down the criminals responsible for the anthrax attack. Pence strongly suspected Middle Eastern terrorists; ultimately, the FBI concluded the sole perpetrator was likely an army biodefense researcher by the name of Bruce Ivins. No evidence ever linked Ivins to the crime, and he committed suicide in 2008 after learning criminal charges were about to be filed against him.

Through the fall of 2001, Pence had little time for politicking, occupied as he was by a full plate of congressional and family responsibilities. By December, however, a reelection year loomed, and he turned his attention back to the campaign trail. Much had changed in Indiana since the last election. Although Indiana's population increased 9.3 percent from 1990 to 2000, its growth fell short of the national average. Reapportionment after the 2000 Census meant Indiana would lose a congressional seat, dropping from ten US House members to nine. In May, a state commission approved a plan that put two of Indiana's Republican House members, Steve Buyer and Brian Kerns, in the same district. Pence was spared a primary fight, but he knew he quickly needed to meet the voters in his new territory, which extended from south of Fort Wayne to Dearborn County near the Ohio River. "We did not take anything for granted," Bill Smith said. "We said we will run the campaign as if we are ten points behind."[22] The new Sixth District included Pence's home in Bartholomew County as well as parts of the old Second, Fourth, Fifth, and Ninth Districts.

In December, the DCCC named Pence as one of twenty-four Republicans it considered vulnerable in the upcoming election. Democratic spokesperson Kim Rubey said Pence made the cut because he was an "extreme conservative" and more concerned with tax cuts for corporations than helping hardworking middle-income Americans.[23] Pence reacted to the news with characteristic humor, declaring he was proud to be on such a distinguished list of candidates. "He was targeted because they thought he was too conservative for the district, which meant they didn't understand the district," Smith said.[24] The first-term congressman had nothing to fear. Pence enjoyed strong name recognition and a half-million-dollar campaign war chest with the election still eleven months away. More important, his tough foreign policy stands and outspoken conservatism were proving extremely popular in post 9/11 Indiana.

# 10

★ ★ ★

## "TAKEN TO THE WOODSHED"

DURING A HEATED DEBATE IN CONGRESS ON LEGISLATION that would increase the budget deficit, Mike Pence called his friend Chuck Mosey for a reality check. "I was determined to take a stand for fiscal responsibility, and I figured he was the right guy to call to get a good perspective from home," Pence said. A resident of Richmond, Indiana, Mosey was a business owner, family man, and volunteer for his church and Junior Achievement. He was the "Will Rogers of eastern Indiana," known for his quick wit and common sense. Mosey listened attentively to Pence's Capitol Hill update and then answered, "Don't those people know how much money we don't have?" The two men erupted in laughter. Pence liked the punch line so much he used it later in the floor debate on the bill.[1]

Few issues consumed Pence quite like deficit spending, the long-standing policy of Congress to write budgets that spend more money than they take in. Throughout his congressional career, Pence fought against earmarks and entitlements—programs that he said would burden his children's generation with a "mountain range of debt"—and he pushed relentlessly for a balanced budget amendment to the US Constitution. What made the fight perplexing to Pence was that, in most cases, he battled his own party.

"By the time he got to Congress," observed longtime friend Jeff Cardwell, "it was not the party of Ronald Reagan."[2] Pence made no secret of his disillusion, describing himself variously as a minuteman who arrived late to the Revolution and a frozen man brought back to life to find a world changed beyond recognition. Old-fashioned though he was, his devotion to Reagan-era policies and values made him an effective spokesman for conservatism. As such, he was embraced by national conservative groups and pundits, including Cal Tomas, George Will, and others who would eventually float his name as a presidential prospect.

It would be a few years before Pence seriously entertained the notion of running for president. First, he needed to solidify his base and prove to voters of the new Sixth District that he understood the issues that concerned them. The district spanned nineteen eastern Indiana counties. Largely rural, its two largest cities, Muncie and Anderson, faced serious economic troubles due to three decades of job loss and factory closings. Pence's opposition to taxpayer-funded projects, called earmarks, and his reluctance to pursue them for his district meant that he would not be able to spend his way to popularity; he would have to persuade constituents of the merits of his political views.

Pence's first reelection campaign pitted him against Melina Fox, a lifelong Hoosier, farmer, and Democrat with deep political roots. Ezra Butler, one of her ancestors, had served in the US House of Representatives and as the governor of Vermont. Two others were delegates to the Indiana Constitutional Convention of 1816. Democrats united early behind Fox to maximize her fund-raising, but Pence had an unbeatable head start with $337,000 in the bank at the end of 2001. He would go on to outspend her three to one.

Fox spoke passionately on the stump about affordable health care, her opposition to trade agreements like NAFTA, and early childhood education. These were issues she believed would resonate with women, who made up more than half the Sixth District, and farmers and blue-collar workers, who made up 38 percent.[3] "Then the major turning point of our campaign happened: September 11th," Fox recalled. "I suspended fund-raising efforts. And voters after that horrific act seemed reluctant for change."[4]

The war on terror overshadowed domestic issues leading up to November 5. President Bush called for the disarming of Saddam Hussein, citing intelligence reports—later discredited—that Iraq had reconstituted its chemical and biological weapons inventory. On October 10, with the election less than a month away, the House voted 296–133 for House Joint Resolution 114, authorizing military force against Iraq. The Senate voted 77–33 for the resolution the next day. "I grieve at the thought of the United States at war and am not anxious to see it," Pence said of the measure he cosponsored with 135 others. "But Saddam Hussein is a threat to America's national security and to world security."[5] Fox opposed the resolution absent more proof of Iraq's arsenal and "a clear-cut military objective."[6]

Unusual for a midterm election, the party of the president picked up seats in both the Senate and the House. Pence defeated Fox handily with 64 percent of the vote, a margin that belied the high caliber of their matchup. Newspapers praised both candidates for constructive messaging, the *Indianapolis Star* calling the race "a model of an issue-oriented, clean, and courteous campaign" even as it endorsed the more budget-conscious Pence.[7] In defeat, Fox declared, "I think we set the standard for how to run a campaign in Indiana."[8] In four subsequent reelection bids, Pence's margin of victory would never fall below the 60 percent mark, and in each, he kept his promise not to go negative.

To Pence's dismay, the increase in Republican seats in the 108th Congress did nothing to advance the conservative cause. When President Bush moved forward on a campaign pledge to cover prescription costs for the elderly, Pence was not surprised. But when House and Senate leadership suggested bigger benefits than proposed by Bush, he was incredulous. "I think I've made it very clear to leadership since last spring that I didn't come to Washington to create new entitlements," he explained.[9]

The GOP majority wanted to extend drug coverage to forty million elderly and disabled Americans at an estimated cost of $400 billion. Pence and other members of the conservative caucus, known as the Republican Study Committee, preferred a limited benefit for low-income seniors, the one in three who had no access to prescription drugs or who faced out-of-pocket expenses of more than $4,000 a year. On November

18, Pence took to the House floor to voice his objections to "the largest expansion of Medicare in 35 years."[10]

Speaker of the House Dennis Hastert was committed to the bill's passage in 2003 to give Republicans a domestic policy victory to brag about in the 2004 elections. There were 229 Republicans in the House, and he needed 218 votes. Although Democrats supported the idea of the new entitlement, they had a plan of their own and were unlikely to cross over in large numbers. Hastert could not afford to lose many Republicans.

On November 21, the day before the House vote, President Bush summoned Pence and a few other dissenters to the Oval Office to appeal for their support. Jeff Cardwell learned of the meeting that morning while reading the *Wall Street Journal*. Certain that Pence would be agonizing over challenging the president, Cardwell fired off an encouraging 5:30 a.m. email urging Pence to stand his ground. "Mike, just remember, good men can disagree." Pence immediately wrote back: "Thanks. I appreciate your prayers."[11]

President Bush opened the meeting with a blunt question: "Pence, what's your problem with this bill?" The Indiana congressman stood his ground: it made no sense to create a new entitlement when the government faced a $430 billion deficit. Pence told the president that he was going straight from the White House to his daughter Charlotte's tenth birthday party and that he would be voting no on the legislation so he would be welcomed at her thirtieth.[12] "He didn't care what the political consequences would be going against the majority and his own White House," remembered Bill Smith, Pence's chief of staff. "At the same time, he had this great affection for President Bush, and that's what made it difficult."[13]

The arm-twisting continued all day and through the night. At one point, Pence told reporters that the "hard-core" conservative bloc had grown to twenty-six, enough to defeat the bill. But Democrats were dealing, too, and some said they were willing to vote yes on the bill, endorsed by the lobbying group AARP, if Republicans could get within a dozen or so votes of passage. Hastert scheduled the vote for 3:00 a.m. with a fifteen-minute window for House members to get from their offices to the electronic voting stations in the chamber. As voting began, seventeen House Republicans immediately cast nay votes. Hastert extended the time frame as he continued to canvass members. As of 3:48 a.m., there were 218 opposed and 215 in favor.[14]

Rather than admit defeat, Hastert kept the voting machine open and launched another offensive, convincing a few members to change their no votes to yes. President Bush telephoned the holdout Republicans while Health and Human Services Secretary Tommy Thompson lobbied them personally on the House floor, a violation of House protocol. Leadership froze C-SPAN television cameras so no one outside the chamber could see what was happening.[15] At one point, Hastert asked Pence what it would take to get a yes vote. Pence replied, "Means test the entitlement." "Impossible," Hastert responded.[16]

The longest roll call in House history ended at 5:53 a.m. with the victorious Republicans cheering the razor-thin 220–215 victory.[17] Twenty-five Republicans voted no, sixteen Democrats voted yes, and Pence and his allies were "taken to the woodshed" by House leadership.[18] They were told in blunt terms "they were not team players and their careers would suffer if they continued to obstruct the leadership's wishes."[19]

The vote demoralized Pence and the Republican Study Committee, which looked for lessons to apply to the next confrontation. "We were wiped out. There was nothing victorious about the Medicare bill. They won, we lost, that's how it works," Pence said. "Sometimes even in defeat, good things can come from people taking a principled stance." In the ensuing months, some colleagues confided to Pence that they would stick with him in the next face-off between politics and principle.[20] The episode also served to elevate Pence's national profile. "That's when the chatter started that this guy could be president," Cardwell said.[21]

In the meantime, there was a presidential election pending. Polling by Gallup suggested that voters' foremost concerns were terrorism and the economy and that this election would be a referendum on Bush's leadership.[22] The Iraq War had been under way since March 2003, and Americans had not yet begun to question the administration's foreign policy. Although the margin of victory was slim, Bush won both the popular and Electoral College vote, and Republicans picked up a few more seats in both the Senate and the House. On the surface, the win appeared to vindicate Republican policies of the previous four years.

Under the surface, conservative frustration with the party's direction continued to build. Pence's leadership opposing the Medicare drug bill had propelled him to the chairmanship of the Republican Study Committee, the largest caucus on Capitol Hill, whose 106 members supported a conservative economic and social agenda. In a breakfast speech at the National Press Club in January 2005, Pence said his priorities were rescinding the Medicare prescription law and the No Child Left Behind Act, the two signature accomplishments of Bush's first term as president. Pence understood he was bucking the establishment, dubbing himself "the skunk at the garden party."[23]

The next showdown came eight months into the 109th Congress, prompted by Hurricane Katrina, the worst natural disaster in US history. On September 15, President Bush delivered a live television address from Jackson Square in New Orleans pledging "we will do what it takes" to rebuild the Gulf Coast region, which had been devastated by storm surge, flooding, and a levee breach that put 20 percent of New Orleans under water.[24] A week later, Pence held a news conference on Capitol Hill proposing Operation Offset. Rebuild New Orleans, Pence said, but cover the costs by finding comparable cuts elsewhere in the budget. Among the possibilities: delay the Medicare prescription drug benefit by a year and ask representatives to give up pet spending projects in the highway funding bill. There were plenty from which to choose. President Reagan had vetoed a highway funding bill in 1987 because it contained two hundred earmarks. The most recent highway bill had twenty thousand earmarks, Pence pointed out in an interview with fellow Hoosier Brian Lamb of C-SPAN.[25]

Democrats labeled his proposal hard-hearted, especially since dead bodies were still being recovered from floodwaters. Republican leaders were riled. Speaker Hastert chastised Pence for his audacity and then invited study committee members to a closed-door meeting where "Republican leaders made clear they would not tolerate criticism of their spending." It was a "scandalous browbeating," syndicated columnist Robert Novak reported.[26] Two weeks later, with a serious split brewing in Republican ranks, Hastert reversed course and proposed cuts of at least $50 billion to offset the hurricane recovery costs. Clearly, the Republican Study Committee was making an impact. A few months

later, Congress passed the Deficit Reduction Act, calling for $40 billion
in budget cuts over five years. Declaring Pence its Man of the Year, the
conservative magazine *Human Events* said the Republican Study Committee had "almost single-handedly stopped the chronic GOP over-
spending of the past five years and forced the first full-fledged budget-
cutting bill since 1997."[27]

Pence's rebellion reached a zenith in 2006 with his decision to challenge John Boehner for the position of minority leader. Democrats had
regained control of the House of Representatives and Senate in the
midterm elections, and Nancy Pelosi was poised to take over as speaker
of the House. Pollsters attributed the election's outcome to public discomfort with the flagging war effort and a congressional corruption
scandal involving a Republican lobbyist. Pence blamed congressional
Republicans for acting like Democrats, saying, "We didn't just lose our
majority, we lost our way."[28]

As the House majority leader under Speaker Hastert, Boehner was
the obvious choice to lead the delegation in their new minority status.
Pence, who easily withstood at the polls the anti-Republican backlash
that claimed three Indiana colleagues, argued it was time for new blood.
He announced his candidacy at 8:00 a.m. on November 8, the day after
the elections. "Let me quote Peyton Manning," he said, referencing the
popular quarterback of the Indianapolis Colts. "It's never good to lose.
There's nothing good about us yielding the House of Representatives
to a liberal Democratic majority."[29]

Pence personally met or spoke by telephone with more than 120
members during the days leading up to the vote, and four of Indiana's
largest newspapers endorsed his bid. So did the advocacy group Club
for Growth, which ranked Pence fifth out of all 435 House members for
his free-market leanings. Conservative talk radio host Laura Ingraham
said of Pence, "If there is a God in heaven, he will be the next House
minority leader."[30]

In the end, it wasn't close. Pence had misjudged the members' readi-
ness for change. The vote was 168–27 for Boehner, who thanked Pence
for his attention to the party's future and committed House Republicans to a "return to our core principles" of fiscal discipline and limited

government.[31] The two men maintained a cordial working relationship, and Boehner asked Pence to serve as lead Republican on a select committee investigating claims that Democrats had rigged a vote on the House floor.[32]

Pence waged one more battle against the establishment during the 110th Congress. In the midst of the economic recession that struck in late 2008, Pence voted against the Bush-backed $700 billion bailout of floundering financial institutions under the Troubled Asset Relief Program, known as TARP. It was "the largest corporate bailout in American history," Pence claimed on the floor.[33] Economists generally deemed the program a necessary evil—necessary because it rescued the financial system from collapse, evil because it rewarded institutions whose lending practices had caused the crisis in the first place. Pence declared it flat-out wrong to make taxpayers pay the price.

Despite his adversarial ways, Pence's career did not suffer the fate threatened by Hastert during the Medicare entitlement debate of 2003. On the contrary, he continued to move up the ladder. Colleagues attributed this to his never-failing cheerfulness, the "happy warrior" approach that defined his twelve years in Congress. As often as he disagreed, he was never disagreeable.[34]

In 2006, President Bush invited Pence to the White House to hear his ideas for an immigration reform plan and to thank him for trying to find a solution to what seemed to be an insoluble issue.[35] Pence's plan, to allow illegal immigrants to return to their native countries and then come back legally to the United States as part of a guest worker program, attracted substantial support from colleagues but not enough to advance to a congressional vote.

Following the 2008 election of President Barack Obama, Pence was elected chair of the House Republican Conference, the third-highest-ranking member in GOP leadership. Boehner had encouraged Pence to run following back-to-back electoral losses by Republicans. "There is no one in our ranks who does a better job of articulating the GOP message of freedom and smaller government," Boehner said.[36]

With his radio and think tank background, Pence was suited for the role. The conference, the organizational body for all GOP members of the House, employed a staff of twenty to help with briefings, talking points, and media events. Pence pushed them to make increased use of social media—YouTube, Twitter, and Facebook—to spread the Republican message.[37] In his new role strategizing for colleagues, Pence pledged, "I will be loyal to the cause of returning our party to the ideals of Lincoln and Reagan, the ideals that most Republican voters embrace—defending our nation, our treasury and our values with everything we've got. And I'm going to be loyal to the cause of returning a Republican majority to Capitol Hill in 2010."[38]

In the same way that he challenged government expansion under President Bush, Pence fought President Obama's two major initiatives: a $787 billion economic stimulus package and the "government takeover of health care" brought about by the Patient Protection and Affordable Care Act.[39] Nicknamed Obamacare, the law consisted of 1,990 pages and required all Americans to be enrolled in a health-care plan, whether offered by a private employer or subsidized by the government. Many Americans shared Pence's concerns about the cost and reach of the law, and Republicans quickly committed to overturning it.

On September 12, 2009, tens of thousands of protesters jammed the National Mall in DC chanting slogans and carrying signs that declared, "Obamacare makes me sick" and "I'm not your ATM." It was a telling sign of the power of the growing Tea Party (short for "taxed enough already") movement, which embraced Pence as an ex officio leader. Pence was one of a handful of congressmen who accepted an invitation to speak at the event. It was a Saturday, and he came straight from his daughter's cross country meet in Northern Virginia, parked at his office garage, and then walked out the west front of the Capitol. He was stunned by the size of the crowd.[40]

Just as he hoped, a Republican majority regained control of Congress in the 2010 midterm elections. Pence won reelection with a commanding 67 percent majority. Two days later, he gave up his leadership position and hinted strongly that the 112th Congress would be his last. It was a decisive moment on his path to national prominence. Should he run for Indiana governor—or for president?

# 11

★ ★ ★

## GREGG VERSUS PENCE

JOHN GREGG WENT TO BED ON ELECTION EVE BELIEVING HE had a good chance of beating Mike Pence. His campaign's final poll showed him trailing Pence by four points in the race for governor, with a margin of error of three, and last-minute trends favored Democrats. The statewide Republican ticket had lost momentum since late October, when Tea Party–backed senate candidate Richard Mourdock declared that pregnancy resulting from rape was something God intended. The comment stirred up a firestorm, especially among moderate Republicans still sour over Mourdock's defeat of veteran senator Richard Lugar in the May primary. Presidential candidate Mitt Romney distanced himself from Mourdock, and pro-life Pence called on him to apologize.[1] Republicans approached Election Day with trepidation.

Up before dawn on November 6, Gregg arrived at his polling place at the Sandborn Community Building with his two sons, the younger one casting a ballot for the first time. That night, they joined Democrats in Indianapolis at the Marriott on West Maryland Street to watch returns. Party leaders were in high spirits and predicting upsets when the polls closed at 6:00 p.m. At 9:36, TV stations declared Democrat Joe Donnelly a six-point winner over Mourdock in the senate race. Democrat Glenda Ritz claimed victory next, beating Tony Bennett, the incumbent state superintendent of public instruction.

For Gregg, the upset was not to be. Around 10:30 p.m., with most key precincts having reported, Joe Champion, Gregg's law partner, pulled him aside to give him an update. "We've looked at the numbers. You can't come back."[2] The candidate sat his family down to tell them the news. Since his 1986 primary win over incumbent state representative Bill Roach of Terre Haute, Gregg had never lost an election. This one had been an uphill fight. As his sons' faces fell with disappointment, Gregg reassured them that he'd be fine. "Boys, the sun is going to come up tomorrow," he said. "I'm going to call Mike Pence."[3]

In the fall of 2010, immediately after his reelection to a sixth term in Congress, Pence gathered with top advisers at the Abe Martin Lodge in Brown County for a retreat to discuss his political future. Participants included chief of staff Bill Smith, district director Lani Czarniecki, campaign chairman Van Smith, pollster Kellyanne Conway, and fund-raiser Marty Obst. The daylong session was not out of the ordinary; the team held annual or biannual strategy meetings to brainstorm and plan the year ahead.

The high stakes made this meeting different. Pence was on the verge of making the choice between running for president, a gamble under the best of circumstances, and running for governor, an almost-sure thing if he entered the race early enough to dissuade other Republican hopefuls.

National conservative leaders had floated Pence's name as a presidential prospect for years—as far back as 2005 when Stephen Moore of the Free Enterprise Fund referred to him as "someone who could fill the Gipper's shoes, even though he's still young and a relative political newcomer."[4] The reference to President Ronald Reagan alluded to Pence's political ideology of limited government and fiscal responsibility. His positions on social issues such as abortion were what mattered to evangelical Christians who took part in the Family Research Council's Values Voter Summit in September 2010, ranking Pence first in a presidential straw poll. "He had some very prominent people who were talking to him about running for president, and it would make anyone feel good about their prospects," said Jeff Brown, a close Columbus friend.[5]

There was even a short-lived draft-Pence movement led by former Reagan administration official Ralph Benko and former congressman Jim Ryun, who were looking for a Reagan-style conservative to challenge President Barack Obama in 2012. The two established a political action committee in early 2011 and invited voters to go online to sign a petition urging Pence to run. Reporter Kathryn Jean Lopez of the *National Review* asked Benko in an interview, "Why shouldn't he run for governor instead?" Benko replied, "Mike Pence is presidential, and his issues are presidential. America needs such a person now."[6]

Those closest to Pence were acutely aware of the challenge of running for president from the House. The only sitting US representative to win the presidency was James Garfield of Ohio, and he didn't seek the position; it came to him. In 1880, after the Ohio legislature elected him to the Senate, Garfield attended the Republican National Convention to nominate Treasury Secretary John Sherman of Ohio for president. The convention couldn't decide between Sherman, James Blaine of Maine, and Ulysses Grant of Ohio, so, on the thirty-sixth ballot, Garfield was nominated as a compromise candidate.

Governors seemed to have a clearer path. Seventeen presidents had served previously as state governors, including four of the previous six: Jimmy Carter, Ronald Reagan, Bill Clinton, and George W. Bush. Jeff Cardwell, a Pence supporter going back to the 1988 campaign, didn't hesitate to share his opinion that Pence "needs executive experience if he ever wants to run for president."[7]

Early media speculation in Indiana ranked Pence first among GOP candidates to succeed Governor Mitch Daniels, who was limited by the state constitution to two consecutive terms.[8] Timing mattered because a deep GOP bench was waiting for Pence to make up his mind. Daniels's lieutenant governor, Becky Skillman, put out feelers to potential donors—and would have received substantial support from Republican women eager for the first female governor—but "minor health problems" caused her to rethink priorities, and she backed out before Christmas.[9] House Speaker Brian Bosma made no secret of his guber-

natorial ambition after Republicans won back the House from Democratic control in 2010 but was at a distinct disadvantage. Pence had been
lining up endorsements for months while Bosma was preoccupied with
the budget-making session of the legislature.

The working assumption at the Brown County retreat was that Pence
would run for governor. "It was in the spirit of, 'Look, I'm making the
decision to go for governor. Now what does that mean?'" recalled Van
Smith, a Muncie businessman who'd chaired Pence's congressional
campaigns since 2000.[10] Conversation focused on what Pence's policy agenda should be. In Congress, Pence made a name for himself by
challenging GOP leadership when it veered off conservative course
and by championing pro-life views on abortion, Planned Parenthood,
and embryonic stem cell research. These weren't issues that concerned
governors. Daniels, himself mentioned as a possible presidential candidate, had urged Republicans to declare a temporary truce on social
issues to focus on economic matters, and his counsel seemed apropos.
"Mike made the decision that the major issues in the campaign for
governor in 2012 should be and must be jobs and education," Van Smith
remembered.[11]

Alumni of the Phoenix Group, the de facto fund-raising arm of the
Republican Party for a brief period in the early 2000s, backed Pence
early, which helped clear the field for Pence. The political action committee was formed in 2001 by businessman Jim Kittle and attorney Bob
Grand, among others, to reinvigorate the party after a string of lost
elections. Republicans were shut out of the governor's office after Evan
Bayh's win in 1988, and donors of influence wanted it back. The Phoenix
Group recruited candidates, raised money, and managed donor data-
bases, and it propelled Kittle to become Republican state chairman in
2002. The group's strategy paid off handsomely two years later with
the election of Daniels, who had served President George W. Bush as
budget director.

Because Pence had never run a statewide campaign, the group introduced him to a wider swath of donors and briefed him on governance issues important around the state. On a visit to his hometown in
Lake County, Grand took Pence to see the Calumet Avenue Overpass,

a state-funded highway project and an example of the nuts-and-bolts affairs of concern to ordinary Hoosiers.[12] Lake County also provided Pence with his most generous and enthusiastic donor. Dean White of Crown Point, a hotel and billboard magnate, contributed $200,000 to Mike Pence for Indiana in 2011 and $350,000 two years later. "He saw in Mike the same thing I did," said Fred Klipsch, Mike Pence for Indiana treasurer. "He saw a politician who was both smart and ethical."[13] (White died in 2016 at age ninety-three.)

Although donors knew his plans, Pence strung out the announcements about his political future over a six-month period. Pence reached a final decision that he would not run for president on the night of January 26 after speaking with leaders of the Republican Governors Association, who offered their support and $1 million in PAC money to help finance his campaign. Pence then embarked on a listening tour around the state to "learn about how Hoosiers think we might best contribute in the years ahead."[14] He officially announced his candidacy by video conference on May 5, a month shy of his fifty-second birthday.

From his first campaign comments, it was clear that Pence planned a positive campaign and would avoid the kinds of negative attacks that got him into trouble back in 1990. It was also evident that following Daniels would require a delicate balancing act: offering Hoosiers a vision for Indiana's future without suggesting that he could do better than the popular outgoing governor. "For the first time in my lifetime, Indiana is essentially the lead car under the yellow light economically in the Midwest," Pence said, invoking one of the race car metaphors that he would occasionally sprinkle into his speeches. Acknowledging Daniels's excellent work, Pence said his campaign theme would be: "How do you build an even better Indiana?"[15]

One more announcement was planned for his hometown of Columbus to set the tone for his campaign. A crowd of about one thousand gathered at The Commons on June 11 for a Hoosier feast of fried chicken, baked beans, potato salad, and fried biscuits. "I love this state, and I believe Hoosiers are the best people in America," Pence told the audience. Photographs of cornfields, basketball, and the Indy 500 played on flat-screen TVs, and country music blared over loudspeakers.[16] The message could not have been clearer: Mike Pence did not see the governor's office as a mere stepping-stone to a higher office.

John Gregg wasn't buying it. "Mike Pence doesn't want to be your governor," he'd say on the campaign trail, reminding folks that Pence had initially flirted seriously with running for president.[17] He hoped to paint Pence as an opportunist who worked harder on the campaign trail than in Congress. Gregg's TV ads noted that Pence earned $174,000 a year, yet he had missed 86 percent of his committee votes and hadn't passed a single bill since he was first elected.[18]

A winding road had led Gregg to the governor's race. He had retired from politics in 2002 after sixteen years in the Indiana house and "never thought I would run for office again."[19] He was practicing law in 2007 when Senator Evan Bayh telephoned him and asked him to serve as honorary chairman of Hillary Clinton's Indiana presidential campaign. Gregg agreed and spent four days campaigning with President Bill Clinton and two days with Hillary Clinton, which "got me back in the political stuff."[20]

On election night 2010, Gregg was watching midterm election returns at home with his sons when he took a call from Tim Jeffers, his former chief of staff, seeking to commiserate about Republican gains in both houses of Congress, including Dan Coats's election to Evan Bayh's old Senate seat. "You're the type of Democrat who can win—a pro-business moderate," Jeffers told him before suggesting that Gregg consider running for governor in 2012.

"I told him to go to hell and hung up on him," Gregg quipped.[21]

By February 2011, Gregg was laying the groundwork for his candidacy. Bayh, who chose not to seek reelection to the Senate, briefly considered running for a second stint as governor but ruled it out that December. Although Bayh would have been the Democratic dream candidate, Gregg was a strong plan B. Party leaders hoped his record would appeal to moderate and liberal Republicans who found Pence too ideological. Gregg was a Blue Dog Democrat who agreed with Pence on an array of issues—"I was pro-gun, pro-life, pro–death penalty"—and had often appeared on Pence's radio show in the mid-1990s when Gregg served as speaker of the Indiana House of Representatives.[22]

To Gregg's surprise, Pence's campaign hardly mentioned the divisive morality issues on which Democrats hoped to capitalize, instead sticking to tax cuts, education reform, and workforce development. "I kept reminding people, this isn't what Pence is about. Look at Congress and his social record."[23] A newspaper reporter confirmed Gregg's dilemma, noting that "Pence sounded more like an accountant than an ideologue, and it contrasted sharply with the bold and inflexible beliefs he's held throughout his career."[24]

To Republican state legislators' surprise, Pence unveiled his policy agenda without consulting them first. The communication failure suggested to House Speaker Bosma that Pence was following a consultant's script and did not understand the political realities at the statehouse. "The tax cut announcement was the one that kind of brought it to a head," Bosma said.[25] On July 31, Pence proposed cutting the individual tax rate by 10 percent over two years, a move that would reduce revenue by $533 million, 7 percent of the state budget. Bosma and Senator Luke Kenley, chair of the appropriations committee, were skeptical and didn't hesitate to share their opinions with the media. The legislature had just cut taxes the previous year, and Indiana already had one of the lowest income tax rates in the nation.

Bosma was right about Pence's reliance on national political advisers. One of them was Kellyanne Conway, who had worked as his pollster since 2009 and would go on to manage Donald Trump's campaign for president. A more recent hire was David Kensinger, former chief of staff to Governor Sam Brownback of Kansas. When running for governor in the summer of 2010, Brownback had issued a "Road Map for Kansas" that set forth key goals for his administration should he win the election. These included cutting taxes, increasing employment, and reforming the state's school funding formula. In 2012, Kensinger left his position with Brownback to work for Pence's campaign, which paid Kensinger & Associates $90,000 for services.[26] In the summer of 2012, Pence issued his "Roadmap for Indiana," using the Kansas template, which advocated tax cuts, spending limits, and education reform. Although Bosma considered the Pence agenda to be boilerplate campaign promises, Bill Smith said it was based on "best practices from around the country" and research by senior policy adviser Chris Atkins, who would later become Pence's budget director.[27]

Both candidates tried to out-Hoosier the other. Pence campaigned in a red Chevy Silverado wearing a bomber jacket on what he called the Big Red Truck Tour. Gregg filmed television ads on the streets of Sandborn—at Carol's Clip & Curl, the First Christian Church, and the Blue Jay Junction Convenience Store. Gregg joked that both had Washington DC experience. "He was familiar with the broken-down Washington, the nation's capital. I was familiar with Washington in Daviess County, Indiana."[28]

Both also selected as running mates female legislators who added gender, geographic, and, in Gregg's case, ideological diversity to their tickets. As the second-highest position in state government, the lieutenant governor oversaw a $1 billion budget that included the departments of agriculture, tourism, and community and rural affairs. Pence tapped freshman state representative Sue Ellspermann of Ferdinand in rural southwestern Indiana, the founding director of the University of Southern Indiana's Center for Applied Research. Gregg chose state senator Vi Simpson of Bloomington, a veteran lawmaker with more liberal views than Gregg on abortion, gun control, and same-sex marriage.

As the election drew near, the candidates agreed to three debates—in Zionsville, South Bend, and Fort Wayne. Sponsored by the Indiana Debate Commission, the televised discussions included Rupert Boneham, an alumnus of the CBS reality show *Survivor*, who was running as a Libertarian, the only third party on the ballot. The first two debates were predictable affairs with the candidates reiterating already advertised campaign slogans. By the third debate, on October 25, the Mourdock controversy had erupted, and Gregg looked to capitalize. One minute into his first chance to speak, the Democrat mentioned Mourdock's comment about God and rape and claimed Pence's views were no different. "As governor I'll keep our state from being controlled by the Tea Party," Gregg said, a reference to the most conservative wing of the Republican Party. "He can't separate himself from the Tea Party because he is the Tea Party."[29] The disciplined Pence did not respond, restricting his comments to jobs, tax cuts, and education. Post-debate commentary declared the debate a draw although a headline in the *Times* of Northwest Indiana said, "Gregg pummels Pence in final debate."[30] Reflecting later on the outcome, Gregg wished he'd been more aggressive about Pence's extreme abortion views. "I could never get him off message."[31]

With the election twelve days away, Democrats continued to push the Mourdock story line. The party spent $1.1 million on last-minute ads in Indiana, airing footage of Mourdock's by then infamous comment that "even when life begins in that horrible situation of rape, that it is something that God intended to happen."[32] Because Gallup surveys showed 77 percent of Americans believed abortion should be legal in all or certain circumstances, such as incest or rape, Democrats hoped Mourdock's statement would show Republicans as unsympathetic or extreme. Eleventh-hour movement toward Democrats indicated the strategy was working.

Republicans had booked the end zone at Lucas Oil Stadium for their election night party. When Fox News, airing live on giant video screens, announced Mourdock's defeat, disappointed Tea Party supporters started trickling out of the stadium. Claiming victory barely in time for the 11:00 p.m. news, Pence first acknowledged "the role of providence in my life" and offered "thanks to God who gave us the strength and the grace these past two years."[33] He then thanked Gregg, Boneham, and those who did not vote for him, saying he would respect their opinions and work together to make Indiana more prosperous for all. His win was closer than expected, considering he'd outspent Gregg two to one. That Pence failed to capture a majority of ballots cast—49 percent to Gregg's 47 percent—prompted some Democrats to say he lacked a mandate to govern. "I don't think many remember how close it was," Gregg reflected. "But I do."[34]

Despite losing two statewide races, Republicans were optimistic. When the Indiana General Assembly convened later that month, Pence would enjoy Republican supermajorities in both houses of the legislature, a promising sign he'd be able to accomplish his agenda.

During a July 2016 fund-raiser at the Columbia Club, Donald Trump sought advice about potential running mates from Republican state chairman Jeff Cardwell. Cardwell told Trump he should choose Pence. *(Photo courtesy of Jeff Cardwell.)*

Jeff Cardwell, standing with Ed Simcox and Rex Early to his right, cast the Indiana delegation vote for the Trump-Pence ticket at the Republican National Convention, July 19, 2016. *(Photo courtesy of Jeff Cardwell.)*

Pence practiced the time-honored political custom of kissing babies on Landry Marshall, infant grandson of Republican state chairman Jeff Cardwell, during a breakfast for the Pences sponsored by the Indiana delegation at the Republican National Convention in July 2016. *(Photo courtesy of Jeff Cardwell.)*

*Overleaf*: Ed Simcox and Victor Smith talked strategy on the campaign plane with Governor Pence in September 2016. *(Photo courtesy of Ed Simcox.)*

Vice President Pence invited family and friends, including Hoosiers
Bill Stephan and Jay Steger, to a reception at his home at the Naval
Observatory following the National Prayer Service on Jan. 21, 2017.
*(Photo courtesy of Jay Steger.)*

*Facing top,* Jeff Cardwell welcomed Mike Pence home upon his return to
Indianapolis November 10, 2016, two days after his election as vice president.
*(Photo courtesy of Jeff Cardwell.)*

*Facing bottom,* On January 6, 2017, his last business day as governor,
Pence dropped by his statehouse office to say goodbye and reminisce
with staff, including Jim Atterholt, chief of staff, on Pence's immediate
right; and Lani Czarniecki, director of inter-governmental affairs,
to his left. *(Governor Mike Pence @GovPenceIN.)*

Pence greeted tourists in the Capitol Rotunda in June 2017. *(Photo courtesy of Deidre Lindsey.)*

Donald Trump announced Governor Mike Pence as his vice presidential candidate running mate at the Midtown New York Hilton on July 16, 2016. *(Courtesy Alamy Live News.)*

*Facing top,* Pence was weighing two political options as the year 2015 arrived: seek a second term as governor in 2016 or make a bid for the presidency. Indianapolis Star cartoonist Gary Varvel illustrated the dilemma on the eve of the governor's State of the State Address. *(By permission Gary Varvel and Creators Syndicate, Inc.)*

*Facing bottom,* Following Donald Trump's announcement of Mike Pence as his running mate, cartoonists were quick to seize upon the pictorial possibilities. Gary Varvel of the Indianapolis Star showed Pence dutifully following behind Trump with a shovel. *(By permission Gary Varvel and Creators Syndicate, Inc.)*

President-elect Donald Trump and Vice President-elect Mike Pence took the stage during a "Thank You Tour" rally on December 16, 2016, at the Central Florida Fairgrounds in Orlando, Florida. *(Courtesy Alamy Live News.)*

*Facing top,* As delegates gathered for the Republican National Convention, GOP presidential nominee Donald Trump and Indiana governor Mike Pence attended a Family and Friends Welcome Rally in Cleveland, Ohio, on July 20, 2016. *(Courtesy Alamy Live News.)*

*Facing bottom,* President-elect Donald Trump conferred with House Speaker Paul Ryan and Vice President-elect Mike Pence in Washington DC on November 10, 2016. *(Courtesy Alamy Live News.)*

# 12

★ ★ ★

# TIPTOEING THROUGH
# THE MINEFIELDS

MIKE PENCE KNEW MITCH DANIELS WOULD BE A HARD ACT to follow.

Elected governor in 2004 in his first try at elective office, Daniels led the state to its first balanced budget in eight years. He fixed the broken license branch system. He expanded access to higher education. Re-elected in 2008, he received more votes than any candidate in Indiana history. By the time he left office four years later, Indiana enjoyed a budget surplus and a first-ever AAA credit rating.

Consultants offered this advice to Pence as he took office on January 14, 2013: Focus on jobs and education. Keep the Daniels momentum going. Downplay social issues. Avoid controversy at all costs. This last piece of advice would prove to be an impossible task considering the myriad political minefields standing in his way.

Mike Pence recited the gubernatorial oath with his left hand on the Bible that had belonged to President Benjamin Harrison, the nation's twenty-third and Indiana's only president. When Harrison took the presidential oath in 1889, his hand was on Psalm 121: "I will lift up mine eyes unto the hills, from whence cometh my help." Pence turned to 1 Kings, chapter 3: "Give therefore thy servant an understanding heart to judge thy people, that I may discern between good and bad; for who is able to govern so great a people?"[1] During the ceremony on the west steps of the statehouse, Pence sat in a hickory Windsor chair that dated to the eighteenth century and was owned by Benjamin Harrison's grandfather William Henry Harrison, the first territorial governor of Indiana and the ninth president. As a history buff, Pence understood the value of symbolism. He was the fiftieth governor. In the final year of his term, Indiana would celebrate its bicentennial. There were personal touches to the day, as well. Volunteers passed out hot chocolate and hand warmers to combat the subfreezing temperatures. Forty fourth graders from Pence's old elementary school in Columbus led the Pledge of Allegiance.

Pence opened his inaugural address by acknowledging those who had come before. He singled out by name previous governors, highlighting the signature accomplishment of each: Doc Bowen for tax reform, Frank O'Bannon for civility and goodwill, and Evan Bayh for "youthful energy and frugality." He reserved his highest praise for Daniels "for leaving our state the fiscal and administrative envy of the nation." Turning to Daniels, he said, "It's a good thing I am only succeeding you because no one will ever replace you."[2] The tone of the day was gracious, bipartisan, and collaborative. As Associated Press reporter Tom LoBianco observed that morning, "It looks like Mike Pence is hanging up his mitts after more than a decade of leading religious conservatives in fights against abortion, gay marriage, and President Barack Obama in Washington."[3]

No sooner than he took office, Pence found himself in a fight—with his own party leadership over his tax-cut proposal. During the campaign, Pence had promised to cut personal income taxes by 10 percent from 3.4 to 3.06 percent. It was one of several policy announcements that caught legislative leaders off guard and put them in a defensive posture before the session convened. "There's a built-in tension between executive and legislative branch leadership," noted Brian Bosma, speaker of the house.[4] The battle would continue until the final day of the budget-writing session, with Pence getting only half of what he wanted. It was an early lesson for Pence in state government dynamics, and it taught the governor and his staff to be less presumptuous in dealing with legislative leaders who had their own agendas to consider, not to mention egos.

The quarrel reached an apex midway through the session when a national conservative group called Americans for Prosperity launched a statewide advertising campaign to boost support for Pence's tax plan. The group, funded by the billionaire brothers David and Charles Koch, ran radio and TV ads that attacked house Republicans as big spenders. The accusation miffed Bosma, who said he'd been the "biggest ally in the building" of the free-market policies advocated by the Kochs.[5] The controversy reinforced the impression among Republican leaders that Pence, who received $200,000 from David Koch in his 2012 campaign for governor, was more interested in building a national profile to run for president than doing what was best for the state. In an unusual move, Bosma sent a letter to Republican county chairmen saying it would be better to phase out the inheritance tax than lower income tax rates, already among the nation's lowest. Some Pence staffers dismissed Bosma's objections as sour grapes, noting he'd given serious thought to running for governor in 2012.

Pence continued to press his plan up until the next-to-last day of the session but in the end agreed to concessions that allowed him to claim a partial victory. The compromise plan cut the income tax in two stages, to 3.3 percent in 2015 and to 3.23 in 2017—a 5 percent cut. It also eliminated the state's inheritance tax retroactively to the first day of the year, a priority of lawmakers. "At the end of the day I think the tax relief that we crafted together is better than what I was proposing," Pence said, extending an olive branch to legislative leaders.[6] Bosma was similarly positive about the outcome. "We were able to link arms at the end and say everybody won."[7] Going forward, Pence and top staff agreed to meet with legislative leaders in advance of the session to ensure a unified front.

While the tax quarrel was of Pence's own making, the next controversy was inevitable: a looming showdown over gay marriage that pitted traditional views of marriage against a rapidly changing society. Indiana lawmakers had been trying since 2011 to amend Indiana's constitution to define marriage as between one man and one woman. State law already defined it that way, but legislators thought constitutional language would have a better chance of withstanding legal challenge from gay couples seeking to wed in Indiana or moving to Indiana with licenses from other states. If Pence's political advisers had hoped the governor could sidestep this debate, they quickly learned otherwise.

On June 26, 2013, the Supreme Court added urgency to the matter with two rulings that, while not legalizing gay marriage, foreshadowed what was to come. The first struck down a provision in the federal Defense of Marriage Act that barred same-sex couples from receiving tax, health, and pension benefits. The second allowed gay weddings to resume in California, where a trial court had invalidated Proposition 8, a constitutional amendment passed by voters there that permitted only heterosexual unions.

Indiana's proposed amendment was similar to Proposition 8, but it was still in the early stages of the lengthy amendment process that required action by two consecutive assemblies followed by a vote of the citizenry. When reporters asked Pence for his position, he minced no words. Speaking on the issue for the first time as governor, he said, "I believe marriage is the union between a man and a woman and is a unique institution worth defending in our state and nation. For thousands of years, marriage has served as the glue that holds families and societies together, and so it should ever be."[8] Pence went on to say that he favored letting Hoosiers decide the issue in a statewide vote.

Public opinion had shifted dramatically since the early 2000s when an overwhelming majority of Hoosiers opposed gay marriage. A 2012 poll by WISH-TV and Ball State University showed Hoosiers were evenly divided on the matter at 45 percent; one year later, 48 percent favored it and 46 percent said no.[9] But there would be no vote by the citizens.

During the 2014 legislative session, lawmakers found themselves under intense pressure from a new pro-gay marriage alliance that included two of Indiana's Fortune 500 companies: Cummins of Columbus, Pence's hometown, and pharmaceutical giant Eli Lilly and Company of Indianapolis, one of the state's biggest employers. The legislature rewrote its proposed amendment to satisfy some of the coalition's concerns, which started the amendment process from scratch. For all practical purposes, the issue was dead.

On June 25, 2014, US District Judge Richard Young held that marriage was a "fundamental right" that could not be denied to gay couples and nullified Indiana's law defining marriage. One year later, the Supreme Court in *Obergefell v. Hodges* struck down all state laws and state constitutions that banned the practice, thus legalizing gay marriage in the fifty states.

Pence promised that Indiana would "uphold the rule of law" and comply fully with the court decision,[10] but his belief in traditional marriage marked him as anti-gay. For Kevin Warren, an Indianapolis real estate agent who campaigned against the constitutional amendment, a more accurate word was *homophobic*. "When Mike Pence became governor, it was like these red flags kept jumping up at me, and I said, 'We've got to watch this person.'"[11] During the debate over House Joint Resolution 3, Warren gave away yard signs opposing the amendment. As demand for the blue and yellow signs boomed, he began charging ten dollars and turned his informal campaign into a registered political action committee called Pence Must Go. Proceeds went to the civil rights group Lambda Legal. "We raised $70,000 off our front porch," he said.[12] Over the next two years, the posters addressed an increasing range of topics, bearing such slogans as "Women's Health Matters," "Cast the First Stone," and "Separation of Church & State." Underlying many of the messages was Warren's number-one grievance: Pence wanted to impose his religious agenda on the rest of the populace.

The accusation had followed Pence through much of his political life, in large part because of his "outspoken Christian witness," said friend Ed Simcox. Since his days at Hanover, Pence routinely practiced the disciplines of prayer, Bible study, and worship. As a member of Greenwood Christian Church in the 1990s, he took part in a weekly accountability group with Pastor Jim Dodson and two other participants who would share personal joys and challenges and ways to faithfully deal with them. In Washington DC, Pence belonged to the Congressional Prayer Caucus, a bipartisan group of sixty that gathered before important votes in Room 219 of the US Capitol. Following his election as governor, Pence asked Simcox to lead a weekly covenant group that met every Tuesday morning at the governor's residence. The group of six would read scripture or a devotional text and discuss life events using a biblical lens. "Living out a strong personal faith in public life is tricky business," observed Simcox, a former Indiana secretary of state known for his thirty-year service in prison ministry. "Mike talks the talk, but he also walks the walk, not with a hard edge or judgmental spirit but with kindness, gentleness, and civility."[13] From the vantage of critics like Warren, Pence's many public statements of Christian faith called into question his commitment to freedom of religion and the First Amendment.

A math problem on an eight-year-old's homework kindled the next issue to trouble the Pence administration. Indiana had adopted the Common Core academic standards in 2010 at the direction of Governor Daniels and school superintendent Tony Bennett. The Common Core was a set of learning guidelines for math and language arts designed to standardize what was taught in K–12 classrooms across the country. There was no debate and almost no news coverage when the Indiana State Board of Education approved the standards, so few Hoosiers knew that the state's previous, highly ranked academic standards had been replaced by a national boilerplate that would eventually be adopted by forty-six states.

A public backlash erupted just in time for the 2012 election. During the 2011–12 school year, Heather Crossin, a concerned parent and conservative Republican, saw a change in the math problems her daughter was bringing home from her Indianapolis school. "Instead of many arithmetic problems, the homework would contain only three or four questions, and two of those would be 'explain your answer.' Like, 'One bridge is 412 feet long and the other bridge is 206 feet long. Which bridge is longer? How do you know?'"[14] With just a little digging, she found that the bewildering new questions were the result of Common Core and its emphasis on "understanding of numbers" over process mastery.[15]

Crossin teamed up with Erin Tuttle, a like-minded mother, to found Hoosiers against Common Core. Like Crossin, Tuttle had noticed "fuzzy math" problems in her child's third-grade textbook. Their crusade was widely credited with Democrat Glenda Ritz's defeat of incumbent Republican Tony Bennett in the school superintendent's race that year.

The two advocates found an enthusiastic ally in state senator Scott Schneider, who opposed any national initiative that stripped states of their power to set education policy. In 2013, the legislature delayed implementation of the standards pending further study. In 2014, lawmakers passed a bill that required the State Board of Education to rescind Common Core and adopt "the highest standards in the United States."[16]

As a strong believer in federalism and state authority over education, Pence was expected to encourage the writing of unique Indiana standards that could be the envy of the nation. But equal pressure was coming at him from education reform groups and the Indiana Chamber of Commerce, which favored Common Core and the uniformity it would bring to schools. The chamber spent more than $100,000 on ads opposing Schneider's bill and questioned the influence of two activists with "no educational backgrounds." In a blog post, a staff member wrote: "Two moms from Indianapolis, a handful of their friends, and a couple dozen small but vocal Tea Party groups. That's the entire Indiana movement that is advocating for a halt to the Common Core State Standards."[17] The blogger was wrong on that score; during the standards-writing process, more than two thousand Hoosiers posted online comments, most of them critical, and hundreds more attended public meetings.[18] Yet the chamber's perspective carried the day. Pence's education staff backed a modest rewrite of the Common Core standards, just enough to rename them the Indiana Academic Standards. One critic branded them "a cut and paste job from the Common Core," full of "circumlocutory edu-speak."[19]

Pence convened the Indiana Education Roundtable on April 21 to approve the standards, a necessary step before forwarding them to the state education board for final action. More than two hundred people packed a statehouse hallway that morning to urge the governor to reject the draft and start over. Many held signs that said, "Governor Pence, are you listening?" Following the rally, protesters walked across the street to the meeting in the State Office Building. When Pence entered the conference room, he was surprised by the standing-room-only crowd. He had not realized the intensity of the opposition. "What's going on? Why are all these people here?" he asked a staff member.[20]

As chair of the roundtable, Pence spoke first in favor of the proposed standards, drawing jeers and laughter from the crowd when he declared, "Clearly these standards were written by Hoosiers and for Hoosiers."[21] The roundtable, representing business, labor, and academia, approved the standards with little dissent. The State Board of Education followed suit a week later on a 10–1 vote with Democratic school superintendent Glenda Ritz siding with Pence.

Much like what occurred in the tax-hike debate, Pence claimed political victory. National headlines credited Indiana as the first state to withdraw from the Common Core, which emboldened other states to do the same. Crossin was disillusioned by what appeared to be a sham process overseen by the governor. "He lacked the strength to buck some of the people whispering in his ear," she observed.[22] Nationally syndicated columnist Michelle Malkin offered a more scathing assessment: "Pence's attempt to mollify critics by rebranding and repackaging shoddy Common Core standards is fooling no one," she wrote.[23] Later in the year, Pence made up with his right-wing base by halting the state's application for an $80 million federal grant for early childhood education, citing concerns about federal intrusion. Although the idea of universal preschool was popular with voters in both parties, social conservatives pointed to decades of research showing only temporary academic gain from government-run preschools and negative behavioral outcomes. Despite the political fallout that came with his decision, Pence had reassured his most loyal constituency.

In the middle of Pence's term, longtime chief of staff Bill Smith stepped down to start a political consulting firm. Smith, who'd been with Pence since his first successful campaign for Congress, had been commuting to the statehouse each day from Elwood, and the sixty-five-minute drive was taxing. Smith intended to play a new role as political adviser to Pence, whom pundits assumed would either seek a second term as governor in 2016 or pursue the presidency.

Jim Atterholt, a former state representative and chair of the Indiana Utility Regulatory Commission, was on the short list to replace Smith, but Pence was in no hurry to decide. A month-long interview process ensued with much of the conversation focused on faith and family. The two men golfed, and they met later with their wives for lunch at the governor's residence. This was Pence's standard practice when hiring key advisers; he considered personal chemistry and family buy-in essential to a successful political career. "I checked the boxes," Atterholt said. "A believer. A conservative record in the legislature. With ten years of executive branch experience, somebody who had strong relationships with the statehouse community."[24] Pence offered him the position and then urged him to go home, discuss it with his wife, and pray over it before accepting. Atterholt did. He moved into his new office in May 2014.

As the two men got to know each other, Pence confessed to Atterholt that he was overwhelmed with the minutiae that came with being governor. "He was overscheduled, making too many small decisions, couldn't think, couldn't breathe."[25] Atterholt's first suggestion was to take better advantage of Sue Ellspermann, who, as lieutenant governor, could make public appearances and assume ceremonial obligations on his behalf. His next solution was to empower staff to make more of the day-to-day decisions that did not entail policy. On his first day in the office, Atterholt met with staff to introduce himself and review procedures. He reminded them of the long-standing office policy of "no surprises."[26]

Ironically, the next controversy to befall the Pence administration came as a surprise to all involved and threatened to steal headlines from what was to be Pence's signature accomplishment as governor. Pence was poised to announce the Obama administration's approval of the Healthy Indiana Plan (HIP) 2.0, a state-led expansion of Medicaid that would provide health-care coverage to 350,000 uninsured Hoosiers. He'd been working for months to obtain a waiver of federal rules, even lobbying President Obama personally on the tarmac of the Evansville airport during his visit to Indiana in October of 2014.

On the morning of Pence's announcement, *Indianapolis Star* reporter Tom LoBianco broke a page-one story about the administration's plans for a state-run website and media service that would generate news and feature stories about the executive branch for statewide distribution. A state employee had leaked to LoBianco a question-and-answer sheet sent from Pence communications director Christy Denault to state agency officials explaining the new service, to be called Just IN.[27] LoBianco's story quoted journalism experts questioning the use of tax dollars to write news stories with a pro-Pence slant. "A state-run news agency?" asked *Indianapolis Star* columnist Matt Tully. "What in the name of Vladimir Putin is the administration thinking?"[28] Once the Gannett news wire picked up the piece, coverage went national. The *Atlantic* joked about "Pravda on the Plains," a reference to the mouthpiece of the Communist Party in the old Soviet Union.[29] Even House Speaker Bosma, a fellow Republican, used his weekly press briefing to poke fun at the notion of a government-run news agency while wearing a Russian-style hat.

Former *Indianapolis Star* reporter Bill McCleery, hired as managing editor, said Just IN was not intended to be a competitive news agency but rather a one-stop shop for citizens seeking information about state government services.[30] No explanation could stanch the unfolding public relations disaster. Four days after the story broke, Pence killed the idea. "The demagoguery had reached a fever pitch," Atterholt said. "It was stepping on the HIP 2.0 announcement—one of our key policies. It just had to be triaged."[31]

HIP 2.0 was the evolution of a low-cost health-insurance program enacted during the Daniels administration. Pence wanted to use the program to expand Medicaid coverage in Indiana—on his terms rather than under the conditions of the Affordable Care Act, the law he'd so vigorously opposed as a congressman. Pence asked health-care advisers Seema Verma and Brian Neale to craft a program that would give consumers a choice of health-care providers and offer financial incentives to use preventative care that would save taxpayers money in the long run. "It was really pretty revolutionary," Atterholt said.[32]

The Pence plan required participants to pay a small premium, up to $25 a month, in exchange for coverage. That was the sticking point for the federal government. Beneficiaries in the traditional Medicaid program pay nothing, but Pence thought it critical that recipients have skin in the game.

In contrast to other issues, which the governor delegated to staff, he got into the granular details of this one.[33] He wrote letters, lobbied, and flew to Washington several times to negotiate with officials at the US Department of Health and Human Services. In the end, the Obama administration approved the waiver. Critics on both right and left complained that the program was too generous or too punitive, a good indication of Pence's political astuteness. As even the liberal *Slate* news magazine noted, Pence had found a way to frame an expanded entitlement program "in free-market and personal responsibility terms while he was actually strengthening the social safety net."[34]

By this time, Pence had figured out the difference between being a congressman and being a governor. In Washington, he had seen his role as obstructionist—fighting bad bills, holding leadership accountable, and reminding colleagues of Republican principles of limited government. As governor, he had to lead. That meant setting a vision and winning over the public and lawmakers. Pence's 2015 State of the State Address was a veritable Christmas list of aspirations: end the war on coal, wage a war on infant mortality, enact a state balanced budget amendment, expand private school choice, give more money to charter schools, and guarantee vocational education in every Indiana high school. Some of the goals were realistic, others clearly aimed at scoring political points. "I guess we heard something today that is going to sound good for voters outside Indiana," responded Democratic minority leader Scott Pelath of Michigan City, who took particular aim at the balanced budget proposal.[35] He noted that Indiana's constitution already kept the state from incurring debt so Hoosiers hardly needed an additional requirement. It seemed obvious to Pelath that Pence was gearing up for a run at national office. But there was one legislative proposal Pence didn't mention that would prove to be a land mine. The Religious Freedom Restoration Act was already making its way through the General Assembly. It made a shambles of Pelath's prediction and would forever alter Indiana's political landscape.

# 13

★ ★ ★

## CRISIS AT THE CAPITOL

A FEW MINUTES INTO GEORGE STEPHANOPOULOS'S ELEVEN-minute grilling of Governor Mike Pence, supporters knew Senate Enrolled Act 101 was toast. Pence had agreed to appear on ABC's Sunday morning show *This Week with George Stephanopoulos* to clarify "misinformation and misunderstanding" about the Indiana religious freedom law that was under national attack as a license to discriminate against gays and lesbians. Pence, who had signed the measure into law, wanted viewers to know that it merely gave individuals a chance to go to court if they felt the government infringed on religious liberty. He went on the air to correct the "gross mischaracterization" of the law by the media. "This is not about discrimination. This is about empowering people to confront government overreach," Pence said.[1]

Over the next few minutes, Stephanopoulos asked Pence a series of yes-or-no questions: "Can a florist refuse to serve a gay couple at their wedding?" "Would the law protect such refusal?" "Do you think it should be legal in the state of Indiana to discriminate against gays or lesbians?" No matter how Stephanopoulos phrased it, Pence dodged. The law did not apply to disputes between individuals unless government action was involved, Pence insisted. There are no kinder, more generous, more welcoming people than Hoosiers, and Hoosiers don't believe in discrimination. An exasperated Stephanopoulos ended the interview without getting the answer he wanted.

The controversy over Indiana's Religious Freedom Restoration Act was the single biggest crisis of Pence's tenure as governor. Critics thought the incident might end his career in politics, believing they'd exposed Pence as a hypocrite who wanted to deny basic rights to homosexuals. Supporters blamed Pence for failing to adequately defend a law that did nothing more than create a new standard of judicial review in religious practice lawsuits.

As the saga unfolded, neither side missed the irony. Congress had passed similar federal legislation in 1993, cosponsored by Democrats Ted Kennedy and Charles Schumer and signed into law by President Clinton, with nary a protest. The federal law was in reaction to a 1990 Supreme Court ruling that, in the eyes of Congress, misinterpreted the First Amendment's free exercise clause. Two Native Americans had been fired from their jobs and denied unemployment benefits because they used peyote, a hallucinogenic drug, in their religious rituals.[2] After the high court denied their request for a religious exemption to Oregon's controlled substance law, Congress—almost unanimously—enacted the Religious Freedom Restoration Act (RFRA). The law stated, "Government shall not substantially burden a person's exercise of religion even if the burden results from a rule of general applicability,"[3] for example, a narcotics law. Nineteen states followed suit with similar legislation.

Society had changed in the twenty-five years since the peyote case. On June 25, 2014, a federal judge struck down an Indiana law defining marriage as between one man and one woman.[4] Efforts to place a gay marriage ban into the state constitution had failed, and the US Supreme Court was poised to decide if gays had a right to marriage under the US Constitution, an idea that would have been unimaginable a quarter century earlier. Conservative Christians were looking for new ways to defend their biblically based views about the institution of marriage, and religious liberty litigation seemed a promising avenue. Liberal groups such as the Indiana Civil Liberties Union, which had previously backed RFRA laws to protect minority religious groups from oppression, now feared those laws could be applied by those who opposed same-sex marriage to deny services to gays. This was the backdrop for the 2015

Indiana General Assembly when it convened in January to consider the RFRA.

Its author was Scott Schneider, a Republican state senator who represented the north side of Indianapolis. Schneider was a small-business owner who had previously served on the Indianapolis's city-county council. Reflective of many conservative Hoosiers, he opposed abortion and gay marriage, preferred state over federal control of health care and education, and advocated tax cuts for businesses and individuals. He had recently led the fight to repeal the Common Core, the untested national K–12 academic standards that many considered an unwarranted interference with state education policy.

Schneider had begun working on the legislation right after the US Supreme Court issued its June 2014 ruling in another religious freedom case, *Burwell v. Hobby Lobby Stores*. Under the Patient Protection and Affordable Care Act, signed into law by President Obama in 2010, companies were required to cover contraceptives in their insurance plans or face steep financial penalties. The Green family, owners of a national chain of arts and crafts shops with thirteen thousand workers, objected on religious grounds to paying for birth control in the group health plan they offered employees. The Greens claimed the mandate violated both the free exercise clause of the First Amendment and the federal RFRA. Similar suits had been filed across the country, including one in Southern Indiana where Madison-based Grote Industries, owned by a Roman Catholic family, objected to subsidizing morning-after pills, contraceptives, and sterilization.

The issue deeply divided the Supreme Court. Under RFRA, a government action that imposes a "substantial burden" on religious exercise must serve a compelling government interest. In this instance, the compelling interest was universal access to health care, including birth control. But in order for the government mandate to stand, it must be the least restrictive means of serving that interest, and "the mandate plainly fails that test," the court found. Writing for a 5–4 majority, Justice Samuel Alito said, "There are other ways in which Congress or HHS (the Department of Health and Human Services) could equally ensure that every woman has cost-free access to the particular contraceptives at issue here and, indeed, to all FDA-approved contraceptives."[5] The decision was controversial because it extended RFRA protections to family businesses like Hobby Lobby as well as individuals.

Because the decision hinged on federal law, and not the First Amendment, Schneider worried about the security of religious liberties in Indiana. "Although there is strong religious freedom language in the state constitution, there is nothing that protects an entity from government action," he observed.[6] Schneider consulted with local attorneys and law professors and decided that a state version of RFRA would be a worthwhile safeguard. He contacted senate president pro tempore David Long, a Republican from Fort Wayne, to tell him he was drafting a bill. He also met with Jim Atterholt, Governor Pence's chief of staff, to brief him on the legislation he expected to file in the upcoming session, though he did not ask for the governor's endorsement. Senators Dennis Kruse and Brent Steele signed on as coauthors.

Pence made no mention of RFRA, or any divisive social issue, in his January 13 State of the State Address, maintaining his promise to stay focused on jobs, fiscal health, and education. In the only surprise of the night, he asked the Indiana General Assembly to begin the process of amending the constitution to insert a balanced budget requirement. The Indiana Constitution already limited the state's ability to take on debt, so Democrats dismissed the idea as a "parlor trick" designed to hide the fact Pence had nothing new to say.[7] Other than that, Pence's vision for 2015 drew virtually no criticism.

Controversy was just around the corner. On January 20, 2015, Schneider introduced Senate Bill 568, later merged into Kruse's Senate Bill 101. It provided that government "may not substantially burden a person's right to the exercise of religion"—unless it can show that there is a compelling reason to do so and that it is the least restrictive method. The bill's language applied to people engaged in business as well as individuals in private lawsuits.[8] To ordinary citizens, the bill was so much gobbledygook. To activists on both sides, every word counted.

Because the bill closely followed the federal RFRA, Schneider did not expect heavy opposition. Yet even before he filed the measure with the senate clerk, the headlines suggested otherwise. Around Christmas, a reporter for the *Indianapolis Star* telephoned Micah Clark, director of the American Family Association of Indiana, to see what bills they were following. Clark, whose organization advocated values based on biblical principles, said he'd heard mention of a bill that would allow bakeries, caterers, florists, and wedding chapels to refuse service to gay couples based on their religious beliefs. The Associated Press picked up the story, which appeared in the Indiana edition of the Louisville *Courier Journal* under the headline "Bill would let businesses refuse service to gays."[9] In Schneider's opinion, both Clark and the headline writer missed the point of the legislation, which was to protect the free exercise of religion from government interference.

On February 9, the Senate Committee on the Judiciary heard five hours of testimony. A Baptist pastor expressed concerns he might be forced by the government to officiate at a gay wedding. A chamber of commerce spokeswoman warned of damage to Indiana tourism and employee recruitment. GOP lawmakers were reassured when Indiana University law professor Daniel Conkle, who supported gay marriage, endorsed the bill. He testified that it would give valuable guidance to Indiana courts weighing religious freedom claims against other competing interests. "There have been suggestions that this legislation would be a 'license to discriminate' that would undermine gay rights and same-sex marriage," Conkle said. "In my judgment it is no such thing. If I thought it would, I would not be here testifying in support of this legislation."[10] Conkle's support carried extra weight with many of the lawyer-lawmakers who had taken his constitutional law class at Indiana University.

On the senate floor, Democrats tried unsuccessfully to amend the measure to make clear that it could not be used as a tool to discriminate against gays. Republicans defeated four amendments, including one pointedly offered by Senator Karen Tallian that would have required businesses refusing service to post a sign explaining their prejudice. The predominantly Republican senate remained steadfast that the bill had no discriminatory intent and passed the bill on February 24 on a 40–10 party line vote.

When the measure reached the house, Speaker Brian Bosma of Indianapolis looked it over and green-lighted it for consideration. "I concluded as a practicing lawyer that all we're talking about is a judicial review standard," Bosma recalled. "We weren't talking about discrimination."[11] Many of the witnesses who testified before the Senate judiciary committee returned for a four-hour hearing before the House Committee on the Judiciary. Sponsoring representative Tim Wesco of Osceola painstakingly explained his reason for carrying the bill in the house. He told the story of a church in his district that wanted to relocate to downtown Goshen to an area zoned for commercial use but was opposed by businesses wanting to preserve storefronts for retail activity. "The Board of Zoning Appeals should not discriminate against that church simply because they are religious," he argued.[12] The committee approved the measure 9–4 on March 16 with Republicans voting yes and Democrats no.

Up to this point, nothing about the bill's progression through the legislature raised red flags for Senator Schneider. Both sides testified in an open hearing. Democrats proposed amendments. With supermajorities in both the house and the senate, Republicans felt no pressure to accept them. The first clue that things might play out differently than usual came a few days before the house vote when Scott McCorkle, CEO of Salesforce Marketing Cloud, addressed a letter to the Indiana General Assembly warning of economic backlash if the bill passed.

Salesforce was a big player in Indiana's high-tech world. The San Francisco–based cloud computing company had purchased ExactTarget of Indianapolis for $2.5 billion in July 2013. The company's success, McCorkle said, was tied directly to its ability to attract highly skilled employees, regardless of gender, religious affiliation, ethnicity, or sexual orientation. RFRA jeopardized all that. "Without an open business environment that welcomes all residents and visitors, Salesforce will be unable to continue building on its tradition of marketing innovation in Indianapolis," he said.[13] With 1,700 Indiana employees, promises to grow, and a forty-eight-story downtown high-rise to manage, Salesforce had clout to accompany its threat.

On March 23, the house passed Senate Bill 101 63–31. Still, it was not a done deal. The bill had to return to the senate for lawmakers' consent to minor wording changes made in the house. The same day, in the first sign of the intensive social media campaign to come, Yahoo sports analyst Jason Collins posted on Twitter: "@GovPenceIN, is it going to be legal for someone to discriminate against me & others when we come to the #FinalFour?"[14] The tweet from Collins, who came out in 2013 as the first openly gay player in the NBA, galvanized others coming to Indianapolis for the NCAA men's basketball tournament the first week in April. The hashtag #Fina14Fairness exploded across social media.

The pressure continued. On March 24, the senate concurred with the house changes and sent the bill to the governor. Lobbying efforts instantly switched from the legislature to the governor's office, with groups now calling on Pence to veto the measure. Gen Con, a four-day gaming convention held annually in Indianapolis, threatened to relocate future events, prompting Indianapolis mayor Greg Ballard into action. Ballard, a Republican, said the bill sent the "wrong signal" about Indiana's openness to diversity and proclaimed his city welcoming to all.[15] Gen Con was the city's single largest convention, attracting fifty-six thousand visitors and generating fifty million in tourism dollars each year. On March 25, the Christian Church (Disciples of Christ) said it would cancel its 2017 convention in Indianapolis, which was expected to draw six thousand attendees. The ultimatums alarmed officials at Visit Indy, the city's convention and tourism bureau, which moved into damage control to reassure clients of Hoosier hospitality.

Despite the growing pressure to veto Senate Bill 101, Pence didn't hesitate. He favored the bill on the merits and saw no reason to second-guess the legislative process. The governor's office invited bill sponsors and advocates to a ceremonial signing on the morning of March 26. More than eighty people attended the event, which was closed to media. "I'd never seen the governor's office so packed for a signing ceremony," Atterholt recalled.[16] Among the guests were Curt Smith of the Indiana Family Institute and the American Family Association's Clark, both leaders of pro-family groups whose members lobbied intensively for the bill.

Yet even as people squeezed into the lobby waiting to be admitted, Schneider felt apprehensive: "There was excitement in the room for our accomplishment, but there was also an underlying thickness in the air, a sense of a building tension or nervousness, like waiting for an impending storm. It was not a pleasant feeling." Office phones rang incessantly, and staffers struggled to answer callers' questions. "Yes, the governor plans on signing the bill this morning." "No, the bill does not allow discrimination." From what he overheard, it was clear to Schneider the public did not understand the bill's intent.[17]

Pence signed the bill and autographed several copies of it, giving one signing pen to each of the three primary legislative sponsors and a fourth to Curt Smith, a trusted friend. Cameras recorded a moment right after the signing when a smiling Pence posed with the bill's authors alongside monks, nuns, and orthodox rabbis wearing religious garb. Pence's media staff posted the picture on his official Twitter account, thinking the racial and religious variety in the group would send a message of inclusion. Instead, house speaker Bosma noted, "that photo went viral and then the issue went viral."[18] Immediately following the ceremony, the governor headed to a news conference to field questions about the law. As Senator Schneider exited the governor's office with Pence aide Jackie Cissell, they discussed the unforeseen firestorm. "Jackie, the truth of the bill is not getting out; it is not being heard." Cissell pounded her fist into her palm. "We are going to fix that right now. The governor is headed to a presser (news conference) upstairs to set the record straight."[19]

Pence spent the remainder of the day attempting to allay concerns. He planned to speak personally to organizations and businesses worried about the bill's effect. "I'll call them. I'll talk to them," he insisted. "This is not about legalizing discrimination." In a radio interview that afternoon, Pence blamed media for misrepresenting the law. "If you read the bill instead of reading the papers, you would see that the Religious Freedom Restoration Act, which is now law in Indiana, is simply about giving the courts guidance and establishing the same standards that have existed at the federal level for more than 20 years," he said.[20]

Within hours of the signing, organized economic and travel boycotts of Indiana erupted—seemingly out of nowhere. Salesforce said it would no longer require customers or employees to travel to Indiana for business. Angie's List canceled plans to pursue a $40 million expansion in Indianapolis. The state of Connecticut and the cities of San Francisco and Seattle banned travel to Indiana by state employees. Jennifer Pizer of Lambda Legal, the oldest civil rights organization for gays, warned that the "economic and legal consequences for Indiana will unfold with time."[21]

Senator Schneider recognized the breadth of the campaign when colleagues outside Indianapolis began reporting economic threats in their districts, reaching into rural counties. A California company contacted a little-known copper wire maker to say it would no longer do business with it because it was based in Indiana.[22] The attacks were personal, too. Schneider faced death threats, and his family's commercial ice business was blacklisted locally. All signs pointed to an organized national campaign that was "pre-loaded to unleash" on whichever state passed the first RFRA of 2015.[23] Legislatures in Arkansas and Georgia monitored the Indiana situation closely and reacted accordingly. After Governor Asa Hutchinson threatened a veto, the Arkansas bill was amended to meet objections and signed into law on April 2. The Georgia bill, which easily passed the state senate, was tabled in a house committee on March 26.

The frenzy continued into the weekend. On Saturday, March 28, Pence met with friends and advisers to consider next steps. The governor's staff and legislators had already raised the possibility of rewriting the new law. Curt Smith, in two separate phone calls with Pence staff, adamantly opposed the idea and suggested that the governor instead issue an executive order making clear that RFRA did not allow discrimination.[24] Also under discussion was whether Pence should go on national television to try to clarify matters. The press office had fielded numerous requests, and opinion was divided. Bill Smith counseled against any national interviews, but Pence wanted to defend the citizens of Indiana, whom he felt were getting a bad rap from the negative publicity. "He was angry that it was turning out to be a case against Indiana in addition to being a case against Mike Pence," Smith recalled.[25] The next decision was whether Pence should appear with Stephanopoulos of ABC or FOX's Megyn Kelly.[26] With Stephanopoulos, he would reach a broader audience; on the conservative FOX network, he would be preaching to the choir.

For all of his polish and experience on broadcast media, Pence was not prepared for the onslaught of questions from Stephanopoulos, a former aide to President Bill Clinton. Out of the gate, the host asked, "So was it a mistake to sign this law?"

"Absolutely not," Pence answered. "I was proud to sign it into law last week."

Repeatedly, Stephanopoulos asked Pence if critics, and some supporters, were correct in saying the law would allow refusal of services to gays. Indiana antidiscrimination laws, he pointed out, did not treat gays and lesbians as a protected class. Might they be vulnerable to discrimination under RFRA? Each time, Pence changed the subject. He decried the baseless "avalanche" of condemnation Indiana had suffered and called out the left for its hypocrisy on matters of religious diversity, noting that "tolerance is a two-way street." Midway through the interview, Pence awkwardly suggested that the act could be rewritten. "We're not going to change the law, OK?" he said. "But if the General Assembly in Indiana sends me a bill that adds a section that reiterates and amplifies and clarifies what the law really is and what it has been for the last twenty years, then I'm open to that."[27]

Curt Smith watched with dismay, wondering why the governor did not flatly deny that the bill was a license to discriminate.[28] Jeff Cardwell, just days away from his election to become Republican state chairman, was attending worship services that morning and did not see the show live, but by the time he got home from church, text messages on his cell phone told the story: "You have to watch it. The interview did not go well."[29]

The TV appearance that intended to clarify the law had only intensified debate. The next day, a letter signed by executives of nine of Indiana's largest employers was hand-delivered to Pence, Bosma, and Long, demanding "immediate action to ensure that the Religious Freedom Restoration Act will not sanction or encourage discrimination against any residents or visitors to our state by anyone."[30] The signers included CEOs of three Fortune 500 companies: Joseph Swedish of Anthem, John Lechleiter of Eli Lilly and Company, and Tom Linebarger of Cummins, the international engine manufacturer based in Pence's hometown of Columbus. Another signer was Dan Evans of Indiana University Health, a lifelong Republican, who registered his objections personally with Pence and Bosma. "I was getting calls from mid-level gay employees who wondered if Indiana was a safe place to live," Evans said.[31]

On March 31, the *Indianapolis Star* ran a full-page editorial on page one under the headline "FIX THIS NOW." "Governor, Indiana is in a state of crisis. It is worse than you seem to understand."[32] The editorial called for a new state law prohibiting discrimination on the basis of sexual orientation or gender identity. The bold treatment stunned longtime subscribers to the paper, now part of the Gannett chain but previously owned by the family of legendary conservative publisher Eugene C. Pulliam.

With or without the newspaper's urging, a fix had become inevitable. Pence knew it, but he felt trapped between personal conviction and political reality. "This was a serious economic threat," Atterholt explained. "He had to look out for the best interests of the state over his own ideological concerns. All of the economic development and job growth progress we had made was in jeopardy."[33] Bosma agreed there was no other way out. "There would have been such a continued hue and cry—inaccurately—it would have continued to be a daily issue in Indiana and badly diminish our state's reputation in the country."[34]

Negotiations ensued among key legislators, business and sports leaders, and members of the governor's staff. It was Wednesday, April 1, and the NCAA national semifinals were just three days away. All the Final Four television coverage seemed focused with laser intensity on RFRA and whether the NCAA would keep its headquarters or future tournaments in Indianapolis. Tension mounted. After a marathon session, participants agreed to add to the law language stating that RFRA did not "authorize a provider to refuse to offer or provide services, facilities, goods, employment, housing, or public accommodation to any member of the public based on sexual orientation or gender identity." A provider was defined as an individual, business, or organization. Churches and nonprofit religious organizations were exempted.[35]

Democrats who had hoped to take advantage of the crisis to enact a statewide antidiscrimination law to protect the LGBT community did not get their way. But conservative Republicans, who had pushed for the law in the first place, felt betrayed. The proposed fix "completely and utterly reversed the protections RFRA had just created for individuals of faith whose commercial enterprises came in conflict with same-sex couples seeking marriage services or just about anything else," Curt Smith argued.[36]

After suspending all rules to push the bill through immediately, the senate voted 66–30 and the house 34–16 to send the bill to Governor Pence. Pressed by some of his most loyal supporters to veto or amend the fix, Pence briefly wavered. "Legislative leadership will make no further changes," Atterholt told him. "There is no more negotiation."[37] Pence signed Senate Bill 50 into law that afternoon.

Although the threats of economic sanctions died out quickly, Democrats put Pence in their crosshairs. "Pence Must Go" signs began appearing in Indianapolis and around the state. "We knew he was a wolf in sheep's clothing," said Kevin Warren, the Indianapolis Democrat and gay rights activist who sold anti-Pence signs from his front porch. Although a gubernatorial election was more than nineteen months away, Warren's aim was to keep Pence from a second term.[38]

Tim Swarens, editor of the editorial page of the *Indianapolis Star*, sat down with Pence to ask what he had learned. "I certainly learned—again—that I'm not perfect. If I have a regret, I regret that we didn't spend more time listening before the bill got to my desk." Swarens, among others, predicted the episode might be Pence's undoing. "His mishandling of RFRA provides Democrats with the best opportunity in 12 years to win back the governor's office and even raises the potential for a challenge in the Republican primary."[39]

That Pence would find himself in such a predicament would have been unthinkable a few short months earlier. The governor had tiptoed carefully around social issues since his 2012 campaign, partly out of principle and partly out of self-preservation. He had always believed that in his role as governor he should not be overly aggressive in pushing social policy; that job belonged more appropriately to the legislative branch. If a bill came to him, he would sign it, but he would not initiate. Looking ahead to presidential possibilities, he'd been advised by his consultants to avoid making waves that could affect his political ambitions. The RFRA proved to be a tidal wave. Although it was not a part of the governor's agenda, by signing it into law he had become its most visible champion. It was yet another irony of the RFRA debacle that Pence became—virtually overnight—the face of homophobia. The reputation was undeserved in the eyes of his supporters, but it was much too soon to say whether it would be his political undoing.

# 14

★ ★ ★

# THE HOLCOMB EFFECT

INDIANA'S TWO HUNDREDTH BIRTHDAY PROVIDED A WEL-
come respite from the trials of being governor. Although "Pence Must
Go" signs dotted the landscape, the hubbub over the Religious Freedom
Restoration Act died down quickly, thanks to a host of distractions.
Dozens of projects were under way to mark the anniversary of Indiana's
first constitution, penned in the hot summer of 1816 by forty-three delegates famously meeting in Corydon under a shady elm tree.

Nearly two thousand Hoosier torchbearers from all ninety-two
counties were taking part in a 3,200-mile relay across Indiana. Con-
struction workers converted the street west of the statehouse into a
Bicentennial Plaza with two competitively chosen sculptures and a
water fountain appropriately ringed by Indiana limestone. Lieutenant
Governor Sue Ellspermann and former congressman Lee Hamilton led
notable Hoosiers in a planning process projecting big ideas for Indiana's
third century.

In January, Pence used his State of the State Address to applaud the
latest economic data—numbers that could serve as the backbone for
his reelection campaign: 139,000 new jobs, unemployment down from
8 to 4.4 percent, 34,000 fewer Hoosiers on unemployment insurance.
"Here in our bicentennial year, there are more Hoosiers going to work
than ever before in our history," he said.[1] In the same address, he asked
lawmakers for a billion dollars in new money to spend on highways,

bridges, and local roads. Infrastructure was one taxpayer investment that proved popular with voters across the political spectrum.

Behind the scenes, Indiana Republicans had personnel matters to resolve. Jeff Cardwell, who'd been with Pence in various capacities since the 1988 campaign, now held the post of Republican state chairman. For him, this was not just the bicentennial year but a high-stakes election year with president, governor, and US Senate races all on the ballot. "As state chairman, my job was to keep the base energized," he recalled.[2]

Three Republicans were pursuing the open US Senate seat created by Dan Coats's retirement, and the race was dividing the rank and file, not to mention eating up precious campaign dollars that might otherwise be spent in the general election. Each of the three candidates presented worthy credentials. Eric Holcomb, who headed Coats's Indiana office, had a head start, having launched his campaign just two days after his boss said he would not seek another term. Representative Todd Young enjoyed strong financial support from Washington DC pro-business groups, and Representative Marlin Stutzman was favored among Tea Party Republicans. Democrats, in contrast, had rallied behind a single candidate, former congressman Baron Hill—at least for the moment. (As the race took on urgency later in the year, Hill would dramatically and sacrificially step away so Evan Bayh could replace him on the ballot.)

At the state level, there was a growing rift between the Pence campaign and Ellspermann, who did not want to play attack dog in the reprise of the 2012 Pence versus Gregg election. John Gregg had decided to take on Pence once more, encouraged that fallout from the RFRA episode would bolster his fund-raising and popularity among moderate voters. "In our polls, Mike's negatives were in the low to mid forties," Gregg said. "And we had money this time."[3] In fact, Gregg had $17 million at his disposal, almost three times what he spent in 2012.

Longtime political columnist Brian Howey dated the tension between Pence and Ellspermann to the fall of 2015 when she publicly advocated an expansion of state civil rights law to include the LGBT community, which was not on Pence's legislative agenda.[4] Jim Atterholt, Pence's chief of staff, attributed the disagreement to a debate over campaign strategy.[5] Pence defeated Gregg by a modest 2 percent four years earlier after a sentimental campaign that highlighted their Hoosier heritage as much as policy differences. John Gregg had promoted himself as "the guy with two first names" and extolled the virtues of an Indiana where "people look out for each other."[6] Pence responded by walking hand in hand with Karen alongside cornstalks higher than fence posts and praising "the strong and good people of Indiana."[7] For the 2016 campaign, campaign advisers Marty Obst and Nick Ayers insisted that the ticket more vigorously attack Gregg's legislative record, which made Ellspermann uneasy.[8]

An opening for the position of president at Ivy Tech Community College offered a convenient solution. This would be a plum career move for Ellspermann, whose work experience and doctoral degree in industrial engineering qualified her for one of the highest-paying jobs in all of state government—at more than $350,000 a year. Ivy Tech was the largest public postsecondary institution in Indiana and one of the largest in the country.

Pence suggested that his lieutenant governor would be an "ideal" candidate for the job,[9] and Ellspermann resigned in March to pursue it aggressively. "I initiated it," Ellspermann said.[10] At the risk of being accused of strong-arm methods, Pence nevertheless penned a four-page letter to the fourteen-member Ivy Tech Board of Trustees endorsing her candidacy. On May 18, the trustees, all appointed by Pence or his Republican predecessor, unanimously approved Ellspermann from a field of more than one hundred candidates. On July 1, she became the ninth president and first female to head Indiana's community college system.

In the meantime, Pence had methodically gone about the task of finding Ellspermann's replacement. His close advisers had narrowed the list of possibilities to three, each with distinctive political attributes that would complement Pence's profile. Connie Lawson was a former state senator of sixteen years and the first woman to serve as majority floor leader, elected secretary of state in 2012. Alex Azar was president of Lilly USA, the largest affiliate of Eli Lilly and Company, a lawyer by education who had clerked for US Supreme Court Justice Antonin Scalia. Eric Holcomb, candidate for US Senate, was a Navy veteran, former aide to Governor Mitch Daniels, and a past Republican state chair.

In a process resembling the one Atterholt experienced when he became chief of staff, the governor carved out time to get to know each candidate personally. In the end, it came down to chemistry. Pence and Holcomb clicked. They had much in common as both were Hanover graduates, and both served as president of the same fraternity. A final interview to decide the next lieutenant governor took place at the governor's residence with the spouses in attendance. "I said that I would be willing to serve in that capacity if he couldn't do any better," Holcomb remembered. Pence replied that he was nearing the end of the process and would spend a bit more time in thought and prayer before making a decision. Aware of a looming February 8 deadline if her husband were to withdraw his name from the senate primary ballot, Janet Holcomb asked quizzically, "Do you think your decision can be made by Monday at noon?"[11]

Pence promised to make up his mind by February 7, which happened to be Super Bowl Sunday. The Denver Broncos were scheduled to take on the Carolina Panthers, and Holcomb was booked to appear at the Cass County Lincoln Day Dinner, always a popular event for grassroots Republicans. Aware that guests wanted to get home by game time, state senator Randy Head "swore it would be the fastest Lincoln Day Dinner in the history of the county."[12] The three senate candidates were allotted five minutes each to share their vision for Indiana's future, and the dinner adjourned by 5:30 p.m. Holcomb was in the car driving back to Indianapolis with Republican field director Joe Elsener when his cell phone rang. Elsener pulled over so Holcomb could get out of the car and talk privately. Pence was on the other end. "We just feel the right way forward would be to saddle up with you," Pence said.[13]

"I'm honored and willing to serve," Holcomb replied.[14] As was his custom, Pence refused to accept Holcomb's answer until he talked it over one more time with his wife. The decision was finalized the next morning, and Holcomb filed the necessary candidate withdrawal form at the secretary of state's office.

A resignation of a lieutenant governor was unusual, and Democrats denounced it. The last lieutenant governor to step down had been Democrat Joe Kernan in 2003, in order to succeed Governor Frank O'Bannon, who died suddenly while in office. "This is unprecedented," senate Democratic leader Tim Lanane warned. "With Lieutenant Governor Ellspermann's sudden departure, state government is less diverse." Indiana Democratic Party spokesman Drew Anderson blasted what he called "a back room deal."[15] Gregg spokesman Jeff Harris accused Pence of "shoving aside an accomplished businesswoman" in favor of "a longtime political operative who will be in lockstep with him."[16] With solid Republican majorities in both houses, there was no threat to Holcomb's nomination. On March 3, the senate voted unanimously and the house 91–3 to approve Holcomb, who took the oath of office a few hours later.

In the end, the arrangement made good sense for all involved. It eclipsed any perception that Pence had pushed Ellspermann out of office to advance his own reelection chances. Holcomb's exit from the senate race simplified the GOP primary choice for voters, who favored Young overwhelmingly on May 3. It reenergized the base, which had been looking to move beyond RFRA and get behind a unified team of statewide candidates in the fall elections. "Eric's spirit and loyalty energized the campaign," Atterholt said. "Mike was having fun again."[17]

Pence now had at his side a "happy warrior" who was willing to assume the attack dog role in order to beat the Democratic ticket of John Gregg and lieutenant governor candidate Christina Hale, Brian Howey observed.[18] Holcomb would indeed need to marshal his partisans because, in a matter of four short months, he would be the Republican candidate for governor.

# 15

★ ★ ★

# TRUMP COMES
# A-COURTING

THE FIRST INDICATION THAT DONALD TRUMP WAS CONSID-
ering Mike Pence as his vice-presidential running mate came in a text
message to Pence from Stephen Hilbert, former CEO of Indianapolis-
based life insurance giant Conseco. It was Friday, June 10, the eve of
the Republican State Convention, and Pence's campaign was hosting a
reception at a banquet hall steps away from Lucas Oil Stadium, home
of the Indianapolis Colts.

Pence and Karen had been making the rounds chatting with Republican delegates when Pence spotted Jim Atterholt, his gubernatorial
chief of staff. "Jim, I need to talk to you right now," Pence told him.

The Pences walked with Atterholt outdoors to the alley off Merrill
Street, accompanied by the two Indiana state police officers assigned
to the governor's security detail. Pence, wanting privacy, gestured for
the troopers to go back inside. Certain that no one could overhear the
conversation, the governor pulled out his cell phone and showed Hilbert's message to Atterholt. It read: "If you were to be considered for
vice president would you be open to it?"

Atterholt's eyes widened at the prospect. Coming from Hilbert, this
had to be a serious inquiry. Hilbert had been close friends with Trump
for two decades, having partnered in the 1998 purchase and renovation
of the iconic fifty-story General Motors Building on Fifth Avenue in
New York City. Hilbert had known Pence for years, too. They'd met

in 1996 when Pence and a film crew arrived at the Hilberts' sprawling estate in Carmel, Indiana, to tape an episode of *Indy-TV After Dinner* about successful Central Indiana entrepreneurs. Three years later, Hilbert and his wife, Tomisue, wrote $1,000 checks to the Mike Pence Committee, the first of a half dozen contributions they would make in support of Pence's political ambitions. In the vice-presidential courting process, it made perfect sense that Hilbert would serve as go-between.

"So, what do you think?" Pence asked his trusted adviser.

Atterholt, known by grassroots Republicans for his wise counsel and calm disposition, couldn't contain his emotion. "My goodness, Governor. It's vice president of the United States of America. You have to at least consider it."[1]

As the year 2015 began, Pence was carefully weighing his political future. Two options lay before him: run for a second term as governor or seek the Republican nomination for president, an option he'd dismissed as premature four years earlier.

He was leaning toward a reelection campaign, in part because he had unfinished business in the statehouse and in part because his name was not rising to the top of a crowded field of potential presidential candidates. On February 1, the *Des Moines Register* published the Iowa Poll, an early sign of Republican preferences. Leading the poll were Wisconsin governor Scott Walker and US senator Rand Paul of Kentucky, followed closely by Ben Carson and Mike Huckabee. Donald Trump was the first or second choice of a mere 2 percent of the respondents, while no one named Pence as a first or second choice. The more problematic poll numbers suggested Pence lacked the national profile needed to be competitive. When asked whether the Indiana governor's political views were too conservative, too moderate, or "about right," 77 percent said they didn't know enough about him to form an opinion.[2]

That same month, columnist George Will, a Pence enthusiast during his congressional years, wrote that being governor worked at cross-purposes with presidential ambition. As a congressman, Will noted, Pence pursued ideological purity without concern for political consequences, which endeared him to the conservative movement. As a governor, he had to govern, which meant tough choices and compromises on issues such as federal education mandates and Medicaid expansion that didn't always set well with the base. When Pence decided to defer an announcement about his political future until after the Indiana General Assembly adjourned in April, Will wrote him off as a serious contender, noting that his timing was "perilously late in the scramble for major donors and seasoned staff."[3]

In fact, the GOP establishment had already put its money behind former Florida governor Jeb Bush and New Jersey governor Chris Christie, while Rand Paul and Scott Walker had emerged as favorites on the right. Although Pence delivered the keynote address at the Conservative Political Action Conference annual meeting on February 27, his name was left off the group's straw poll, a telling omission considering its stature among conservatives. "We were asked if his name should be on the ballot. We said no. We thought it would be a distraction," adviser and Pence confidant Bill Smith recalled. "We were preparing for a reelection bid."[4] Even Pence's mother thought the timing was wrong to run for president. As she told a student reporter from her alma mater, St. Mary of the Woods College, "I want him as my governor. My feeling is he is a good governor."[5]

By early April, the decision had been made for him. The debacle over the Religious Freedom Restoration Act ended all presidential discussion among Pence and his team of advisers, so the governor focused his attention on seeking a second term.[6] During a meeting with reporters on May 12, GOP state chairman Jeff Cardwell confirmed Pence's candidacy, although Pence waited for more time to pass before making a formal announcement. He chose his audience carefully: a June 1 Republican Party fund-raising dinner, where he confronted RFRA's fallout head-on, dismissing critics who had accused him of anti-gay bigotry. Speaking to about eight hundred party faithful, Pence took responsibility for the hit the state's image had suffered and insisted Indiana would not tolerate discrimination. But he said religious liberty must also be protected. "We will find our way forward as a state that respects the dignity and worth of every individual, and we will ensure that no government intervention, no government coercion, will interfere with the freedom of conscience and the freedom of religion," Pence said.[7] The conciliatory message rang hollow with several dozen protesters outside the banquet hall carrying "Fire Mike Pence" signs.

The protesters were part of a larger movement to end Pence's political career and were led by Bill Oesterle, the former CEO of Angie's List, who opposed the RFRA and remained dissatisfied with its fix. Oesterle was a Republican who had managed Mitch Daniels's first gubernatorial campaign in 2004, raising $18 million, a record for an Indiana governor's race. Oesterle had left Angie's List in April 2015, explaining at the time that he wanted to get more involved in Indiana politics, which he couldn't do while heading a business. The explanation provided timely cover for Oesterle to step away from the financially struggling online consumer review company that would later be purchased by IAC, the owner of rival HomeAdvisor. The intensity of his opposition to Pence surprised acquaintances, especially in light of Oesterle's $150,000 donation to Pence's first gubernatorial campaign.

Although Oesterle hinted at running for governor himself, his primary objective was to unseat Pence. In a rare move for a solitary citizen, he commissioned an opinion poll by Christine Matthews of Bellwether Research & Consulting to gauge Pence's popularity. The results, released on the eve of Pence's reelection announcement, showed that 54 percent of one thousand registered voters wanted a new governor, while under a third said they would vote to reelect Pence. In a one-on-one against Democratic challenger John Gregg, Pence fared better, deadlocked with Gregg at about 40 percent.[8] Democrats, eager to retake the governor's office after twelve years out of power, cheered the findings, while GOP operatives questioned the reliability of Matthews's polling. Said Cardwell, "We didn't pay a lot of attention to it because of the way it came about and who funded it."[9]

As Pence was kicking off his campaign, the presidential contest was taking unexpected turns. All predictions to the contrary, Donald Trump had shot up in the polls. He was second behind Bush in a CNN/ORC (Opinion Research Corporation) national poll on Republican presidential candidates released in early July, though few pollsters thought the trajectory would continue. "Will Trump fizzle?" pollster

John Zogby asked in a July 8 article in *USA Today*. "I'd bet the Iowa farm on it."[10] Within four months, Trump had moved into first place. A Washington Post / ABC News poll released in late November showed him with 32 percent, leading Ben Carson at second place with 22 percent. Far behind were Marco Rubio at 11 percent, Ted Cruz at 8 percent, and Jeb Bush at 6 percent.[11]

The momentum was enough to bring former Republican state chairman Rex Early out of retirement to chair Trump's Indiana campaign. Early was a legendary figure in Indiana politics due to his plainspoken speaking style and irreverent sense of humor. Chair of the Republican State Central Committee from 1991 to 1993, Early had attended eleven Republican National Conventions, competed in the May 1996 primary for governor, and been through enough elections to recognize a winner.

The idea to contact the Trump campaign came to Early while eating lunch in March at the Antelope Club, a private club in Downtown Indianapolis where elected officials, media, and pundits often gathered to assess the political landscape. On this particular day, Early was sharing predictions with a half dozen fellow Republicans, including lawyers Henry Dean and John Forbes. "Let's call Trump's office and say we want to be for him," Early suggested.[12] The others agreed; Forbes retrieved his cell phone and dialed the number for the Trump for President office in New York City, reaching Michael Glassner, Trump's national political director. Early called Glassner back a few days later to share dates on the Indiana political calendar and contact information for delegates to the 2012 national convention, many of whom were likely to be delegates again in 2016.

In early April, Trump named Early chair of his Indiana campaign. "I think Trump is going to carry Indiana real big," Early predicted in the *Indianapolis Star* story announcing his appointment.[13] On Early's recommendation, Trump hired as his state director Suzanne Jaworowski, who had co-chaired Carly Fiorina's Indiana campaign until the former Hewett-Packard chairwoman dropped out of the race in February.

Though he'd met Trump only once in person, Early admired the real estate mogul's chutzpah. Their previous encounter had been brief but memorable. The occasion was the February 13, 1996, Indianapolis Press

Club Gridiron Dinner, a fund-raiser for the now-defunct journalists' group. Both men attended a VIP cocktail party at the Hyatt Regency Hotel and were among the roasted that evening before a crowd of nine hundred at the Indiana Convention Center. Trump, in attendance with his second wife, Marla Maples, held a press conference earlier in the day to discuss his plans for a riverboat casino set to open in Gary, Indiana, later that year—a boat he proclaimed "the world's largest and most exciting," with 2,100 gaming positions and Strauss crystal chandeliers.[14] The casino became the butt of jokes by emcees Jim Shella and Mike McDaniel, who poked fun at Trump's ego, hairstyle, and business acumen, having chosen as the location for his new venture a city considered the murder capital of Indiana. "This guy's a big deal, and he dreams big dreams, and he makes those dreams come true," McDaniel quipped. "It takes vision to build a classy gaming establishment in Gary. Someday soon people around the world will be dreaming of vacationing in Monaco, Nassau, Las Vegas, Gary." Trump smiled cordially at the joke while the crowd roared.[15]

The next time Early met Trump was at a rally at the Indiana State Fairgrounds on April 20, 2016, two weeks before the May 3 Indiana presidential primary election. "We had thousands of people. It was unbelievable," Early recalled. Early briefly spoke at the affair while the crowd waited for Trump's arrival. "I've got eight grandchildren, and I'm very concerned about their well-being and what President Obama has done to weaken the military," he told the assembly.[16]

Trump had begun his Indianapolis visit at the governor's residence, where he asked for Pence's primary endorsement, and then traveled by motorcade to the fairgrounds, where he spoke for the better part of an hour. Trump had won the New York primary the day before and was feeling confident. The focus of his comments was lost manufacturing jobs. He used the occasion to blast the air-conditioning manufacturer Carrier, which had recently announced it was cutting 2,100 Indiana jobs so it could move its production facility to Mexico. Trump said he would "tax the hell" out of companies that did that. His comments drew cheers from the audience that had been waiting for hours to hear him speak. "Everybody was in the greatest mood," recalled Nancy Meek, a real estate agent who decided spur-of-the-moment to attend the rally with her son and a friend. "People were wild to see him. It didn't matter what he said. Everybody loved it."[17]

A similar rally in Evansville on April 28 drew over twelve thousand people to the Old National Events Plaza. Thousands were turned away at the door but remained standing outdoors listening over loudspeakers in a celebratory spirit.

No one had expected Pence to endorse Donald Trump, whose womanizing reputation and extravagant lifestyle seemed contrary to the Christian values Pence championed. Because of Trump's obvious popularity with Hoosiers, Pence's advisers hoped, and assumed, the Indiana governor would stay neutral. In a surprising move even to Republican state chairman Jeff Cardwell, Pence, the day after the Evansville rally, announced on the Greg Garrison radio show (WIBC-FM) that he planned to vote for "principled conservative" Ted Cruz. In the same announcement, Pence praised Trump, who "has given voice to the frustrations of millions of working Americans."[18]

"Why endorse anybody?" Cardwell thought to himself at the time. "Mike has nothing to gain here. Nobody's calling Republican headquarters about Ted Cruz. Nobody's calling about John Kasich. Every phone call that came in was 'When and where is Donald Trump going to be?'"[19]

Rex Early was equally shocked and called Jim Atterholt in frustration. "What in the hell? Is it true that Mike is going to endorse Cruz?"[20] Advisers feared Pence might suffer a backlash from Trump voters come November and were pleased he worded his endorsement carefully enough to avoid alienating anyone. "Much like he did in Congress, Mike was able to disagree without being offensive," Cardwell said. "There were several people around him telling him not to do it. But Mike stood his ground."[21]

Trump returned to Indiana on primary eve, with the party's nomination clearly in his sight. Though Hoosiers typically have no say in the presidential nominating process due to the lateness of the Indiana primary on the calendar, 2016 was a different story. The campaign season, which had begun with seventeen Republicans, was down to three. The others—a who's who of Republican politics—had dropped out, one by one, as they ran out of money or support: Rick Perry, Scott Walker, Rand Paul, Chris Christie, Jeb Bush, and Marco Rubio. The delegate count now stood at 996 for Trump, 565 for Cruz, and 153 for Ohio governor Kasich, who had stayed in the race in the event of a contest at the Republican National Convention in Cleveland. Even establishment Republicans admitted that Trump might claim the 1,237 delegates he needed to win the nomination outright. Indiana was Cruz's last chance.

Despite an eleventh-hour, multimillion-dollar ad buy for Cruz in the days leading up to the primary, it turned out to be no contest. On election night, Rex Early, Steve Hilbert, and other Trump supporters gathered at the Sheraton at Keystone Crossing to watch returns, with Hilbert updating Trump from time to time by cell phone. "The numbers we were seeing were unbelievable," Early said.[22] The Associated Press called the race at 7:00 p.m., earlier than any had predicted. Trump beat Cruz 591,514 to 406,783, winning every congressional district and all fifty-seven delegates. From his election night headquarters at Union Station, Cruz announced he was suspending his campaign. "We left it all on the field in Indiana, we gave it everything we've got, but the voters chose another path," he told supporters.[23] Early said Cruz's decision was critical to unifying the party. "If he hadn't thrown in the towel, I am pretty sure neither one of them would have had 1,237 votes. It would have been a bloodbath at the convention."[24]

With Trump the presumptive nominee, speculation immediately turned to his vice-presidential options. Interviewed May 4 by phone on MSNBC's *Morning Joe*, Trump indicated that he wanted a political insider who could balance out his lack of experience in Washington: "Somebody that can help me with legislation and somebody that can help me get things passed and somebody that's been friends with the senators and the congressmen and all."[25] Although Pence fit the description, early speculation did not list him. Other Midwestern governors—Rob Portman of Ohio and Joni Ernst of Iowa—were prominently mentioned. It was not until Pence opened his text message from Hilbert that he had any idea he was under consideration.

The inquiry from Hilbert pushed Pence into a period of introspection and prayer. After telling only a few confidants about what he figured was an outside chance of joining Trump on the ticket, Pence went about business as usual. In his address to the state convention on June 11, he urged Hoosier Republicans to unite behind Trump or forgo key party priorities including abortion, the Supreme Court makeup, and the Second Amendment. "It's time to come together around the people who were the people's choice," Pence told the convention. "We must resolve today that Indiana will be the first state on the board to make Donald Trump the 45th president of the United States of America."[26]

Though Pence's nomination became official on primary day, the other statewide offices, including lieutenant governor, secretary of state, and attorney general, were subject to majority vote at the convention. The 1,731 delegates, drawn from all ninety-two counties, unanimously nominated Eric Holcomb to be Pence's running mate, not imagining he would eventually replace Pence as the gubernatorial nominee.

Within a few weeks, Pence's name started to surface in media reports. When asked by reporters on June 30 whether he would accept an invitation to become Trump's running mate, Pence said he "wouldn't speak to a hypothetical." A May poll had showed Pence in a dead heat with Democratic challenger John Gregg, 40 percent to 36 percent, with a 4 percent margin of error. With his reelection bid "no sure thing," the Indianapolis Star concluded that Pence was "weighing his political future in Indiana against national aspirations."[27]

In the weeks following Hilbert's text message, signs increasingly pointed to Pence as a finalist in the vice-presidential courting process. Vaughn Hillyard, the NBC reporter embedded with the Trump campaign, called Republican state chairman Jeff Cardwell "out of the blue" and asked if they could meet for lunch when he came to town July Fourth weekend. Cardwell thought he wanted to talk about Pence's reelection campaign. Instead, Hillyard informed Cardwell that Pence was on the "short list" for vice president.[28] Fourth of July weekend, Pence and Karen flew to New Jersey, where Pence joined Trump for a round of golf at the Trump National Golf Club in Bedminster. Afterward, Pence told reporters in typical self-effacing fashion, "He's a very good golfer. He beat me like a drum."[29]

About the same time, names of prospective candidates being vetted by Washington lawyer Arthur B. Culvahouse started to surface in media reports. In addition to Pence, they included Senator Bob Corker of Tennessee, New Jersey governor Chris Christie, and former speaker of the House Newt Gingrich. Culvahouse, counsel to President Ronald Reagan from 1987 to 1989, had faced criticism in 2008 after playing the same role in John McCain's presidential campaign and giving the green light to Sarah Palin. The Alaska governor, whom Culvahouse described to McCain as "high risk, high reward,"[30] proved to be woefully unprepared for the rigorous policy questions asked of her on the campaign trail.

Pence, in contrast, posed minimal risk to Trump's victory prospects and potentially high reward. The 2016 vetting process required candidates to hand over medical histories and financial and tax records and to answer questions about their professional and private lives. Pence retained lawyers Bob Grand and Matt Morgan of Barnes & Thornburg LLP in Indianapolis to manage the response process on his behalf. Grand, managing partner with more than thirty years of Republican campaign experience, called Pence "probably the easiest person I've vetted" due to the limited scope of his personal and financial dealings. When Culvahouse's staff asked about Pence's relationships on K Street, Grand chuckled. He understood that they were digging for dirt—any signs of undue influence from donors or special interests. K Street, the Washington address of countless think tanks and advocacy groups, is the nickname for the lobbying industry. "Mike Pence was not a person who spent a lot of time on K Street or with lobbyists. He was known for doing his job, voting, and then spending as much time as possible with his family," Grand explained.[31]

Pence, meanwhile, had started to gather input from trusted friends about the risks and rewards of running for vice president. "My advice was emphatically yes," said David McIntosh, the former congressman who headed Club for Growth, a free-enterprise lobbying group that opposed Trump in the primary. "If you don't win, you will be the national leader of the party. You win, and you're vice president of the United States."[32] At no point did Pence express reluctance to align himself with a candidate rejected by some within his own party, a group that came to be known as Never Trumpers. "Are you kidding?" quipped Rex Early. "At this point in his career, how many chances is Pence going to get?"[33]

Throughout the vetting process, Culvahouse told Grand that Pence was "a frontrunner."[34] The final audition was to take place July 12, when Trump was scheduled to go to Indianapolis for a private fund-raiser and a public rally. Donors paid between $2,700 for a ballroom reception to $250,000 for an exclusive private meeting with Trump at the members-only Columbia Club on Monument Circle. The club, founded in 1889 by Republican backers of President Benjamin Harrison, offered both historic ambience and privacy from scores of reporters following Trump to his campaign stops.

Trump's Boeing 757 flew into Signature Flight Support, the Indianapolis terminal serving business and private aviation, where motorcade drivers were stationed to carry the entourage to the Columbia Club. Kevin Eck, a Republican volunteer who'd worked with Rex Early since his campaign for governor, was parked at the front of the line. As Trump's jet taxied to a stop, Eck noticed a flat tire on the right side and alerted the Secret Service agent in the car behind him. "Holy shit," the agent said, before radioing up to a colleague on board the plane. "Somebody tell the pilot he's got a flat tire down here."[35]

The flat tire launched a chain of events that would keep Trump in Indianapolis overnight, a delay that many credited with sealing the deal. Having more time with Pence, Trump became increasingly comfortable with Pence's style and ability. Republican state chairman Cardwell believes Trump had been leaning toward Gingrich until he was won over by Hoosier supporters and Pence himself.

During the Columbia Club reception, Trump pulled Cardwell aside to speak privately about the choice. "I understand you've known Mike Pence for a long time," Trump said. Cardwell nodded.

"Off the record, it's down to two people: Newt Gingrich or Mike Pence. Who would you pick?"

Cardwell didn't hesitate. "Of course I'd pick Mike Pence."

"Why?" Trump demanded.

"You don't need another lightning rod at the top of the ticket," Cardwell explained. "Mike Pence can deliver what Newt Gingrich can't. Mike can deliver the Rust Belt. Mike is well known within the Republican Governors Association. He's friends with Scott Walker, Rick Snyder, and Matt Bevin (governors of Wisconsin, Michigan, and Kentucky). Mike can deliver the evangelical community. It is a win-win combination."

Cardwell pressed his case for a few more minutes, pointing out that Pence had experience in legislative and executive branches, which would complement Trump's business résumé. "You've got fifty years of private sector experience. Mike's got sixteen years of public sector experience. You guys will be a fantastic public-private partnership creating jobs for America."[36]

Pence made a strong impression at the rally later that day. In a five-minute introduction of Trump at the Grand Park Events Center in Westfield, Pence wowed the crowd of 6,500. He delivered a scathing attack on Democratic presidential candidate and former secretary of state Hillary Clinton, whom he faulted for the 2012 terrorist attack on the US mission in Benghazi, Libya. "As the proud father of a United States Marine, let me say from my heart we don't need a president that took 13 hours to send help to Americans under fire. Anyone who did that should be disqualified from ever being commander in chief of the armed forces of the United States of America."[37]

Pence's change in tone did not go unnoticed. *Indianapolis Star* reporter Chris Sikich wrote the next day, "The attacks on Clinton were uncharacteristically fierce for Pence, who has eschewed negative campaigning in the past. But the comments are typical for vice presidential candidates, who are often called upon to act as attack dogs on the campaign trail." One person in the crowd echoed Sikich's conclusion. "That's the most exciting I'd ever heard or seen the man," said Lyle Enyeart, a Pence supporter from Warsaw. "Man, what a ball of fire there."[38]

Rex Early did not attend the Westfield rally. He had received a call from hospice staff at Community Hospital North inquiring if Trump could pay a visit to a twenty-four-year-old patient who was a huge Trump booster and had just days to live. Trump's schedule was too tight to alter, but when Early explained the situation, the candidate took off the red "Make America Great Again" hat he was wearing, signed it, and added an encouraging note in black marker. Early went straight to the hospital to deliver the hat and Trump's best wishes. The patient, Shawn Edward Duncan, died nine days later.[39]

The rest of July 12 was a blur as campaign staff hustled to rearrange Trump's schedule. Once the decision was made to spend the night, rooms were booked at the Conrad, dinner reservations made for the Pences and Trump at The Capital Grille, and Trump team members summoned from New York City. Daughter Ivanka Trump and her husband, Jared Kushner, son Donald Trump Jr., and campaign manager Paul Manafort made plans to fly into Indianapolis to join the Pences for breakfast at the governor's residence. Trump's son Eric, already in Indianapolis, joined his father for dinner with the Pences.

On the morning of July 13, Eck, the motorcade driver, returned to the airport to retrieve the other Trump family members, while Karen Pence picked up a breakfast casserole from the Illinois Street Food Emporium restaurant three minutes away. Eck, noting that the Trump plane was still parked on the tarmac with its flat tire unrepaired, had been told by Secret Service that a faulty brake caused the flat and a repair part had been ordered.

Once guests arrived at the residence, Pence poured the coffee, and Karen served the food, which caught Trump's attention. Aware that the Pences owned no property, not even a home, and had limited financial resources, Trump at one point asked the governor, "How do you live like that?" Pence replied, "God has always provided."[40]

To the press, it increasingly looked like Pence was the choice. Sean Hannity, the Fox news host who had been vocally pushing for Gingrich, provided a private jet to fly the former House speaker to Indianapolis in a last-ditch appeal over lunch at the Conrad. Although Trump had narrowed his list to Pence and Gingrich, New Jersey governor Christie also continued to press his case. As Eck drove Eric and Ivanka Trump and Jared Kushner back to the airport, Eric, sitting in the front seat, turned to Ivanka and said, "Chris tried to call Dad five times during lunch. Dad didn't answer." Eric phoned Christie, whose voice was animated on the other end of the line, and tried to reassure him. "I can promise you no decision has been made," Eric told him.[41]

That evening, Pence invited Atterholt, campaign manager Marty Obst, and political consultant Nick Ayers to a meeting in the guesthouse adjacent to the governor's residence. He wanted to discuss strategy and logistics going forward. Timing was tricky. Should Pence join the Trump ticket, he would have to file a candidate withdrawal form by noon on Friday, the statutory deadline to remove his name from the general election ballot. There were other candidates to consider, too. Pence's exit from the gubernatorial ballot would create a mad dash for his successor. The Republican State Committee would have thirty days to choose his ballot replacement. But the three likely candidates—Lieutenant Governor Eric Holcomb and US representatives Susan Brooks and Todd Rokita—were already on the ballot for other offices and would have to remove their names by noon Friday, too.

About an hour into the meeting, Ayers took a call from a Trump campaign official. In a few minutes, Trump would be calling to invite Governor Pence to join him on the ticket. "After Nick told the governor, I suggested we all pray together, which we did," Atterholt recalled. "The governor asked me to lead the prayer, and I prayed for wisdom, for a peace that surpasses all understanding, and for a hedge of protection to be placed around the governor and his family. The governor then left the guesthouse and went to the residence as he wanted to be with Karen when he got the call from Trump."[42]

Trump intended to make his decision public the next day, July 14, but things did not go as planned. A tweet that morning from CBS News reporter Major Garrett spoiled any remaining element of surprise. Garrett was returning to New York City from assignment in Indianapolis and happened to notice Pence's press secretary Marc Lotter on the same plane. "I'm sure just coincidence," Garrett tweeted using the hashtag #veepstakes.[43] In no time, the tweet went viral.

Meanwhile, tragedy in France prompted Trump to delay all campaign announcements. A terrorist had plowed a truck into crowds celebrating Bastille Day on the French Riviera, killing eighty-five people. The Islamic State claimed responsibility. Foreign policy replaced vice-presidential speculation as the day's headline news. In an interview with Fox's Bill O'Reilly, Trump said if elected president he'd be willing to ask Congress for a declaration of war against ISIS. As it turned out, the vice-presidential sweepstakes winner was announced not with a bang but with a whimper. On the morning of July 15, Donald Trump sent out a twenty-four-word tweet: "I am pleased to announce that I have chosen Governor Mike Pence as my Vice Presidential running mate. News conference tomorrow at 11:00 A.M."[44]

The flashy New York City billionaire had cast his lot with the humble Hoosier governor who prayed not just at mealtime but before every big decision. "Pence will be salt to Trump's pepper," predicted conservative columnist Cal Thomas.[45] It was a union of two men who could not have been more different, but somehow the unlikely combination worked.

# 16

★ ★ ★

## "BUDDY,
## THE BALL GAME
## IS OVER"

IF NATIONAL PUNDITS HAD SPENT MORE TIME FOLLOWING Jeff Cardwell and Rex Early around Indiana and less time talking to pollsters, they would have seen Donald Trump's election coming. Cardwell and Early predicted it, and not out of wishful thinking. For months leading up to the November 8 election, Republican chairman Cardwell could hardly keep up with the demand for yard signs, which he disbursed by the thousands. When Cardwell and Early, Trump's Indiana campaign chair, visited small Hoosier towns on a Trump-Pence tour that fall, hundreds of Republicans came out—to see *them*. Hillary Clinton and Tim Kaine signs were nowhere in sight. With a combined eighty years in Republican politics, the two men had never experienced anything like it. "They were taking pictures of Rex and me holding Trump-Pence signs as if we were the candidates," Cardwell said. "There were traffic jams in little towns when we came through. We were like rock stars."[1]

The Trump-Pence ticket made its official debut on July 16 at the New York Hilton Midtown Hotel. "I found the leader who will help us deliver a safe society and a prosperous, really prosperous, society for all Americans," Trump said in his introduction of Pence. He praised Pence's economic record as governor, the same statistics that Pence had mentioned six months earlier in his State of the State Address. Sensitive to media reports that his delayed announcement was caused not by the terror attack in Nice but second thoughts about the Hoosier governor, Trump made a point of adding, "Indiana governor Mike Pence was my first choice."[2]

Reaction to the selection was overwhelmingly positive, with even Trump doubters feeling reassured. The congressional relationships Pence had so carefully nurtured on the Hill paid off in congenial endorsements. Arizona's Jeff Flake called Pence the "best choice Donald Trump's made so far."[3] Marco Rubio tweeted: "Great pick. @mike_pence is rock solid."[4] Speaker of the House Paul Ryan, one of Pence's closest friends in Washington, said, "I can think of no better choice for our vice-presidential candidate."[5]

The choice opened lines of communication with big money conservative donors that had scorned Trump in the primaries, including Club for Growth, which had spent $10 million on ad buys declaring "there's nothing conservative about Donald Trump."[6] Club president David McIntosh, who had held Pence's old congressional seat, said his friend's addition to the ticket gave him hope that Trump would move "toward economic conservatism and limited government."[7] Although the group declined to finance the Trump-Pence effort, it spent millions on down-ticket races that helped ensure Trump a majority in both houses of Congress. The same applied to Freedom Partners, a conservative advocacy group backed by the billionaire owners of Koch Industries, the second-largest privately held company in the country. "The Kochs were very excited about the vice presidential pick," said Marc Short, who had served as a top aide to Pence on the Hill before joining the Kochs as head of Freedom Partners.[8] Though the Kochs remained "at odds" with Trump on some issues, their connection to him grew stronger thanks to Pence, who, after the election, brought key Koch staff members including Short into the administration.[9]

Democrats sought to paint Pence as a right-wing ideologue out of touch with the American mainstream. John Podesta, chair of the Clinton campaign, called him the "most extreme pick in a generation."[10] For evidence, they looked to Pence's record in Congress, where he had relentlessly pushed legislation to undo the 1973 Supreme Court ruling that legalized abortion. One Clinton campaign video cited Pence's effort to shut down the federal government in an unsuccessful attempt to end taxpayer funding of Planned Parenthood in 2011.

But not all of the criticism came from the left. The columnist George Will, a fan of Pence in his congressional days, quickly turned on him for teaming up with a man Will would come to call the worst-ever president. In a column bearing the headline "Pence, the pliable," Will wondered how a conservative who strongly backed free trade could tie his fortunes to a candidate who deemed the North American Free Trade Agreement "the worst economic deal in the history of our country."[11]

By the time Trump made his announcement, Republicans were already gathering in Cleveland for their national convention, where delegates were to formally nominate Pence on July 19. Indiana Lieutenant Governor Eric Holcomb was eating lunch at an event in Independence, Ohio, when he received an urgent phone call from Marc Lotter, Pence's press secretary and a longtime Republican communications strategist. "Governor Pence would like you to nominate him tonight," Lotter said. "What time can you be at the hall?"

"I'm in a golf shirt and khaki pants," Holcomb replied. "I need to get a tie on and shower."

"OK," Lotter said. "Get here as soon as you can. By the way, we need your speech to download into the teleprompter."[12]

Holcomb ended up dictating his remarks as Lotter typed. When he arrived at Quicken Loans Arena later that afternoon, Holcomb practiced the speech in a small room off the main hall and then joined House Speaker Paul Ryan and Senate Majority Leader Mitch McConnell backstage in the Green Room. Now wearing a blue suit jacket and red tie, Holcomb stepped confidently to the podium and declared with uncharacteristic exuberance, "On behalf of the great state of Indiana, I proudly nominate a great man of integrity, a proven conservative, an incredible husband and father, and one of my best friends."[13] That evening, an emotional Jeff Cardwell cast Indiana's fifty-seven delegate votes for the Trump ticket, which he called the "greatest honor of my life."[14]

The next night, Governor Pence presented himself to a national TV audience estimated at twenty million people.[15] As he waited backstage before his address, a Republican stalwart gave him this suggestion: "When you walk out on that big stage with all the television cameras and the thousands of people in the stadium, what you ought to do is stop for a minute and find the Hoosiers in the crowd." After a brief introduction by Paul Ryan, Pence entered stage right, walked toward the Indiana delegation, pointed, fist pumped, and put his hand on his heart. Later he reflected, "There was Jeff Cardwell, and there were all my fellow Hoosier Republicans cheering me on. And it gave me such a lift of confidence as I stepped out on that national stage."[16] In his half-hour speech, Pence introduced his family, bragged about Indiana's business climate, and previewed the campaign message as delegates occasionally interrupted with chants of "We like Mike."[17]

On the final night of the convention, Trump accepted his party's nomination, pledging to be tough on crime at home and on terrorists abroad. The Pence family joined the Trumps on stage for the finale— a downpour of 125,000 red, white, and blue balloons amidst flashing strobe lights, the song "All Right Now" blasting over the speakers.

Pence, always agile on the campaign trail, proved equally comfortable attacking Hillary Clinton or cleaning up after Trump's unforced errors. After Trump disparaged Khizr and Ghazala Khan, a Gold Star family who spoke against his immigration policy at the Democratic National Convention, Pence clarified the matter. He said their son, killed in the Iraq War, was a hero, and his family should be cherished by every American. On September 10, at the Values Voter Summit in Washington, Pence responded directly to Clinton's comment that half of Trump supporters were racist, sexist, homophobic, or otherwise prejudiced and belonged in a basket of deplorables. "Hillary: They are not a basket of anything; they are Americans, and they deserve your respect," Pence said.[18]

At the October 4 debate against his Democratic vice-presidential counterpart, Tim Kaine, moderated by Elaine Quijano of CBS News, Pence put his high school extemporaneous speech skills to use. While Kaine frequently interrupted during the ninety-minute session, Pence remained patient and unruffled. The next day, as good reviews came in, Pence deflected the praise to his boss. "From where I sat Donald Trump won the debate," he said. In a snap poll by CNN, 48 percent declared Pence the winner compared to 42 percent for Kaine.[19]

Three days later, a bombshell report created what one reporter called "an existential crisis" for the Trump campaign,[20] but this time, Pence offered no excuse for his running mate's conduct. The *Washington Post* reported on a Friday that Trump made lewd and offensive remarks about women during a 2005 conversation with Billy Bush, a coanchor of the television show *Access Hollywood*. Trump's comments were captured on an open mike and saved on videotape. The revelation threatened to destroy the fragile Republican unity that had developed around the Trump-Pence team since the convention, and some GOP lawmakers and leaders called for Trump to step aside and let Pence take his place.[21]

Meeting with top campaign staff at Trump's residence in New York City, GOP national chair Reince Priebus bluntly told the candidate, "You have two choices. One, you lose the biggest electoral landslide in American history and take everybody with you, or two, you can drop out of the race and let someone else be the nominee." Trump, looking straight at Priebus with jaw set, declared he would not only stay in the race but also "I'm going to win."[22]

Trump issued a televised apology and, in a debate that Sunday against Hillary Clinton, characterized his poor choice of words to Billy Bush as "locker room talk."[23] As for Pence, he briefly withdrew from the campaign trail and issued a statement: "I do not condone his remarks and cannot defend them."[24] But he was back on the speaking circuit by Monday and "proud to stand with Donald Trump." He squashed as "absolutely false" reports that he had considered dropping off the ticket, telling a rally in Charlotte, North Carolina, that as a Christian he was obliged to show grace. "I've received it. I believe in it. I believe in forgiveness."[25]

As a result of such professions of faith, the independent evangelical churches claimed Pence as their own, and he made a special effort to court them. They, too, were forgiving of Trump's indiscretions. With abortion the only litmus test for many pro-life voters and an open seat on the US Supreme Court, it was a low-cost, high-return strategy. In a video message distributed via Pat Robertson's Christian Broadcasting

Network, Pence promised that a president Trump would appoint justices to the Supreme Court "who will uphold our Constitution and the rights of the unborn." He also signaled an effort to repeal the Johnson Amendment, which prevents churches from taking political stands or raising money for candidates. The law was designed as a barrier between church and state entanglement but viewed by many religious leaders as a restriction of their free speech rights.[26]

Pence continued to serve as governor throughout the campaign, checking in daily with chief of staff Jim Atterholt and going to the office most Fridays. He attended the Indiana State Fair in August, as was his custom, and spoke at bicentennial events as his schedule allowed. Critics charged he was neglecting the more substantive duties of state with the controversial case of Keith Cooper drawing headlines amid charges that Pence cared more about politics than compassion. Wrongly convicted of armed robbery and released from prison in 2006 in a deal with prosecutors, Cooper had petitioned Pence for a pardon that would dissolve his conviction, clean his record, and help him find better work. The Indiana Parole Board recommended a pardon, yet Cooper's petition had been pending for more than two hundred days.[27] A spokesman said Pence did not want to intervene until Cooper had exhausted remedies in the judicial branch.[28] In February 2017, Governor Eric Holcomb pardoned Cooper as one of his first acts as governor.

Pence faced similar criticism for failing to go to East Chicago after the Environmental Protection Agency identified high levels of lead and arsenic in the soil underneath a public housing complex, forcing the relocation of 1,200. An editorial in the *Times* of Northwest Indiana attacked Pence and other statewide candidates from both parties for a "woeful" lack of compassion.[29] Atterholt said Pence did not want to politicize the situation with his presence but assigned a team of staff members to work on the crisis.[30]

One other issue dogged Pence throughout the election year or, more accurately, "thoroughly exasperated" his receptionists and social media staff.[31] Near the end of the 2016 legislative session, Pence signed into law "with a prayer" what was labeled one of the most restrictive abortion laws in the country.[32] House Enrolled Act 1337 prohibited abortions sought for reasons of race, gender, or fetal abnormality such as Down syndrome and required the burial or cremation of the remains of miscarried and aborted fetuses. Planned Parenthood and the American Civil Liberties Union of Indiana filed suit to overturn the law, arguing that a woman's right to an abortion in the first trimester of pregnancy was absolute under *Roe v. Wade*.

As the legal arguments worked their way through the courts, opponents made their way to the governor's office with daily phone calls updating Pence on the status of their reproductive cycles. "Good morning. I just wanted to call and let the good Governor know that I am still not pregnant, since he seems to be so worried about women's reproductive rights," one caller reported.[33] Protesters also jammed the governor's social media accounts with personal and deliberately graphic briefings. Laura Shanley, organizer of what she called "Periods for Pence," said participants were trying to make the point that women's health-care decisions weren't anybody's business. "I understand why he feels the way he does. I was raised in a conservative church. I know the basis of where he's coming from. But there has got to be a point where empathy overrides theocracy."[34] When Pence joined the Trump ticket, Shanley broadened the campaign's Facebook page to apply to other antiabortion politicians, too, attracting almost one hundred thousand followers. On the legal front, US District Court judge Tanya Walton Pratt halted the Indiana law's enforcement, promising a protracted court battle. (A federal appeals court struck down the law as unconstitutional in April 2018.)

In the final month of the campaign, Cardwell, Early, and Tony Samuel, vice chair of the Trump Indiana effort, traveled the state again, hitting every congressional district from the Ohio River in the south to Crown Point near Chicago. They did not hear at ground level any of the concerns being discussed by the news media, be it Trump's moral lapses or Pence's so-called war on women's health. They were astonished when five hundred people came out to greet them in Corydon, the state's first capital; when scores showed up at the Bedford GOP headquarters; when dozens found their way to Trump Hill in Cicero, where a homeowner had cut the name TRUMP into the grass with his lawnmower. The experience was consistent from town to town, leading the men to conclude that professional pollsters were missing something. Virtually all national polls showed Hillary Clinton with a sizable lead over Trump up until the last ten days. "When I was listening to radio or watching TV, nobody was capturing what we were seeing on the road," Cardwell said.[35]

He and Bill Smith, Pence's longtime aide and political adviser, accompanied Pence on a swing through Colorado and Arizona and found the same response, people lining the motorcade route all the way to the venues, cheering and waving Trump-Pence signs. Ed Simcox told a similar story from Iowa, where he spent a day on the campaign trail with Pence in October. A polite Republican gathering of farm families met them at their first stop, Mason City. In Dubuque, a blue-collar, industrial community on the Mississippi River, Pence addressed a lively and cheering crowd of 350 at Giese Manufacturing, a metal fabrication shop. As he walked across a vacated factory floor on the way to the rally site, Simcox noticed Trump bumper stickers stuck to all manner of toolboxes and equipment. "This kind of crowd I had never seen in all my years for a Republican candidate for office," Simcox said. "Right then and there, I knew there was something special going on, something unique."[36] Early, always an astute analyst of the political scene, claimed to know before the Indiana May primary that Trump would be the forty-fifth president. Trump was a phenomenon that could not be explained away. "When you hold a rally in Evansville and twenty-five thousand people show up to hear Donald Trump, then, buddy, the ball game is over," Early said.[37]

As of November 2, with the election a week away, polls showed Republicans still trailing, although by shrinking margins. Hillary Clinton would later blame two October surprises for the trends. First, the anti-secrecy website Wikileaks began releasing emails allegedly stolen from Clinton campaign chairman John Podesta's account, some aimed at showing Clinton as out of touch and in the pocket of Wall Street firms and donors. The email theft and allegations of Russian hackers would lead to an independent counsel probe of Russian interference in the 2016 election. Then, on October 29, FBI director James Comey sent a letter to Congress informing members that his agency had reopened an investigation into Clinton's improper use of a private email server during her time as secretary of state. A few days later, Comey reiterated an earlier conclusion that she had done nothing to warrant criminal charges. "I remember the Comey letter and Wikileaks dump happening," Cardwell said. "This was all that the news media cared about, but voters didn't seem to notice."[38] The effect on the electorate's choices would prove impossible to quantify; polling experts found "mixed evidence" of any impact.[39]

On election night, Pence and Karen joined the Trumps at the Hilton Midtown Hotel in Manhattan for what they fully expected to be a celebration. Twenty-six Pence family members were there, including two of the three children (Audrey was abroad), all five siblings, mother Nancy and stepfather Basil, and numerous nieces and nephews. "Michael had me convinced they would win," his brother Ed Pence recalled. "He had this confidence that they were going to win, despite what the polls said."[40] At no point during the evening did Pence envision defeat, even texting to some friends the famous picture of President Harry Truman waving the "Dewey defeats Truman" headline.[41]

As the hour grew late, national media called the crucial swing states for Trump one by one: Ohio, North Carolina, Florida, Wisconsin, Pennsylvania. At 3:04 a.m., the Republican ticket crossed the threshold to claim a majority of Electoral College votes. Pence offered brief victory remarks before introducing the president-elect. "This is a historic night. The American people have spoken, and the American people have elected their new champion. America has elected a new president, and it's almost hard for me to express the honor that I and my family feel that we will have the privilege to serve as your vice president of the United States of America."[42]

As Trump strode onto the stage, ABC's George Stephanopoulos, the newsman whose grilling of Pence one year earlier had seemed to dash his political hopes, said of Trump: "There he is. . . . The man who has just pulled off the most stunning, unbelievable upset in American political history."[43]

Pence family members left the ballroom around 3:30 a.m. too excited to sleep. Brother Gregory and his wife, Denise, invited the crew to their hotel room for an hour to unwind. In the meantime, they had received a text message from kin in Doonbeg, Ireland, who'd awakened to the news that their relative had been elected vice president. The message included a photo of a distinctive red Trump hat on their door knocker with a note: "Gone celebrating."[44]

Back home in Indiana, Republicans held their election night party in the ballroom at the JW Marriott in downtown Indianapolis. As happy as he was for the new vice-president-elect, Cardwell had other victories to celebrate. It had been a clean sweep for Indiana Republicans, thanks in no small part to Trump's lengthy coattails. In the US Senate race, Todd Young defeated Evan Bayh, one of the most popular politicians in Indiana history. Eric Holcomb beat John Gregg in the governor's matchup by a wider margin than Pence had four years before. Attorney General Curtis Hill became the highest vote-getter in state history. Jennifer McCormick won back the school superintendent's office from the Democrats. "I'll never forget that night," said Cardwell, who cemented his own reputation as one of the most successful Republican state chairmen in state history.[45]

Busloads of Hoosiers traveled from Indiana to Washington for the inauguration on January 20, 2017. The Columbus North High School Band and the Culver Academies Black Horse Troop marched in the parade. Republicans from Bartholomew County, Pence's childhood home, chartered a two-bus caravan they jokingly called the Roving Elephants. Wayne County state representative Tom Saunders organized a trip for 110 GOP supporters from around the state. More than three hundred Hoosiers sat in the freezing rain to watch the inauguration of their native son.

Under a gray sky, Mike Pence raised his right hand and placed his left hand on top of Ronald Reagan's family Bible, the Pence family Bible beneath it: "I, Michael Richard Pence, do solemnly swear, that I will

support and defend the Constitution of the United States . . . and that I
will well and faithfully discharge the duties of the office on which I am
about to enter. So help me, God."

The forty-eighth vice president shook hands with Supreme Court
justice Clarence Thomas, who had administered the oath, embraced his
wife, Karen, and their three children, and waved to the crowd. Standing
near the podium, where moments before their friend had just assumed
the country's second-highest office, Jeff Cardwell and Ed Simcox took
time to reflect on the occasion. "To see that transition of power, it's one
of those moments that really define America," Cardwell said, "regardless of where you stand on politics."[46]

★ ★ ★

# EPILOGUE:
# A SUBSTANTIAL
# VICE
# PRESIDENCY

IN 1876, DELEGATES TO THE REPUBLICAN NATIONAL CONvention nominated William Wheeler of New York as running mate to Rutherford Hayes, prompting the Ohio presidential candidate to ask his wife, "Who is Wheeler?"[1] John Nance Garner gave up his powerful job as speaker of the House in 1932 to run alongside Franklin Delano Roosevelt, only to be told a year later by his boss, "You tend to your office, and I'll tend to mine."[2] When a government courier knocked on Vice President John Tyler's door to inform him of President William Henry Harrison's passing in 1841, the story goes, he found Tyler kneeling on the floor playing marbles with his sons.[3] Such was the standing of the vice presidency, leading Garner to lament that the job of second-in-command wasn't "worth a bucket of warm spit."[4]

More recently, as the author Jules Witcover noted, "the American vice president has for all practical purposes come to be the de facto assistant president."[5] The job description fittingly applies to Mike Pence, who has achieved more policy victories from his position inside the Trump administration than he accomplished during twelve years on Capitol Hill. Whether casting tie votes as president of the Senate in his official capacity, influencing foreign policy behind the scenes, or luring conservative thinkers into key positions, Pence's vice presidency has promised to be one of the most substantial in US history. As *Politico*'s Tim Alberta wrote, "He is deeply involved with nearly every major decision coming from the White House, whether it be the withdrawal from the Paris climate accord or the appointment of Neil Gorsuch to the Supreme Court."[6]

As the only federal official who straddles two branches, Pence has advanced key goals through his constitutional powers under Article I, Section 3: "The Vice President of the United States shall be President of the Senate, but shall have no vote, unless they be equally divided." Since 1789, vice presidents have cast 263 votes to break ties in a divided Senate.[7] John Calhoun holds the record at thirty-one. Twelve vice presidents, including Pence's immediate predecessor, Joe Biden, cast none. Dick Cheney, in his eight years as vice president under George W. Bush, cast eight. After fourteen months in office, Pence had cast nine, including the first ever on a cabinet nomination.[8] His was the critical fifty-first vote to confirm the nomination of Betsy DeVos as secretary of education.

Pence took satisfaction in his October 2017 tiebreaker on House Joint Resolution 111, which allowed states to withhold federal family planning funds from Planned Parenthood and other abortion providers. Since his first campaign for Congress in 1988, Pence has said he would like to see the Supreme Court's *Roe v. Wade* decision overturned and the issue of abortion returned to the states. It is a position grounded in his reading of scripture and one verse in particular that he cites from Jeremiah: "Before I formed you in the womb I knew you." It is also a reflection of his understanding of federalism and the proper distribution of power between the federal government and states.

Pence's studious approach to Bible study and history has likewise informed his views on Israel, a foreign policy matter on which he has wielded enormous influence inside the White House. In 1995, Congress passed the Jerusalem Embassy Act directing the federal government to relocate its embassy from Tel Aviv to Jerusalem, a holy city whose status is at the heart of the dispute between Israel and Palestinian Arabs. No president dared do it—until Donald Trump, with Pence's endorsement.

In an address to the Knesset in January 2018, Pence promised that the embassy would move by the end of 2019, calling Israel an "inspiration to the world."[9] Several Arab-Israeli Knesset members interrupted his remarks before being forcibly ejected, one of them appearing to shout, "You are free to give up Indiana but not Jerusalem!" The address, which drew on passages from Deuteronomy and Isaiah and referenced predictions from Hebrew scripture, "was one of the most Zionist speeches ever given by a non-Jew in the Knesset," wrote attendee Meir Soloveichik, director of the Straus Center for Torah and Western Thought of Yeshiva University.[10]

Over many years, Pence's friend and policy adviser Tom Rose has offered trusted counsel on the matter of US-Israeli relations. The Indianapolis native, who spent six years as publisher of the conservative *Jerusalem Post*, was among dozens of Pence associates hired by the Trump administration in policymaking roles. Alex Azar, former Eli Lilly executive, was approved to be secretary of health and human services. Seema Verma, who advised Governor Pence in the crafting of his Medicaid waiver, was named administrator of the Centers for Medicare and Medicaid Services. Dr. Jerome Adams, Pence's state health commissioner, became US surgeon general.

As an administration insider, Pence has not been able to escape his share of the seemingly endless strife that roils the Trump White House. Even before taking office, Pence was booed by some in the audience during a family visit to see *Hamilton* on Broadway and scolded by a cast member who declared from the stage, "We, sir, are the diverse America who are alarmed and anxious that your new administration will not protect us—our planet, our children, our parents—or defend us and uphold our inalienable rights, sir." In typical turn-the-other-cheek fashion, Pence took no offense and said the criticism was "what freedom sounds like."[11]

On a more substantive level, political reporters raised questions early in 2017 about what Pence knew—in his role as head of the Trump transition team—about Michael Flynn, the disgraced former Trump national security adviser. Flynn was forced to resign after less than a month in the job for misleading Pence and others in the administration about his ties to the government of Turkey and his postelection conversations with a Russian ambassador. In December 2017, special counsel Robert Mueller charged Flynn with lying to the FBI as part of an investigation into possible collusion between the Russian government and the Trump campaign. There were lesser controversies too, including one involving Pence's tenure as governor when he maintained a personal AOL email account through which he conducted public business. In March 2017, Pence's lawyers delivered the emails to the statehouse in paper form for state government archiving.

Indiana is often called the "mother of vice presidents," having produced six of them since 1868, when Ulysses Grant picked Schuyler Colfax, a little-known founder of the Republican Party. The Indiana town of Colfax was named in his honor, but Hoosiers paid little heed to his historic legacy, and Colfax became famous instead for its fried catfish. The popular Miller's Restaurant closed in 1999, and today, the town's population is under seven hundred. As noted by Indiana University historian James Madison, Pence was chosen for many of the same reasons as the other five. "Pence stands in a long line of Indiana vice presidents chosen less for demonstrated leadership than for their potential to attract a particular segment of the electorate," Madison said.[12]

In contrast to his predecessors, Pence has been allowed to play a meaningful role. According to Tim Alberta, Pence asked Trump during their first meeting prior to joining the ticket "what the job description was, because there's only one person who writes it, and that's the president." Trump's answer, Alberta found out months later, was that Trump wanted "the most consequential vice president ever."[13] Only one other Hoosier came close to wielding the power that Pence has exercised, and not by design of the president. Democrat Thomas R. Marshall was running mate to Woodrow Wilson in 1912 and 1916, though their relationship became so frayed at one point that Wilson asked him to resign. As one would expect of the feisty promoter of the phrase "What the country needs is a really good five-cent cigar,"[14] Marshall refused. In 1919, Wilson suffered a debilitating stroke. Wilson's cabinet and Marshall, with help from Wilson's wife, functioned without a transfer of power.

There are no signs that the Trump-Pence relationship is anything but solid, in part due to Pence's own insistence that his job is to support the president. Newt Gingrich has said that Pence is one of three people with the most policy influence in the administration. The other two are Trump himself and Chief of Staff John Kelly.[15] This influence may shed light on what many consider the biggest enigma of Pence's vice presidency: how could a biblically based Christian so readily align himself with a man prone to flout the most recognized rules of civility?

Considering Pence's calculated approach to his political career, it would be easy to ascribe the unlikely union solely to Pence's own presidential ambition, but the answer is more nuanced than that. For Pence, politics is a calling. In the 1990s, when Pence was a talk radio show host, he would occasionally invite *Indianapolis Star* editorial cartoonist Gary Varvel, an evangelical Christian, to join him on the show to discuss the day's news. Afterward, they would have lunch and sometimes talked about the Bible. A favorite and familiar Old Testament passage tells the story of Esther, an orphan who becomes queen of Persia and intercedes with the king to save the Jewish people from annihilation. As Esther ponders what to do, her cousin asks, "And who knows but that you have come to royal position for such a time as this?"[16] The question is a fitting one for the forty-eighth vice president. "Such a time as this" will test the political skills Pence has developed over a lifetime and the leadership role he has so faithfully pursued.

# NOTES

### INTRODUCTION: "AND THEN THERE'S ME"

1. "VP Mike Pence Shares Testimony at Church by the Glades."
2. George F. Will, "Pence the Pliable," 5C.
3. Jane Mayer, "The President Pence Delusion," 66.
4. Bobby Jindal, "Trump's Style Is His Substance," A17.

### 1. GROWING UP HOOSIER

1. Ralph Gray, *Indiana History*, 256.
2. Jacob Piatt Dunn, "The Word 'Hoosier,'" 61–63.
3. Brenda Maschino, "Pence Encourages Students to Dream," A1.
4. "Vice President Mike Pence Speaks at Latino Coalition."
5. New York, Passenger Lists, 1820–1957.
6. United States Federal Census, 1920 and 1930.
7. "Vice President Pence Wreath Laying."
8. "Vice President Pence Wreath Laying."
9. "Learning from Columbus," 4.
10. Harry McCawley, "The Road to the Governor's Office," G8.
11. Zach Peterson, "Vice President's Mother Discusses Young Mike Pence."
12. Sheryl Gay Stolberg, "'I Am an American Because of Him.'"
13. Boris Ladwig, "Pence Recounts How Hometown Shaped Future," A3.
14. Mike Pence, "Tribute to Dr. Julius Perr."

15. Ladwig, "Pence Recounts," A3.

16. Judith Valente, "Catholic Sister Recalls Her Pupil."

17. McCawley, "The Road," G8.

18. Valente, "Catholic Sister Recalls."

19. Jeff Brown, interview by author, October 19, 2017.

20. Maschino, "Pence Encourages Students," A1.

21. Brown interview.

22. Brown interview.

23. "North Grad Third in NFL Speech Contest," 6.

24. McCawley, "The Road," G8.

25. Tim Grimm, interview by author, August 30, 2017.

26. Steven David, interview by author, February 21, 2018.

27. McCawley, "The Road," G9.

28. "North Grad Third," 6.

29. Grimm interview.

30. Ladwig, "Pence Recounts," A3.

31. Brown interview.

32. Brown interview.

33. Brian Francisco, "2nd District Candidates on Best Behavior," 1A.

34. Jane Mayer, "The President Pence Delusion," 57.

35. Kirk Johannesen, "Belief in the American Dream," A5.

36. McCawley, "The Road," G8.

37. Ladwig, "Pence Recounts," A1.

38. Stolberg, "'I Am an American.'"

39. Stolberg, "'I Am an American.'"

40. Simon Carswell, "Mike Pence and Donald Trump's Irish Connection."

## 2. ON THE BANKS OF THE OHIO

1. Mike Pence, "Commencement Speaker Mike Pence."

2. Daniel P. Murphy, interview by author, July 24 and October 18, 2017.

3. J. C. Steger, "Pence, Parties, and Parents."

4. Murphy interview.

5. Murphy interview.

6. Murphy interview.

7. Steger, "Pence, Parties, and Parents."

8. Mike Pence, "VP Mike Pence Shares Testimony."

9. Murphy interview.

10. Anne Klouman, "Vespers Looking Up," 2.

11. Pence, "VP Mike Pence Shares Testimony."

12. Pence, "VP Mike Pence Shares Testimony."

13. Harry McCawley, "The Road to the Governor's Office," G9.

14. Steve Kukolla, "Penance, Redemption Punctuate Life of Mike," par. 6.

15. Bryan Corbin, "Pence Finally Realizes Dream of Going to Washington," A10.

16. Lake Lambert, interview by author, July 24, 2017.

17. Murphy interview.

18. George M. Curtis III, "History 331."

19. George M. Curtis III, interview by author, January 27, 2018.

20. J. C. Steger, interview by author, June 29, August 3, and December 22, 2017.

21. J. C. Steger, "Consulting All Truth."

22. Michael Richard Pence, "The Religious Expressions of Abraham Lincoln."

23. Pence, "Commencement Speaker Mike Pence."

24. Thomas W. Leyden, "Reagan Aide Explains Rights Policy," 39.

### 3. LAW, MARRIAGE, AND MENTORS

1. Jennifer Mehalik, "Iconic Lawyer Passes Torch."

2. Steve Kukolla, "Penance, Redemption Punctuate Life of Mike."

3. J. C. Steger, interview by author, June 29, August 3, and December 22, 2017.

4. J. C. Steger, "The Gloves Come Off."

5. Ed Simcox, interview by author, August 21, 2017.

6. Kukolla, "Penance, Redemption."

7. "Alumni Spotlights"; Kukolla, "Penance, Redemption."

8. Bill Stephan, interview by author, October 19, 2017.

9. Stephan interview.

10. "Mike Pence Cartoons in *Dictum*."

11. Brian Bosma, interview by author, October 4, 2017.

12. Curtis Shirley, interview by author, March 2, 2018.

13. Carolyn Harvey Lundberg, personal communication, February 28, 2018.

14. Lundberg personal communication.

15. Steger interview.

16. Shari Rudavsky, "She's Right at Home," G11.

17. Jeff Brown, interview by author, October 19, 2017.

18. "Indiana's First Lady Recalls Her Days at Park School," 37.

19. "Whitaker-Batten," 5.

20. Ashley Parker, "Karen Pence Is the Vice President's Prayer Warrior."

21. Rudavsky, "She's Right at Home," G11.

22. Will Maule, "Karen Pence."

23. Rudavsky, "She's Right at Home," G11.

24. Brown interview.

25. Melissa Langsam Braunstein, "Second Lady Karen Pence Opens Up about Her Struggles with Infertility."

26. Mike Pence, "Right to Life Speech."

27. Lundberg personal communication.

28. Lundberg personal communication.

29. "Pence Statement on Passing of Indiana University Professor William F. Harvey."

#### 4. THE FIRST CAMPAIGN

1. John Schorg, "Riding the 2nd District," A11.

2. John Schorg, interview by author, June 27, 2017.

3. J. C. Steger, interview by author, June 29, August 3, and December 22, 2017.

4. Steger interview.

5. Bill Stephan, email to author, February 28, 2018.

6. Harry McCawley, "The Road to the Governor's Office," G9.

7. McCawley, "The Road," G9.

8. John Schorg, "Mike Pence Enters 2nd District Race," A14.

9. Fredreka Schouten, Christopher Schnaars, and Maureen Groppe, "Who's Giving Big Money to Vice President Pence's Leadership PAC?"

10. Brian Francisco, "2nd Best," D1.

11. Steger interview.

12. Steger interview.

13. Steger interview.

14. Steven V. Roberts, "Working Profile."

15. Ken Ward, "A Columbus Connection in the 2nd District?," D6.

16. Schorg, "Mike Pence Enters," A14.

17. Schorg, "Riding the 2nd District," A11.

18. Schorg, "Riding the 2nd District," A11.

19. Schorg interview.

20. Schorg, "Pence 'Lauds' Foe's PAC Funds," A14.

21. Schorg, "Pence Wants Proof of Alleged Lies," A1.

22. James G. Newland Jr., "Politics Serves as a Magnet for Coats' Campaign Chief," B3.

23. Chuck Quilhot, interview by author, August 8, 2017.

24. Jeff Cardwell, interview by author, July 6 and 27, 2017, and January 4, 2018.

25. Cardwell interview.

26. Steve Polston, "Pence Defends Campaign Funding," A1.

27. Polston, "Pence Defends Campaign Funding."

28. Evans Witt, "Young Hoosier Is an Appealing Choice," A2.

29. Schorg, "Pence Says Quayle Gives His Candidacy a Shot of Adrenalin," A3.

30. "Debate News Disappointing," 4.

31. Brian Francisco, "Burton Breezes, Sharp Squeezes to Victory," A1.

32. Cardwell interview.

33. John R. O'Neill, "Pence Isn't Ruling Out Rematch with Sharp," B4.

## 5. THE AGONY OF DEFEAT

1. Patrick J. Traub, "GOP's 1990 Election Roster Still Has a Lot of Holes," F4.

2. Brian Francisco, "Pence Seeks GOP Nod to Challenge 2nd District's Sharp," A2.

3. J. C. Steger, interview by author, June 29, August 3, and December 22, 2017.

4. Steger interview.

5. "Mike Pence to Run against Rep. Sharp," D4.

6. Brian Francisco, "Pence Announces Second Run for Congress," A7.

7. Brian Francisco, "Campaign's Nasty Boys Get in Last Jabs," D1.

8. David Hackett and Jeff Madsen, "Pence Backers Unaware of Spending," A1.

9. "Pence Forms For-Profit Panel," A14.

10. "Pence Accused of Breaking Federal Campaign Fund Law," A3.

11. Richard M. Bates, letter to Federal Election Commission, August 8, 1990.

12. Jeff Owen, "GOP Campaign Misses Important Opportunity," A4

13. Danny Lee, "Pence Says No More Campaign Funds for Personal Expenses," A1.

14. John R. O'Neill, "More Accusations Fly in 2nd District," D2.

15. Brian Francisco, "Prosecutor: Pence Aide Violated Law," 1, 10.

16. John R. O'Neill, "Pence Slings Oil, Not Mud," B1.

17. Associated Press, "Arab-Americans Protest Commercial," 5.

18. Sherman Johnson, interview by author, August 31, 2017.

19. Angela Allen, "200 Arabs Rally to Protest 'Hurtful' Pence Commercial," B17.

20. Dan Carpenter, "Racial Stereotypes," B1.

21. Brian Francisco, "Pence Disagrees with New Taxes," A1, A12.

22. Owen, "GOP Campaign Misses," A4.

23. David Hackett, "Controversial Phone Blitz Attacks Sharp," 1, 12.

24. Hackett, "Controversial Phone Blitz," 12.

25. "Improper Influence?" 3.

26. Jodi Perras, "Pence Acknowledges Staff Was Involved in Phony Phone Poll," A1.

27. Steger interview.

28. Karen Terhune, "Sharp Whips Pence with 62% of Vote," 1.

29. Owen, "GOP Campaign Misses," A4.

30. Terhune, "Sharp Whips Pence," 8.

31. Mike Pence, "Hard-Fought Election," A4.

## 6. FROM REPENTANCE TO REDEMPTION

1. Curt Smith, interview by author, June 28, 2017.

2. Smith interview.

3. Chuck Quilhot, appointment calendar, December 8, 1988.

4. Indiana Review Foundation, *Articles of Incorporation*, January 19, 1989.

5. T. Craig Ladwig, interview by author, June 5, 2017.

6. Chuck Quilhot, interview by author, August 8, 2017.

7. Quilhot interview.

8. Ladwig interview.

9. Mike Pence, "Confessions of a Negative Campaigner."

10. "Political Regrets," A18.

11. "Pence's Apology Helps, but Concerns Remain," A4.

12. Brian Francisco, "Pence Sorry for Negative Campaign," 8.

13. Brian Francisco, "Pence Not Interested in Running for Office," 8.

14. Dan Carpenter, "Fortunately, 'Think Tanks' Keep Dimwits Off the Streets," C1.

15. Bob Massie, "Rash Day-Saving by Dan," A7.

16. T. Craig Ladwig, ed., *Indiana Mandate*.

17. Mike Pence, "By Adopting Term Limits," 31.

18. Ladwig interview.

19. Ladwig interview.

20. "Judge Rejects Challenge to '92 Bill That Raises State Lawmakers' Pensions," C3.

21. Pence v. State, 652 N.E.2d 486 (Supreme Court of Indiana 1995).

22. Pence v. State.

23. Chuck Quilhot, "A Letter to a Senior Senator," 13.

24. Chuck Quilhot, "IPR Inter-Office Memo."

25. Mike Pence, letter to John Andrews, Texas Public Policy Foundation, January 5, 1994.

26. Brian Francisco, "Talk Radio Suits Former Congressional Candidate," 1B.

## 7. "GREETINGS ACROSS THE AMBER WAVES OF GRAIN"

1. David Yepsen and Holli Hartman, "Dole, Buchanan Finish 1–2," A1.
2. Mike Pence, host, *The Mike Pence Show*, February 13, 1996.
3. Craig Fehrman, "Incoming: Mike Pence."
4. Fehrman, "Incoming."
5. Steve Hall, "The Kind Conservative," C2.
6. Ryan Trares, "Pence Used Radio Talk Show to Build Name, Reputation," A6.
7. Bob Lovell, interview by author, November 27, 2017.
8. Steve Hall, "Pence on TV Fuses Sparks, Substance," D7.
9. Brian Blair, "Open Mike," B1.
10. Steve Hall, "If Talk Show Turns You Off, Turn It Off," D5.
11. Kathleen Glenister Roberts and Ronald C. Arnett, *Communication Ethics*, 266.
12. Blair, "Open Mike," B1.
13. Mike Pence, *The Pence Report*.
14. Todd Meyer, interview by author, October 5, 2017.
15. Emily Mantel, interview by author, November 6, 2017.
16. Hall, "The Kind Conservative," C2.
17. Tamara Jones, "The Pilot's Cloudy Future."
18. Chris Pollock, producer, *The Mike Pence Radio Show*.
19. Blair, "Open Mike," B1.
20. Blair, "Open Mike," B1.
21. Blair, "Open Mike," B1.
22. Mantel interview.
23. Russ Dodge, interview by author, November 11, 2017.
24. Jon Quick, interview by author, December 9, 2017.
25. Dave Wilson, interview by author, July 14, 2017.
26. Pence, *The Pence Report*.
27. Hall, "Pence on TV," D7.
28. Hall, "Pence on TV," D7.
29. Mike Pence, "Reflections on GOP Dinner," 5.
30. Lovell interview.

## 8. MR. PENCE GOES TO WASHINGTON

1. David McIntosh, interview by author, October 5, 2017.
2. Brian Blair, "Open Mike," B1.

3. McIntosh interview.

4. McIntosh interview.

5. Bill Smith, interview by author, July 25, 2017, and January 5, 2018.

6. Smith interview.

7. Michele McNeil Solida, "McIntosh's Exit Leaves Door Open for Democrats," A15.

8. Solida, "McIntosh's Exit," A15.

9. Gregory Weaver, "Robert Rock to Face Mike Pence," A6.

10. Seth Slabaugh, "Pence: Global Warming 'a Myth,'" 1A.

11. Slabaugh, "Pence," 6A.

12. Bryan Corbin, "Pence Tries a Third Time," A10.

13. "Pence a Changed Man Since Early Campaigns," D1.

14. Mike Pence, "Candidate Ready to Provide Leadership," 3D.

15. Smith interview.

16. Rick Yencer, "Pence Wins Big, McIntosh Loses Home Precinct," 1A.

17. McIntosh interview.

18. Gannett News Service, "Rep.-Elect Mike Pence Is Learning the Basics," 4A.

19. Dave Evensen, "Constituents Turn Out to Meet Pence," A3.

20. Smith interview.

21. J. C. Steger, interview by author, June 29, August 3, and December 22, 2017.

22. John Clark, "Columbus' Pence Joins 107th Congress," A1.

23. Associated Press, "Indiana Contingent Puts Partisanship Aside for Inauguration," A3.

24. George W. Bush, "Inaugural Address."

## 9. THE UNFORGETTABLE 107TH CONGRESS

1. "Pence Moves to Top of House Class," 3D.

2. "The Unforgettable 107th Congress."

3. Bill Smith, interview by author, July 25, 2017, and January 5, 2018.

4. Maureen Groppe, "For Rep. Mike Pence, the Show Must Go On," B5.

5. Jeff Flake, Conscience of a Conservative, 16.

6. Flake, Conscience of a Conservative, 17.

7. Kirk Johannesen, "House Colleagues Have Fond Memories of Columbus Native," G7.

8. "Small Business Paperwork Relief Act."

9. Johannesen, "House Colleagues," G7.

10. Mike Pence, "Veto Human Embryo Research."

11. Jeff Cardwell, interview by author, July 6 and 27, 2017, and January 4, 2018.

12. Cardwell interview.

13. Janet Hook, "Bush's First Veto," A2.

14. Cardwell interview.

15. Mike Pence, "Pence on 9/11."

16. John Clark, "Pence: Response Must Be Swift and Violent," A7.

17. John Clark, "Hill, Pence Tour Devastation at New York's Ground Zero," A8.

18. "Rep. Pence New Member of Judiciary Committee," A8.

19. Karen Gullo, "Letters Seem Coordinated," 5A.

20. Smith interview.

21. John Clark, "Pence Family Takes Steps vs. 'Poison Powder,'" A1.

22. Smith interview.

23. Rick Yencer, "Pence Targeted by Democrats," 1B.

24. Smith interview.

## 10. "TAKEN TO THE WOODSHED"

1. Mike Pence, "Tribute to Chuck Mosey."

2. Jeff Cardwell, interview by author, July 6 and 27, 2017, and January 4, 2018.

3. Danny J. Ernstes, "The Sixth Congressional District of Indiana," 20, 27.

4. Melina Fox, email to author, October 4, 2017.

5. "Pence Supports President," 5A.

6. Bryan Corbin, "Candidates Answer Questions about Iraq, Medicare," A11.

7. "Pence Deserves 2nd Term in Office," A10.

8. Dan McFeely, "Pence Cruises to Landslide Victory," V2.

9. Maureen Groppe, "Assistance for Wishard in Jeopardy," B3.

10. "House of Representatives."

11. Cardwell interview.

12. Lawrence Kudlow, "2005 Man of the Year: Rep. Mike Pence."

13. Bill Smith, interview by author, July 25, 2017, and January 5, 2018.

14. David Broder, "Bush's Pre-Dawn Lobbying Got Medicare Bill Through House," A4.

15. Bruce Bartlett, "Republican Deficit Hypocrisy."

16. George F. Will, "Tea Party Would Back Pence for President," A10.

17. Broder, "Bush's Pre-Dawn Lobbying," A4.

18. Kudlow, "2005 Man of the Year."

19. Michael D. Tanner, *Leviathan on the Right*, 72.

20. Stephen Dinan, "Medicare Bill Incites House Conservatives."

21. Cardwell interview.

22. Joseph Carroll, "Economy, Terrorism Top Issues in 2004 Election Vote."

23. Will Lester, "Pence Leads Call for Rollback of Bush Initiatives," A1.

24. "Excerpts from Bush's speech," A8.

25. "Q&A with Mike Pence."

26. Robert Novak, "House Leadership Had to Cave on Spending," A4.

27. Kudlow, "2005 Man of the Year."

28. Gannett News Service, "Pence Could Be Spoiler in Race for House GOP Leadership Post," 3A.

29. Andrea Neal, "In GOP Loss, Pence Is Quoting Peyton," A6.

30. Gannett News Service, "Pence Could Be Spoiler," 3A.

31. Malia Rulon, "Republicans Rebuff Pence's Leadership Bid," A8.

32. John Bicknell, "Pence, Mike."

33. "Emergency Economic Stabilization Act of 2008."

34. Cardwell interview.

35. Maureen Groppe, "Bush Takes Interest in Pence's Immigration Plan," A1.

36. Maureen Groppe, "House GOP to Put Hoosier in Charge of Its Message," A9.

37. Bicknell, "Pence, Mike."

38. "Pence Elected House Republican Conference Chairman."

39. "Comments and Statistics on the Health-Care Overhaul," 6A.

40. George Will, "Pence May Be a Favorite for Conservatives in the 2010 Race," A6.

## 11. GREGG VERSUS PENCE

1. Chris Sikich, "Remarks Draw Widespread Rebukes," A9.

2. John Gregg, interview by author, September 11, 2017.

3. Gregg interview.

4. Mike Dorning, "One for the Gipper," 5.

5. Harry McCawley, Kirk Johannesen, and Paul Minnis, "Many Think Pence Could Win Gubernatorial Race," A4.

6. Kathryn Jean Lopez, "Mike Pence for President."

7. Jeff Cardwell, interview by author, July 6 and 27, 2017, and January 4, 2018.

8. Mary Beth Schneider, "Decisions, Decisions. Will Pence and Bayh Run?," A1.

9. Brian Howey, "Skillman's Exit Only a Mild Surprise as Pence Rises," E2.

10. Craig Fehrman, "Incoming: Mike Pence."

11. Fehrman, "Incoming."

12. Robert T. Grand, interview by author, August 14, 2017.

13. Fred Klipsch, interview by author, December 21, 2017.

14. Kirk Johannesen, "Run for Governor to Be Explored," A1.

15. Mary Beth Schneider, "Pence Reveals 'Worst-Kept Secret,'" B3.

16. Kirk Johannesen, "Their Man Mike," A1.

17. Gregg interview.

18. "John Gregg for Indiana Governor: 'Two Kinds.'"

19. Gregg interview.

20. Gregg interview.

21. Gregg interview.

22. Gregg interview.

23. Gregg interview.

24. Fehrman, "Incoming."

25. Brian Bosma, interview by author, October 4, 2017.

26. Dave Helling, "Missouri and Kansas Republicans Like Apparent Pick of Mike Pence for GOP Ticket"; Bryan Lowry, "Trump's Likely VP Pick Has a Connection to Kansas Politics."

27. Bill Smith, interview by author, July 25, 2017, and January 5, 2018.

28. John Gregg, email to author, February 26, 2018.

29. Chris Sikich and Carrie Ritchie, "Gregg, Pence Push for Lasting Impressions," A1.

30. Dan Carden, "Gregg Pummels Pence in Final Debate," A1.

31. Gregg interview.

32. Robert King, "Remark Reflects U.S. Friction over Abortion," A9.

33. Mike Pence, "Mike Pence's Acceptance Speech."

34. Gregg email.

## 12. TIPTOEING THROUGH THE MINEFIELDS

1. James H. Johnson, "Pence Inauguration as Governor Touches on Hoosier History," A4.

2. Mike Pence, "Gov. Mike Pence's Inaugural Speech."

3. Tom LoBianco, "Gov.-Elect Uses Rare Opportunity to Trade Social Crusader Mantle," A3.

4. Brian Bosma, interview by author, October 4, 2017.

5. "Conservative Group That Supports Spending Cuts."

6. Dan Carden, "Pence Claims Tax Cut Victory," A6.

7. Bosma interview.

8. Tom LoBianco, "Rulings Clear Path for Indiana Battle," A8.

9. Jon Murray, "Poll: Marriage Measure Draws Opposition," A3.

10. Maureen Groppe, "Who Gets Boost from Court?" 26A.

11. Kevin Warren, interview by author, September 13, 2017.

12. Warren interview.

13. Ed Simcox, interview by author, August 21, 2017; Ed Simcox, written notes shared with author, August 21, 2017.

14. Maggie Gallagher, "Two Moms vs. Common Core."

15. Alec Torres, "The Ten Dumbest Common Core Problems."

16. Senate Enrolled Act No. 91, 118th General Assembly (2014).

17. Gallagher, "Two Moms vs. Common Core"; Indiana Chamber Staff, "Facts Ignored, Politics Winning on Common Core."

18. Joy Pullman, *The Education Invasion*, 144

19. Pullman, *Education Invasion*, 143.

20. Heather Crossin, interview by author, December 16, 2017.

21. Scott Elliott, "Pence, Ritz Strongly Endorse New Indiana Standards over Objections."

22. Crossin interview.

23. Michelle Malkin, "Common Core Backlash Claims New Casualties," A4.

24. Jim Atterholt, interview by author, November 13 and 30, 2017.

25. Atterholt interview.

26. Atterholt interview.

27. Tom LoBianco, "Pence Team Starting State-Run News Wire," A2.

28. Matt Tully, "Mike Pence's Horrible Idea," A3.

29. Tim Swarens, "Pence's Reputation Bruised by Just IN," A15.

30. William McCleery, interview by author, June 27, 2017.

31. Atterholt interview.

32. Atterholt interview.

33. Atterholt interview.

34. Mark Joseph Stern, "The Most Cynical Republican on Obamacare."

35. Tom Davies, "Pence Touts Plans for Education," 6.

### 13. CRISIS AT THE CAPITOL

1. George Stephanopoulos, "Indiana Gov. Mike Pence Says Religious Freedom Law 'Absolutely Not' a Mistake."

2. Employment Division, Department of Human Resources of Oregon v. Smith. Oyez (Accessed January 12, 2018), https://oyez.org/cases/1989/88–1213.

3. Free Exercise of Religion Protected, 42 U.S. Code § 2000bb-1.

4. Baskin v. Bogan, 766 F.3d 648 (Court of Appeals, 7th Circuit 2014).

5. Burwell v. Hobby Lobby Stores. Oyez (Accessed January 12, 2018), https://www.oyez.org/cases/2013/13–354.

6. Scott Schneider, interview by author, December 28, 2017.

7. Tony Cook, "Pence Calls for Balanced Budget Amendment," A1.

8. Senate Bill No. 568, 119th General Assembly (2015).

9. Associated Press, "Bill Would Let Businesses Refuse Service to Gays," A3.

10. Stephanie Wang, "Law's Roots Tied to Marriage Fight," 4A.

11. Brian Bosma, interview by author, October 4, 2017.

12. Dan Carden, "Panel OKs 'Religious Freedom' Edict," A6.

13. Justin L. Mack and Stephanie Wang, "Salesforce Executive: Bill Would Do Harm," 3A.

14. Jason Collins (@jasoncollins98), "@GovPenceIN, is it going to be legal for someone to discriminate against me & others when we come to the #FinalFour?"

15. "Reaction," 17A.

16. Jim Atterholt, interview by author, November 13 and 30, 2017.

17. Scott Schneider, email to author, January 10, 2018.

18. Bosma interview.

19. Schneider email.

20. Tony Cook, "Pence: SB 101 'Is Not about Legalizing Discrimination,'" 1A, 6A.

21. Jennifer C. Pizer, "Indiana's Rush to Invite Law-Breaking for Religious Reasons."

22. Schneider interview.

23. Bosma interview.

24. Curt Smith, *Deicide*, 72.

25. Bill Smith, interview by author, July 25, 2017, and January 5, 2018.

26. Jeff Cardwell, interview by author, July 6 and 27, 2017, and January 4, 2018.

27. Stephanopoulos, "Indiana Gov. Mike Pence Says Religious Freedom."

28. Smith, *Deicide*, 73.

29. Cardwell interview.

30. Jeff Swiatek and Tim Evans, "9 CEOs Urge Change to RFRA," 3A, 7A.

31. Dan Evans, interview by author, December 21, 2017.

32. "Fix This Now," 1A.

33. Atterholt interview.

34. Bosma interview.

35. Senate Enrolled Act No. 50, 119th General Assembly (2015).

36. Smith, *Deicide*, 75.

37. Atterholt interview.

38. Kevin Warren, interview by author, September 13, 2017.

39. Tim Swarens, "After RFRA, Pence Pledges to Listen More," 5A.

## 14. THE HOLCOMB EFFECT

1. Mike Pence, "2016 State of the State Address."

2. Jeff Cardwell, interview by author, July 6 and 27, 2017, and January 4, 2018.

3. John Gregg, interview by author, September 11, 2017.

4. Brian Howey, "Pence's Shift to Holcomb," D2.

5. Jim Atterholt, interview by author, November 13 and 30, 2017.

6. "John Gregg for Indiana Governor: 'Hobo.'"

7. "Mike Pence for Indiana Governor."

8. Atterholt interview.

9. Tony Cook and Chelsea Schneider, "Ellspermann Eyes Ivy Tech Top Job," 1A.

10. Chelsea Schneider and Stephanie Wang, "Ellspermann Picked to Lead Ivy Tech," 1A.

11. Eric Holcomb, interview by author, January 3, 2014.

12. Holcomb interview.

13. Holcomb interview.

14. Holcomb interview.

15. Dwight Adams, "The State Reacts to Pence's Selection of Holcomb," 8A.

16. Tony Cook and Chelsea Schneider, "Pence Picks New Running Mate," 8A.

17. Atterholt interview.

18. Howey, "Pence's Shift," D2.

## 15. TRUMP COMES A-COURTING

1. Jim Atterholt, interview by author, November 13 and 30, 2017.

2. Jennifer Jacobs, "Walker Has Edge in Tight GOP Field," 12A.

3. George Will, "The Mike Pence Conservative Paradox," B5.

4. Bill Smith, interview by author, July 25, 2017, and January 5, 2018.

5. Kirk Johannesen, "Mom to Mike: Keep Your Day Job," A2.

6. Atterholt interview; Jeff Cardwell, interview by author, July 6 and 27, 2017, and January 4, 2018.

7. Tom Davies, "Governor Defiant over Religious Freedom Legislation during Announcement," A2.

8. Tony Cook, "What Will Pence Say?" 1A.

9. Cardwell interview.

10. Rick Hampson, "What Explains Appeal of Donald Trump?" 1B.

11. Eric Bradner, "Polls: Donald Trump Leads, Ben Carson Slips."

12. Rex Early, interview by author, July 13 and December 28, 2017.

13. Brian Eason, Chelsea Schneider, and Maureen Groppe, "Behind Closed Doors," 11A.

14. Associated Press, "It's Official: Riverboat Casinos Open to the Public," A9.

15. *Donald Trump Roast.*

16. Early interview.

17. Nancy Meek, telephone interview by author, December 23, 2017.

18. Scott Bauer and Steve Peoples, "Governor Endorses 'Principled' Cruz," A8.

19. Cardwell interview.

20. Early interview.

21. Cardwell interview.

22. Early interview.

23. Ted Cruz, "Ted Cruz Drops Out of Presidential Race."

24. Early interview.

25. Noland D. McCaskill, "Trump Says He's Begun Vetting VP Picks."

26. Dan Carden, "Hoosier GOP Makes Picks," A5.

27. James Briggs and Stephanie Wang, "Pence 'Rings the Most Bells,'" A5.

28. Cardwell interview.

29. Mike Pence, "Gov. Pence Talks about Meeting with Donald Trump."

30. United Press International, "Palin Pick Called 'High Risk, High Reward.'"

31. Robert T. Grand, interview by author, August 14, 2017.

32. David McIntosh, telephone interview by author, October 5, 2017.

33. Early interview.

34. Grand interview.

35. Kevin Eck, telephone interview by author, December 11, 2017.

36. Cardwell interview; Jeff Cardwell, journal entry, July 12, 2016.

37. Chelsea Schneider and Tony Cook, "Can GOP Duo Work through Differences?" 8A.

38. Chris Sikich, "Announcement Expected Soon on Trump's Running Mate," 7A.

39. Early interview.

40. Atterholt interview.

41. Eck interview.

42. Jim Atterholt, email to author, January 9, 2018.

43. Major Garrett (@MajorCBS), "#veepstakes mania watch 2."

44. Donald J. Trump (@realDonaldTrump), "I am pleased to announce that I have chosen Governor Mike Pence."

45. Cal Thomas, "Pence Salt to Trump's Pepper," 6A.

### 16. "BUDDY, THE BALL GAME IS OVER"

1. Jeff Cardwell, telephone interview by author, March 5 and March 22, 2018.

2. Donald Trump, "Donald Trump Introduces Running Mate Mike Pence."

3. Louis Nelson, "Sen. Flake: Pence Would Be Trump's 'Best Choice' So Far."

4. Marco Rubio, "@realDonaldTrump Great pick. @mike_pence is rock solid."

5. David Sherfinski, "Paul Ryan on Mike Pence."

6. Club for Growth, "There's Nothing Conservative about Donald Trump."

7. Maureen Groppe, "Pence: I'm Very Excited," 10A.

8. Jane Mayer, "The President Pence Delusion," 56.

9. James Oliphant, "Once on the Outside, Conservative Koch Network Warms to Trump."

10. Nick Gass, "Clinton Campaign: 'Pence Is Most Extreme Pick in a Generation.'"

11. George F. Will, "Pence the Pliable," 5C.

12. Eric Holcomb, interview by author, January 3, 2014.

13. Eric Holcomb, "Lt. Governor Eric Holcomb on Mike Pence."

14. Tony Cook, "Trump, Pence Formally Nominated at Convention," 2A.

15. Dominic Patten, "Republican Convention Night 3 Ratings Down."

16. Todd Scoggins, "Thank you, Chairman Cardwell."

17. Mike Pence, "Vice Presidential Nominee Mike Pence."

18. Seema Mehta, "Clinton Sorry She Labeled 'Half' of Trump Supporters," 26.

19. Alexander Burns, "After Debate, Both Campaigns Say, 'We're No. 1,'" A8.

20. David Jackson, "Trump Resists Pressure from GOP to Step Aside," 7A.

21. "Who Has Pulled Their Support?" 4B.

22. Corey R. Lewandowski and David N. Bossie, *Let Trump Be Trump*, 203.

23. "Full Transcript: Second 2016 Presidential Debate."

24. Jackson, "Trump Resists Pressure," 7A.

25. Maureen Groppe, "Pence Lauds Trump for Admission," 6A.

26. Mike Pence, "Pence Church Message."

27. Madeline Buckley, "Innocent Man Frustrated as He Waits for Pardon," 3A, 5A.

28. Jim Atterholt, interview by author, November 13 and 30, 2017.

29. "Leaders Absent at Lead Crisis," D2.

30. Atterholt interview.

31. Dave Bangert, "Sen. Alting Gets Dose of 'Periods for Pence,'" 1A.

32. Mike Pence, "Governor Pence Statement on HEA 1337."

33. Camila Domonoske, "Periods as Protest."

34. Shari Rudavsky, "Meet Woman behind Periods for Pence," 5E.

35. Cardwell telephone interview.

36. Ed Simcox, telephone interview by author, March 6, 2018.

37. Rex Early, interview by author, July 13 and December 28, 2017.

38. Cardwell telephone interview.

39. Danielle Kurtzleben, "Pollsters Find 'at Best Mixed Evidence' Comey Letter Swayed Election."

40. Kirk Johannesen, "Family: Courage and Conviction Carry Pence to Success," A6.

41. Tim Alberta, "Man on a Wire: Mike Pence's Tightrope Act."

42. Mike Pence, "Mike Pence Introduces President-Elect Trump."

43. Pence, "Mike Pence Introduces."

44. Johannesen, "Family," A6.

45. Jeff Cardwell, interview by author, July 6 and 27, 2017, and January 4, 2018.

46. Cardwell interview.

## EPILOGUE: A SUBSTANTIAL VICE PRESIDENCY

1. Jules Witcover, *The American Vice Presidency*, 185.

2. Witcover, *American Vice Presidency*, 304.

3. Edward P. Crapol, *John Tyler: The Accidental President*, 8.

4. Witcover, *American Vice Presidency*, 298.

5. Witcover, *American Vice Presidency*, ix.

6. Tim Alberta, "Man on a Wire: Mike Pence's Tightrope Act."

7. United States Senate, "Tie Votes."

8. Senate Historical Office, "Occasions When Vice Presidents Have Voted to Break Tie Votes in the Senate."

9. Mike Pence, "VP Pence's Remarks at the Israeli Knesset."

10. Meir Soloveichik, "Pence Visits Israel's Capital."

11. Eric Bradner, "Pence: 'I Wasn't Offended' by Message of 'Hamilton' Cast."

12. James Madison, email to author, March 22, 2018.

13. Alberta, "Man on a Wire."

14. Andrea Neal, *Road Trip: A Pocket History of Indiana*, 186.

15. Jane Mayer, "The President Pence Delusion," 54.

16. Gary Varvel, "What Motivated Pence to Run with Trump?," A22.

# BIBLIOGRAPHY

Adams, Dwight. "The State Reacts to Pence's Selection of Holcomb."
　　*Indianapolis Star*, February 10, 2016, 8A.

Alberta, Tim. "Man on a Wire: Mike Pence's Tightrope Act." *Politico Magazine*,
　　July/August 2017. https://www.politico.com/magazine/story/2017/06/16
　　/vice-president-mike-pence-profile-feature-215257.

Allen, Angela. "200 Arabs Rally to Protest 'Hurtful' Pence Commercial."
　　*Indianapolis Star*, October 14, 1990, B17.

"Alumni Spotlights." Indiana University Robert H. McKinney School of Law.
　　https://mckinneylaw.iu.edu/alumni-donors/alumni-spotlights/Pence-Mike
　　.html.

Associated Press. "Arab-Americans Protest Commercial." *Tribune*, October 15,
　　1990, 5.

Associated Press. "Bill Would Let Businesses Refuse Service to Gays."
　　*Courier-Journal*, January 5, 2015, A3.

Associated Press. "Indiana Contingent Puts Partisanship Aside for Inaugura-
　　tion." *Republic*, January 21, 2001, A3.

Associated Press. "It's Official: Riverboat Casinos Open to the Public."
　　*Daily Journal*, June 12, 1996, A9.

Associated Press. "Linder Demands Equal Air Time to Pence on Radio."
　　*Palladium-Item*, January 8, 2000, A1.

Bangert, Dave. "Sen. Alting Gets Dose of 'Periods for Pence.'" *Journal & Courier*,
　　April 6, 2016, 1A+.

Bartlett, Bruce. "Republican Deficit Hypocrisy." *Forbes*, November 20, 2009. https://www.forbes.com/2009/11/19/republican-budget-hypocrisy-health-care-opinions-columnists-bruce-bartlett/.

Bauer, Scott, and Steve Peoples. "Governor Endorses 'Principled' Cruz." *Tribune*, April 30, 2016, A8.

Behind Closed Doors. "Bosma Quick with Quips about Just IN." *Indianapolis Star*, February 1, 2015, A15.

Bicknell, John. "Pence, Mike." CQ Press Congress Collection, 2011. http://library.cqpress.com/congress/pia112-Pence_Mike.

Blair, Brian. "Open Mike—Columbus Native's Radio Show, Saturday TV Debut Demonstrate He Has Learned Diplomacy." *The Republic*, September 17, 1995, B1.

Bradner, Eric. "Pence: 'I Wasn't Offended' by Message of 'Hamilton' Cast." CNN, November 20, 2016. https://www.cnn.com/2016/11/20/politics/mike-pence-hamilton-message-trump/index.html.

———. "Polls: Donald Trump Leads, Ben Carson Slips." CNN, November 23, 2015. https://www.cnn.com/2015/11/22/politics/donald-trump-leads-ben-carson-two-polls-election-2016/index.html.

Braunstein, Melissa Langsam. "Second Lady Karen Pence Opens Up about Her Struggles with Infertility." *Federalist*, April 25, 2017. http://thefederalist.com/2017/04/25/second-lady-karen-pence-opens-struggles-infertility/.

Briggs, James, and Stephanie Wang. "Pence 'Rings the Most Bells.'" *Indianapolis Star*, July 6, 2016, 1A+.

Brock, Fred. "Peace Is More Than a Passing Fad to Hanover Professor." *Courier-Journal*, December 22, 1970, B1.

Broder, David. "Bush's Pre-Dawn Lobbying Got Medicare Bill through House." *Courier-Journal*, November 23, 2003, A4.

Buckley, Madeline. "Innocent Man Frustrated as He Waits for Pardon." *Indianapolis Star*, August 3, 2016, 3A+.

Buckman, Rebecca. "Lawmakers Served with Suit Claiming Pension Hike Illegal." *Indianapolis Star*, May 5, 1993, B6.

———. "Rethinking the Issues." *Indianapolis Star*, February 7, 1993, F4+.

Burns, Alexander. "After Debate, Both Campaigns Say, 'We're No. 1.'" *Star Tribune*, October 6, 2016, A8.

Burns, Alexander, and Maggie Haberman. "How Donald Trump Finally Settled on Mike Pence." *New York Times*, July 15, 2016. www.nytimes.com/2016/07/16/us/politics/mike-pence-donald-trump-vice-president.html.

Bush, George W. "Inaugural Address." The American Presidency Project, January 20, 2001. http://www.presidency.ucsb.edu/ws/?pid=25853.

Carden, Dan. "Gregg Pummels Pence in Final Debate." *Times*, October 26, 2012, A1+.

———. "Hoosier GOP Makes Picks." *Times*, June 12, 2016, A1+.

———. "Panel OKs 'Religious Freedom' Edict." *Times*, March 17, 2015, A1+.

———. "Pence Claims Tax Cut Victory." *Times*, April 30, 2013, A1+.

Carpenter, Dan. "Fortunately, 'Think Tanks' Keep Dimwits Off the Streets." *Indianapolis Star*, December 1, 1991, C1.

———. "Racial Stereotypes: We've Not Come Such a Long Way, Baby." *Indianapolis Star*, October 14, 1990, B1.

Carroll, Joseph. "Economy, Terrorism Top Issues in 2004 Election Vote." Gallup News Service, September 25, 2003. http://news.gallup.com/poll/9337 /economy-terrorism-top-issues-2004-election-vote.aspx.

Carswell, Simon. "Mike Pence and Donald Trump's Irish Connection: Doonbeg." *Irish Times*, July 14, 2016. https://www.irishtimes.com/news/world/us /mike-pence-and-donald-trump-s-irish-connection-doonbeg-1.2720970.

Clark, John. "Columbus' Pence Joins 107th Congress." *Republic*, January 4, 2001, A1+.

———. "Hill, Pence Tour Devastation at New York's Ground Zero." *Republic*, October 2, 2001, A8.

———. "Hometown Supports Pence." *Republic*, September 26, 2000, A1+.

———. "House Speaker Stumps—Hastert Praises Pence's Attributes at Columbus Stop." *Republic*, September 26, 2000, A1.

———. "Pence Family Takes Steps vs. 'Poison Powder.'" *Republic*, October 28, 2001, A1+.

———. "Pence: Response Must Be Swift and Violent." *Republic*, September 12, 2001, A7.

Club for Growth. "There's Nothing Conservative about Donald Trump." February 12, 2016. https://www.youtube.com/watch?v=CRn_u61lo9E.

Collins, Jason (@jasoncollins98). "@GovPenceIN, is it going to be legal for someone to discriminate against me & others when we come to the #FinalFour?" Twitter, March 23, 2015, 4:12 p.m. https://twitter.com /jasoncollins98/status/580145175726403584.

"Comments and Statistics on the Health-Care Overhaul." *Star Press*, March 20, 2010, 6A.

"Conservative Group That Supports Spending Cuts, Right to Work to Lobby for Pence Tax Cuts." RTV6 The Indy Channel, March 7, 2013. https://www .youtube.com/watch?v=tTodA-HjIDE.

"Conservative Think Tank New Pence Passion." *Republic*, April 9, 1993, A7.

Cook, Tony. "Pence Calls for Balanced Budget Amendment." *Palladium-Item*, January 14, 2015, A1.

———. "Pence: SB 101 'Is Not about Legalizing Discrimination.'" *Indianapolis Star*, March 27, 2015, 1A+.

———. "Trump, Pence Formally Nominated at Convention." *Star Press*, July 20, 2016, 1A+.

———. "What Will Pence Say?" *Indianapolis Star*, June 18, 2015, 1A+.

Cook, Tony, and Chelsea Schneider. "Ellspermann Eyes Ivy Tech Top Job." *Indianapolis Star*, December 22, 2015, 1A+.

———. "Pence Picks New Running Mate." *Indianapolis Star*, February 10, 2016, 1A+.

———. "Surprise, Surprise, Surprise." *Indianapolis Star*, July 14, 2016, 1A+.

Cook, Tony, and Marisa Kwiatkowski. "Religious Freedom Bill Is Drafted." *Indianapolis Star*, December 27, 2014, A1+.

Cook, Tony, and Tom LoBianco. "Deal Is Reached on Law Fix." *Indianapolis Star*, April 2, 2015, 1A+.

Corbin, Bryan. "Candidates Answer Questions about Iraq, Medicare." *Daily Journal*, November 2, 2002, A11.

———. "Pence Finally Realizes Dream of Going to Washington." *Daily Journal*, December 2, 2000, A1+.

———. "Pence Promises to Keep It Clean, to Play It Nice." *Edinburgh Courier*, March 1, 2000, A8.

———. "Pence Tries a Third Time." *Daily Journal*, April 24, 2000, A1+.

Coveney, Anne. "North Assembly Receives 'Thank You' from Africa." *Republic*, April 28, 1975, A2.

Crapol, Edward P. *John Tyler: The Accidental President*. Chapel Hill: University of North Carolina Press, 2012.

Cruz, Ted. "Ted Cruz Drops Out of Presidential Race." Recorded May 3, 2016, by CNN. https://www.youtube.com/watch?v=njlp4AaTwWQ.

Curtis, George M., III. "History 331: American Constitutional and Legal History, 1600–1860." Syllabus, Hanover College, Hanover, IN, 1980.

Davies, Tom. "Governor Defiant over Religious Freedom Legislation during Announcement." *Daily Journal*, June 19, 2015, A2.

———. "Pence Touts Plans for Education." *Post-Tribune*, January 14, 2015, 6.

"Debate News Disappointing." *Daily Journal*, September 30, 1988, 4.

Dinan, Stephen. "Medicare Bill Incites House Conservatives." *Washington Times*, December 23, 2004. https://www.washingtontimes.com/news/2004/dec/23/20041223-122159-6084r/.

Domonoske, Camila. "Periods as Protest: Indiana Women Call Governor to Talk about Menstrual Cycles." National Public Radio, April 8, 2016. https://www.npr.org/sections/thetwo-way/2016/04/08/473518239/periods-as-protest-indiana-women-call-governor-to-talk-about-menstrual-cycles.

*Donald Trump Roast*. Recorded February 1996 at Indianapolis Press Club Gridiron Dinner. DVD duplication by Movietyme Video Productions.

Dorning, Mike. "Pushing Conservative Ideals." *Republic*, November 6, 2005, B1+.

———. "One for the Gipper." *Chicago Tribune*, October 26, 2005, 1+.

Dunn, Jacob Piatt. "The Word 'Hoosier.'" *Indiana Magazine of History* 7, no. 2 (June 1911): 61–63.

Eason, Brian, Chelsea Schneider, and Maureen Groppe. "Behind Closed Doors." *Indianapolis Star*, April 10, 2016, 11A.

Ehlers, Susan. "Politics, Paychecks Don't Mix, Employer Finds." *Republic*, July 6, 1990, A1.

Elliott, Scott. "Pence, Ritz Strongly Endorse New Indiana Standards over Objections." *Chalkbeat*, April 22, 2014. https://www.chalkbeat.org/posts/in/2014/04/22/pence-ritz-strongly-endorse-new-indiana-standards/.

"Emergency Economic Stabilization Act of 2008." *Congressional Record* 154, no. 157 (September 29, 2008).

Ernstes, Danny J. "The Sixth Congressional District of Indiana: An Inside Look at a U.S. Congressional Race." IUPUI, Fall 2002.

Evensen, Dave. "Constituents Turn Out to Meet Pence." *Palladium-Item*, January 13, 2001, A3.

"Excerpts from Bush's Speech." *Indianapolis Star*, September 16, 2005, A8.

Fehrman, Craig. "Incoming: Mike Pence." *Indianapolis Monthly*, January 2, 2013. https://www.indianapolismonthly.com/news-opinion/incoming-mike-pence/.

"Fix This Now." *Indianapolis Star*, March 31, 2015, 1A.

Flake, Jeff. *Conscience of a Conservative*. New York: Random House, 2017.

Francisco, Brian. "Burton Breezes, Sharp Squeezes to Victory." *Muncie Star*, November 9, 1988, A1.

———. "Campaign's Nasty Boys Get in Last Jabs." *Star Press*, November 4, 1990, 1D.

———. "GOP Still Lacks Timing, Candidate to Beat Sharp." *Muncie Star*, November 8, 1990, A11.

———. "Pence Announces Second Run for Congress." *Muncie Star*, February 21, 1990, 7.

———. "Pence Disagrees with New Taxes." *Muncie Star*, June 28, 1990, A1+.

———. "Pence Not Interested in Running for Office." *Muncie Star*, August 15, 1991, A8.

———. "Pence Seeks GOP Nod to Challenge 2nd District's Sharp." *Muncie Star*, February 18, 1990, A2.

———. "Pence Sorry for Negative Campaign." *Star Press*, August 15, 1991, 1+.

———. "Prosecutor: Pence Aide Violated Law." *Muncie Star*, July 6, 1990, 1+.

———. "2nd Best—To Face Phil Sharp You First Have to Win Republican Primary." *Muncie Star*, May 1, 1988, D1.

———. "2nd District Candidates on Best Behavior for Graduation." *Star Press*, August 11, 1990, 1A.

———. "Sharp Farm Plan Rankles Neighbors." *Star Press*, October 14, 1990, A1+.

———. "Talk Radio Suits Former Congressional Candidate." *Star Press*, March 7, 1994, 1B.

"Full Transcript: Second 2016 Presidential Debate." *Politico*, October 10, 2016. https://www.politico.com/story/2016/10/2016-presidential-debate-transcript -229519.

Gallagher, Maggie. "Two Moms vs. Common Core." *National Review*, May 12, 2013. https://www.nationalreview.com/2013/05/two-moms-vs-common -core-maggie-gallagher/.

Gannett News Service. "Pence Could Be Spoiler in Race for House GOP Leadership Post." *Star Press*, November 16, 2006, 3A.

Gannett News Service. "Rep.-Elect Mike Pence Is Learning the Basics." *Star Press*, November 18, 2000, 4A.

Garrett, Major (@MajorCBS). "#veepstakes mania watch 2 -- Marc Lotter, deputy campaign manager for @GovPenceIN on my flight from Indy to NYC. I'm sure just coincidence." Twitter, July 14, 2016, 8:30 a.m.

Gass, Nick. "Clinton Campaign: 'Pence Is Most Extreme Pick in a Generation.'" *Politico*, July 15, 2016. https://www.politico.com/story/2016/07/trump-vp -pick-clinton-react-225606.

Gray, Ralph D., ed. *Indiana History: A Book of Readings*. Bloomington: Indiana University Press, 1994.

Groppe, Maureen. "Assistance for Wishard in Jeopardy." *Indianapolis Star*, November 17, 2003, B1+.

———. "Bush Takes Interest in Pence's Immigration Plan." *Palladium-Item*, June 29, 2006, A1+.

———. "For Rep. Mike Pence, the Show Must Go On." *Indianapolis Star*, March 27, 2001, B5.

———. "House GOP to Put Hoosier in Charge of Its Message." *Indianapolis Star*, November 19, 2008, A1+.

———. "Pence Hires Outside Counsel." *Indianapolis Star*, June 16, 2017, 1A+.

———. "Pence: 'I'm Very Excited.'" *Indianapolis Star*, July 16, 2016, 1A+.

———. "Pence Lauds Trump for Admission." *Indianapolis Star*, October 11, 2016, 1A+.

———. "Pence Served as 'Happy Warrior.'" *Indianapolis Star*, November 9, 2016, A3+.

———. "Pence's Oath Kicks Off Key Moments." *Indianapolis Star*, April 30, 2017, 10A.

———. "Pence Sworn, Family Moves In." *Star Press*, January 4, 2001, 1A.

———. "Pence Ups National Media Exposure." *Lafayette Journal and Courier*, January 4, 2004, C10.

———. "Pitcock Out, Ayers Now in as Chief of Staff for Pence." *Indianapolis Star*, July 1, 2017, 14A.

———. "Who Gets Boost from Court?" *Indianapolis Star*, June 28, 2015, 25A+.

Groppe, Maureen, Fredreka Schouten, and Tony Cook. "Pence Gets Caught in Fray." *Indianapolis Star*, May 19, 2017, 1A+.

Gullo, Karen. "Letters Seem Coordinated." *Argus-Leader*, October 24, 2001, 5A.

Hackett, David. "Controversial Phone Blitz Attacks Sharp." *Daily Journal*, November 6, 1990, A1+.

Hackett, David, and Jeff Madsen. "Pence Backers Unaware of Spending." *Daily Journal*, July 21, 1990, A1.

Hall, Steve. "If Talk Show Turns You Off, Turn It Off." *Indianapolis Star*, November 3, 1995, D5.

———. "The Kind Conservative." *Indianapolis Star*, September 11, 1995, C1+.

———. "Patrick Won't Kick about Trick." *Indianapolis Star*, October 24, 1996, F5.

———. "Pence on TV Fuses Sparks, Substance." *Indianapolis Star*, September 26, 1995, D7.

Hampson, Rick. "What Explains Appeal of Donald Trump?" *Indianapolis Star*, July 8, 2015, 1B+.

Helling, Dave. "Missouri and Kansas Republicans Like Apparent Pick of Mike Pence for GOP Ticket." *Kansas City Star*, July 14, 2016. http://www.kansascity.com/news/politics-government/article89704697.html.

Holcomb, Eric. "Lt. Governor Eric Holcomb on Mike Pence—Republican National Convention." Recorded July 19, 2016, by ABC15 Arizona. https://www.youtube.com/watch?v=s9pgN7SMSls.

Hook, Janet. "Bush's First Veto: Stem Cell Bill 'Crosses Moral Boundary.'" *Morning Call*, July 20, 2006, A1+.

"House of Representatives." *Congressional Record* 149, no. 167 (November 18, 2003).

Howey, Brian. "Pence's Shift to Holcomb." *Times*, February 14, 2016, D2.

———. "Skillman's Exit Only a Mild Surprise as Pence Rises." *Times*, December 26, 2010, E2.

"H.R. 327 – 107th Congress: Small Business Paperwork Relief Act of 2002." www.GovTrack.us. (2001). Accessed January 28, 2018. https://www.govtrack.us/congress/bills/107/hr327.

Hutson, Jeff. "Pence Has Dubious Award for Sharp." *Daily Journal*, July 23, 1988, A1+.

"Improper Influence?" *Star Press*, November 9, 1990, 3.

Indiana Chamber Staff. "Facts Ignored, Politics Winning on Common Core." Indiana Chamber, April 23, 2013. http://www.indianachamberblogs.com /facts-ignored-politics-winning-on-common-core/.

"Indiana Governor Mike Pence's 2015 State of the State Address," January 14, 2015. https://www.youtube.com/watch?v=xO507zePZkQ.

Indiana Review Foundation. *Articles of Incorporation of the Indiana Review Foundation.* January 19, 1989.

"Indiana's First Lady Recalls Her Days at Park School." *Park Tudor School Alumni News* (Summer 2013): 37.

"Iowa Poll—How Each Republican Rates." *Des Moines Register*, February 1, 2015, 12A.

Jackson, David. "Outsider Trump May Pick Insider VP." *Springfield News-Leader*, May 18, 2016, 14A.

———. "Trump Resists Pressure from GOP to Step Aside." *Palladium-Item*, October 16, 2016, 7A.

Jacobs, Jennifer. "Walker Has Edge in Tight GOP Field." *Des Moines Register*, February 1, 2015, 1A+.

Jenkins, Aric. "Official Denies Mike Pence Offered to Replace Trump as the Presidential Nominee." *Time*, December 5, 2017. http://time.com/5049831 /mike-pence-access-hollywood-tape/

Jindal, Bobby. "Trump's Style Is His Substance." *Wall Street Journal*, February 15, 2018, A17.

Johannesen, Kirk. "Belief in the American Dream." *Daily Reporter*, January 18, 2017, A1+.

———. "Family: Courage and Conviction Carry Pence to Success." *Daily Reporter*, January 18, 2017, A1+.

———. "House Colleagues Have Fond Memories of Columbus Native." *Republic*, January 13, 2013, G7.

———. "Mom to Mike: Keep Your Day Job." *Daily Journal*, January 29, 2015, A2.

———. "Run for Governor to Be Explored." *Republic*, January 28, 2011, A1+.

———. "Their Man Mike." *Republic*, June 12, 2011, A1+.

"John Gregg for Indiana Governor: 'Hobo.'" GreggforIndiana, August 13, 2012. https://www.youtube.com/watch?v=9uMT9YrEZiI.

"John Gregg for Indiana Governor: 'Two Kinds.'" GreggforIndiana, September 6, 2012. https://www.youtube.com/watch?v=69wav8ewjPo.

Johnson, James H. "Pence Inauguration as Governor Touches on Hoosier History." *Daily Journal*, January 26, 2013, A4.

Jones, Tamara. "The Pilot's Cloudy Future." *Washington Post*, April 29, 1997. https://www.washingtonpost.com/archive/lifestyle/1997/04/29/the-pilots -cloudy-future/fced3a5d-ce9b-4eb7-bfe6-bb2479103301/?utm_term =.cof8578b7ec2.

"Judge Rejects Challenge to '92 Bill That Raises State Lawmakers' Pensions." *Indianapolis Star*, March 5, 1994, C3.

King, Robert. "Remark Reflects U.S. Friction over Abortion." *Indianapolis Star*, October 25, 2012, A1+.

Klouman, Anne. "Vespers Looking Up." *Triangle* LXXIII, no. 1 (September 27, 1980): 2.

Kudlow, Lawrence. "2005 Man of the Year: Rep. Mike Pence." RealClearPolitics .com, December 24, 2005. https://www.realclearpolitics.com/Commentary /com-12_24_05_LK.html.

Kukolla, Steve. "Penance, Redemption Punctuate Life of Mike." *Indianapolis Business Journal*, January 31, 1994. http://online.wsj.com/public/resources /documents/2016_0713_pence_ibj.pdf.

Kurtzleben, Danielle. "Pollsters Find 'at Best Mixed Evidence' Comey Letter Swayed Election." National Public Radio, May 5, 2017. https://www.npr.org /2017/05/05/526936636/pollsters-find-at-best-mixed-evidence-comey-letter -swayed-election.

Kusmer, Ken. "Pence Puts Social Issues on Table for Statehouse Run." *Republic*, May 7, 2011, A3.

Ladwig, Boris. "Pence Recounts How Hometown Shaped Future." *Daily Journal*, January 14, 2013, A1+.

Ladwig, T. Craig, ed. *Indiana Mandate: An Agenda for the 1990s*. Indianapolis: Indiana Policy Review Foundation, 1992.

"Leaders Absent at Lead Crisis." *Times*, August 28, 2016, D2.

"Learning from Columbus." *Indiana Preservation*, March/April 2018, 4–5.

Lee, Danny. "Pence Says No More Campaign Funds for Personal Expenses." *Republic*, August 17, 1990, A1.

———. "Pence Sees Campaign Changes in Two Tries." *Republic*, November 7, 1990, A4.

Lester, Will. "Pence Leads Call for Rollback of Bush Initiatives." *Republic*, January 6, 2005, A1+.

Lewandowski, Corey R., and David N. Bossie. *Let Trump Be Trump: The Inside Story of His Rise to the Presidency*. New York: Center Street, 2017.

Leyden, Thomas W. "Reagan Aide Explains Rights Policy." *Indianapolis Star*, May 25, 1981, 39.

LoBianco, Tom. "Gov.-Elect Uses Rare Opportunity to Trade Social Crusader Mantle for Broader Appeal." *Daily Journal*, January 14, 2013, A3.

———. "Pence Team Starting State-Run News Wire." *Indianapolis Star*, January 27, 2015, A1+.

———. "Rulings Clear Path for Indiana Battle." *Republic*, June 27, 2013, A8.

———. "Soon Making Another Run?" *Indianapolis Star*, March 2, 2015, A3+.

Lopez, Kathryn Jean. "Mike Pence for President." *National Review*, January 17, 2011. http://www.nationalreview.com/corner/257327/mike-pence-president -kathryn-jean-lopez.

Lowry, Bryan. "Trump's Likely VP Pick Has a Connection to Kansas Politics." *Wichita Eagle*, July 14, 2016. http://www.kansas.com/news/politics -government/election/article89647207.html.

Mack, Justin L., and Stephanie Wang. "Salesforce Executive: Bill Would Do Harm." *Indianapolis Star*, March 20, 2015, 3A.

Madsden, Jeff. "Rematch Turns into Mismatch for Pence as Sharp Wins Again." *Daily Journal*, November 7, 1990, A1.

Malkin, Michelle. "Common Core Backlash Claims New Casualties." *Star-Democrat*, May 20, 2014, A4.

Maschino, Brenda. "Pence Encourages Students to Dream." *Republic*, February 5, 2002, A1+.

Massie, Bob. "Rash Day-Saving by Dan." Letter to the editor. *Indianapolis Star*, December 10, 1991, A7.

Maule, Will. "Karen Pence: 'Mike Told Me, "Jesus Needs to Be Number One in Your Life." hellochristian.com, April 5, 2017. https://hellochristian.com/7091 -karen-pence-mike-told-me-jesus-needs-to-be-number-one-in-your-life.

Mayer, Jane. "The President Pence Delusion." *New Yorker*, October 23, 2017, 54–69.

McCaskill, Nolan D. "Trump Says He's Begun Vetting VP Picks." *Politico*, May 4, 2016. https://www.politico.com/blogs/2016-gop-primary-live-updates-and -results/2016/05/trump-vice-president-pick-222781.

McCawley, Harry. "The Road to the Governor's Office." *Republic*, January 13, 2013, G8+.

McCawley, Harry, Kirk Johannesen, and Paul Minnis. "Many Think Pence Could Win Gubernatorial Race." *Republic*, January 29, 2011, A1+.

McClain, Randy. "Columbus Native Pence Pledges to Serve All Hoosiers." *Republic*, January 15, 2013, A1+.

McFeely, Dan. "Pence Cruises to Landslide Victory." *Indianapolis Star*, November 6, 2002, V2.

Mehalik, Jennifer. "Iconic Lawyer Passes Torch." Harrison & Moberly, LLP, October 23, 2008. http://www.harrisonmoberly.com/news/?id=6.

Mehta, Seema. "Clinton Sorry She Labeled 'Half' of Trump Supporters." *Chicago Tribune*, September 11, 2016, 26.

Memoli, Michael A. "Conservative Summit Picks Pence, Not Palin." *Hartford Courant*, September 19, 2010, A9.

"Mike Pence Cartoons in *Dictum*." Indiana University, August 19, 2016.

"Mike Pence for Indiana Governor." Pence4Indiana, May 4, 2011. https://www .youtube.com/watch?v=HFakXWUUwCY&t=14s.

"Mike Pence to Run against Rep. Sharp." *Indianapolis News*, February 19, 1990, D4.

Miller, William J. *The 2012 Nomination and the Future of the Republican Party*. Lanham, MD: Lexington Books, 2013.

Murray, Jon. "Poll: Marriage Measure Draws Opposition." *Indianapolis Star*, November 14, 2013, A3.

Neal, Andrea. "In GOP Loss, Pence Is Quoting Peyton." *Richmond Palladium-Item*, November 17, 2006, A6.

———. *Road Trip: A Pocket History of Indiana*. Indianapolis: Indiana Historical Society Press, 2016.

Nelson, Louis. "Sen. Flake: Pence Would Be Trump's 'Best Choice' So Far." *Politico*, July 14, 2016. https://www.politico.com/story/2016/07/jeff-flake -pence-vp-pick-225543.

Nesbit, Jeff. *Poison Tea: How Big Oil and Big Tobacco Invented the Tea Party and Captured the GOP*. New York: Thomas Dunne Books, 2016.

Newland, James G., Jr. "Politics Serves as a Magnet for Coats' Campaign Chief." *Indianapolis Star*, August 12, 1990, B3.

New York, Passenger Lists, 1820–1957 (database online). Provo, UT: Ancestry. com Operations, 2010.

"North Grad Third in NFL Speech Contest." *Columbus Herald*, July 1, 1977, 6.

Novak, Robert. "House Leadership Had to Cave on Spending." *News Herald*, October 12, 2005, A4.

Oliphant, James. "Once on the Outside, Conservative Koch Network Warms to Trump." Reuters, June 27, 2017. https://www.reuters.com/article/us-usa -trump-koch/once-on-the-outside-conservative-koch-network-warms-to -trump-idUSKBN19I137.

O'Neill, John R. "More Accusations Fly in 2nd District." *Indianapolis Star*, August 8, 1990, D2.

———. "Pence Isn't Ruling Out Rematch with Sharp." *Indianapolis Star*, November 10, 1988, B4.

———. "Pence Slings Oil, Not Mud." *Indianapolis Star*, October 10, 1990, B1+.

Owen, Jeff. "GOP Campaign Misses Important Opportunity." *Daily Journal*, November 7, 1990, A4.

Parker, Ashley. "Karen Pence Is the Vice President's 'Prayer Warrior,' Gut Check and Shield." *Washington Post*, March 28, 2017.

Patten, Dominic. "Republican Convention Night 3 Ratings Down from 2012 for ABC & CBS as Ted Cruz Shunned and Mike Pence Speaks." Deadline Hollywood, July 21, 2016. http://deadline.com/2016/07/republican-convention -night-3-ratings-fall-from-2012-ted-cruz-mike-pence-americas-got-talent -1201789883/.

"Pence Accused of Breaking Federal Campaign Fund Law." *Republic*, August 10, 1990, A3.

"Pence a Changed Man since Early Campaigns." *Star Press*, November 5, 2000, D1.

"Pence Deserves 2nd Term in Office." *Indianapolis Star*, October 26, 2002, A10.

"Pence Elected House Republican Conference Chairman." News release, November 19, 2008. http://www.standardnewswire.com/news/962183612.html.

"Pence Forms For-Profit Panel." *Republic*, July 26, 1990, A14.

Pence, Michael Richard. "The Religious Expressions of Abraham Lincoln." Hanover College Library, December 14, 1980.

Pence, Mike. "America About to Sign into No-Tell Motel with Clinton." *Daily Journal*, October 21, 1992, A4.

———. "By Adopting Term Limits, Indiana Would Enhance, Not Diminish, the Meaningful Choices of Democracy," in *Indiana Mandate: An Agenda for the 1990s*, ed. T. Craig Ladwig (Indianapolis: The Indiana Policy Review Foundation), 31–32.

———. "Candidate Ready to Provide Leadership." *Star Press*, October 29, 2000, D1+.

———, dir. *Indy TV's After Dinner*. IMS Broadcasting LLC. Aired October 27, 1996, on WNDY, Channel 23, Indianapolis.

———. "Commencement Speaker Mike Pence." Hanover College Commencement Records, HC 31, 2008. Digital Video.

———. "Confessions of a Negative Campaigner." *Indiana Policy Review* 2, no. 7 (October 1991).

———. "Embryonic Stem Cell Research." *Congressional Record*, July 23, 2001.

———. "Governor Pence Statement on HEA 1337." March 24, 2016. http://www .in.gov/activecalendar/EventList.aspx?fromdate=3/21/2016&todate=4/28 /2016&display=Month&type=public&eventidn=244247&view =EventDetails&information_id=240077.

———. "Gov. Mike Pence's Inaugural Speech." Indianapolis, IN. Recorded January 14, 2013, by RTV6 The Indy Channel. https://www.youtube.com /watch?v=NtQhgVlHS1s.

———. "Gov. Pence Talks about Meeting with Donald Trump." Recorded July 4, 2016, RTV6 The Indy Channel. https://www.youtube.com/watch?v =p5LsyLrZIrY.

———. "Hard-Fought Election." Letter to the editor. *The Republic*, November 21, 1990, A4.

———. "Indiana Lawmaker Offers Alternative." *Indianapolis Star*, August 3, 2001, A17.

———. "Mike Pence Introduces President-Elect Trump." Recorded November 9, 2016, by ABC News. http://abcnews.go.com/Politics/video/mike-pence -introduces-president-elect-trump-43409852.

———. "Mike Pence's Acceptance Speech." Indianapolis, IN. Recorded November 6, 2012, by WLKY News Louisville. https://www.youtube.com /watch?v=aawnC1C6AsY&t=372s.

———. "Pence Church Message." GOP TV Clips, November 4, 2016. https:// www.youtube.com/watch?v=0UkdvxqCKtg.

———. "Pence on 9/11: Longest 12 Minutes of My Life." Speech in Shanksville, PA. Recorded September 11, 2017, by CNN. https://www.youtube.com /watch?v=RhhNWTpPIF8.

———. *Pence Report* 2, no. 7 (August 15, 1995).

———. "Reflections on GOP dinner," in *Pence Report*, August 15, 1995, 5.

———. "Renewing our Commitment to Limited Government." Speech to the Heritage Foundation, April 30, 2004. https://www.heritage.org/government -regulation/report/renewing-our-commitment-limited-government.

———. "Right to Life Speech, Tippecanoe County." West Lafayette, IN. November 23, 2010.

———. "Rule of Law Prohibits Harvesting of Stem Cells from Human Embryos." *Congressional Record*, June 27, 2001.

———. "2016 State of the State Address." Recorded January 13, 2016. https:// www.youtube.com/watch?v=kjW2_gs87Pw&t=1025s.

———, host. *The Mike Pence Show*. Network Indiana, February 13, 1996. Audiocassette.

———. "Tribute to Chuck Mosey." *Congressional Record*, September 8, 2004.

———. "Tribute to Dr. Julius Perr." *Congressional Record*, October 20, 2005.

———. "Tribute to Rush Hudson Limbaugh, III." *Congressional Record*, October 16, 2001.

———. "Veto Human Embryo Research." *Congressional Record*, July 19, 2006.

———. "Vice Presidential Nominee Mike Pence, Full Speech." Recorded July 20, 2016, by Republican National Convention. https://www.youtube.com /watch?v=c7oUpJrvoeY.

———. "VP Mike Pence Shares Testimony at Church by the Glades." Recorded April 8, 2017, by VFNKB–VFNtv. https://www.youtube.com/watch?v =5BO6DxuxAFA.

———. "VP Pence's Remarks at the Israeli Knesset." US Embassy Tel Aviv, January 22, 2018. https://www.youtube.com/watch?v=eHqKpCvCMlI.

"Pence Moves to Top of House Class." *Star Press*, February 11, 2001, 3D.

"Pence's Apology Helps, but Concerns Remain." *Daily Journal*, August 17, 1991, A4.

"Pence Statement on Passing of Indiana University Professor William F. Harvey." Press Release. Governor Archives, November 17, 2016. http://www .in.gov/activecalendar/EventList.aspx?view=EventDetails&eventidn =254288&information_id=252916&type=&syndicate=syndicate.

"Pence Supports President." *Star Press*, October 8, 2002, 5A.

"Pence Taps Running Mate." *Tribune*, May 22, 2012, 9A.

"Pence Urged to Enter Race for President in '12 Election." *Republic*, January 18, 2011, A1+.

"Pence Wins Legion Speech Contest." *Republic*, March 16, 1977, A1+.

Perras, Jodi. "Pence Acknowledges Staff Was Involved in Phony Phone Poll." *Star Press*, November 13, 1990, A1.

Peterson, Zach. "Vice President's Mother Discusses Young Mike Pence and Her First Time in Chattanooga." *Times Free Press*, May 20, 2017. http://www .timesfreepress.com/news/local/story/2017/may/20/vice-president-pences -mother-discusses-very-t/429144/.

"Petition for Naturalization. Richard Michael Cawley. No. 214627." U.S. Department of Justice Immigration and Naturalization Service, December 18, 1940.

Pizer, Jennifer C. "Indiana's Rush to Invite Law-Breaking for Religious Reasons." Lambda Legal, March 26, 2015. https://www.lambdalegal.org/blog /20150326_in-rush-to-invite-law-breaking-for-religious-reasons.

"Political Regrets." *Indianapolis Star*, August 16, 1991, A18.

Pollock, Chris, prod. *The Mike Pence Radio Show*. Broadcast Productions, May 23, 2007. DVD.

———. *The Mike Pence Show*. Paramount Stations Group. Aired August 1, 1998, on WNDY, Channel 23, Indianapolis.

———. *The Mike Pence Show*. Paramount Stations Group. Aired December 19, 1998, on WNDY, Channel 23, Indianapolis.

Polston, Steve. "Pence Defends Campaign Funding." *Palladium-Item*, November 3, 1988, A1+.

Potts, Monica. "Thousands of Women Are Calling Vice Presidential Candidate Mike Pence to Update Him on Their Periods." *Vogue*, November 4, 2016. https://www.vogue.com/article/periods-for-politicians-mike-pence.

Pullman, Joy. *The Education Invasion: How Common Core Fights Parents for Control of American Kids.* New York: Encounter Books, 2017.

"Q&A with Mike Pence." C-SPAN, January 19, 2006. https://www.c-span.org /video/?c680443/clip-qa-mike-pence.

Quilhot, Chuck. "A Letter to a Senior Senator." *Indiana Policy Review* 4, no. 7 (December 1993).

"Reaction." *Indianapolis Star*, March 29, 2015, 17A.

"Rep. Pence New Member of Judiciary Committee." *Republic*, October 5, 2001, A8.

"Representative Mike Pence (1959–)." Congress.gov. Accessed June 5, 2017. https://www.congress.gov/member/mike-pence/P000587?q=%7B %22status%22%3A%22Roll+call+votes+on+amendments+in+House%22 %2C%22congress%22%3A%22109%22%7D.

Roberts, Kathleen Glenister, and Ronald C. Arnett. *Communication Ethics: Between Cosmopolitanism and Provinciality.* New York: Peter Lang, 2008.

Roberts, Steven V. "Working Profile; The Life of a 'Watergate Baby': Philip R. Sharp." *New York Times*, May 13, 1986. https://www.nytimes.com/1986/05/13 /us/working-profile-the-life-of-a-watergate-baby-philip-r-sharp.html.

Rubio, Marco (@marcorubio). "@realDonaldTrump Great pick. @mike_pence is rock solid." Twitter, July 15, 2016, 10:01 a.m.

Rudavsky, Shari. "Meet Woman behind Periods for Pence." *Indianapolis Star*, November 6, 2016, 4E+.

———. "She's Right at Home." *Indianapolis Star*, December 9, 2012, G1+.

Rulon, Maria. "Republicans Rebuff Pence's Leadership Bid." *Journal & Courier*, November 18, 2006, A8.

Schmidt, Michael S. "Documents Reveal New Details on What Trump Team Knew about Flynn's Calls with Russian Ambassador." *New York Times*, December 1, 2017. https://www.nytimes.com/2017/12/01/us/politics/flynn -russia-sanctions.html.

Schneider, Chelsea, and Stephanie Wang. "Ellspermann Picked to Lead Ivy Tech." *Indianapolis Star*, May 19, 2016, A1+.

Schneider, Chelsea, and Tony Cook. "Can GOP Duo Work through Differences?" *Indianapolis Star*, July 17, 2016, 1A+.

Schneider, Mary Beth. "Decisions, Decisions. Will Pence and Bayh Run?" *Indianapolis Star*, December 6, 2010, A1+.

———. "100 Days and Counting, What Do Hoosiers Know?" *Indianapolis Star*, April 22, 2013, A1+.

———. "Pence Reveals 'Worst-Kept Secret.'" *Indianapolis Star*, May 6, 2011, B1+.

Schorg, John. "Mike Pence Enters 2nd District Race." *Republic*, February 24, 1988, A14.

———. "Pence 'Lauds' Foe's PAC Funds." *Republic*, July 21, 1988, A14.

———. "Pence Says Quayle Gives His Candidacy a Shot of Adrenaline." *Republic*, August 17, 1988, A3.

———. "Pence Wants Proof of Alleged Lies." *Republic*, October 5, 1988, A1.

———. "Riding the 2nd District—Pence 'Pedals' His Candidacy for Congress." *Republic*, July 10, 1988, A11.

Schouten, Fredreka, Christopher Schnaars, and Maureen Groppe. "Who's Giving Big Money to Vice President Pence's Leadership PAC? Lots of Corporations." *USA Today*, January 31, 2018. https://www.usatoday.com/story/news /politics/onpolitics/2018/01/31/whos-giving-big-money-vice-president -pences-leadership-pac-lots-corporations/1084432001/.

Scoggins, Todd. "Thank You, Chairman Cardwell." January 27, 2017. http:// www.jeffcardwell.com/home.html.

Senate Historical Office. "Occasions When Vice Presidents Have Voted to Break Tie Votes in the Senate." February 2, 2018. https://www.senate.gov /artandhistory/history/resources/pdf/VPTies.pdf

Senate Bill No. 568. Introduced version, 119th General Assembly (2015).

Senate Enrolled Act No. 50, 119th General Assembly (2015).

Senate Enrolled Act No. 91, 118th General Assembly (2014).

"Sharp Has Obligation to File FEC Complaint." Unsigned editorial. *Daily Journal*, December 20, 1990, A4.

Sherfinski, David. "Paul Ryan on Mike Pence: 'I Can Think of No Better Choice' for Our V.P. Candidate." *Washington Times*, July 15, 2016. https://www .washingtontimes.com/news/2016/jul/15/paul-ryan-mike-pence-i-can-think -no-better-choice-/.

Sikich, Chris. "Announcement Expected Soon on Trump's Running Mate." *Indianapolis Star*, July 13, 2016, 1A+.

———. "Remarks Draw Widespread Rebukes." *Indianapolis Star*, October 25, 2012, A9.

Sikich, Chris, and Carrie Ritchie. "Gregg, Pence Push for Lasting Impressions." *Indianapolis Star*, October 26, 2012, A1+.

Slabaugh, Seth. "Pence: Global Warming 'a Myth.'" *Star Press*, October 27, 2000, 1A+.

"Small Business Paperwork Relief Act." *Congressional Record* 147, no. 35 (March 15, 2001).

Smith, Curt. *Deicide: How Eliminating the Deity Is Destroying America*. Zionsville, Indiana: CreateSpace, 2016.

Solida, Michele McNeil. "McIntosh's Exit Leaves Door Open for Democrats." *Indianapolis Star*, April 9, 2000, A1+.

Soloveichik, Meir. "Pence Visits Israel's Capital." *Wall Street Journal*, January 23, 2018. https://www.wsj.com/articles/pence-visits-israels-capital-1516754820.

Steger, J. C. "Consulting All Truth." Memoir shared with author, March 7, 2018.

———. "The Gloves Come Off." Memoir shared with author, March 7, 2018.

———. "Pence, Parties, and Parents." Memoir shared with author, March 7, 2018.

Stephanopoulos, George. "Indiana Gov. Mike Pence Says Religious Freedom Law 'Absolutely Not' a Mistake." *This Week with George Stephanopolous*. ABC-News, March 29, 2015. https://www.youtube.com/watch?v=_-iOtRlDbzQ&t =388s.

Stern, Mark Joseph. "The Most Cynical Republican on Obamacare." *Slate*, September 26, 2017. http://www.slate.com/articles/news_and_politics/politics /2017/09/how_mike_pence_embraced_aca_medicaid_expansion_in _indiana.html#lf_comment=738495197.

Stolberg, Sheryl Gay. "'I Am an American Because of Him': The Journey of Pence's Grandfather from Ireland." *New York Times*, March 16, 2017. https:// www.nytimes.com/2017/03/16/us/politics/mike-pence-immigration -grandfather.html?mtrref=www.google.com&gwh=88499914F8AD3C2 D0F9316890DA24912&gwt=pay.

Swarens, Tim. "After RFRA, Pence Pledges to Listen More." *Indianapolis Star*, May 23, 2015, 5A.

———. "Pence's Reputation Bruised by Just IN." *Indianapolis Star*, January 30, 2015, A15.

Swiatek, Jeff, and Tim Evans. "9 CEOs Urge Change to RFRA." *Indianapolis Star*, March 31, 2015, 3A+.

Syeed, Nafeesa. "D.C. Protesters Blast Obama." *Sentinel*, September 13, 2009, A10.

Tanner, Michael D. *Leviathan on the Right*. Washington DC: Cato Institute, 2007.

Terhune, Karen. "Sharp Whips Pence with 62% of Vote." *Muncie Evening Press*, November 7, 1990, 1+.

"The Pence Agenda for the 107th Congress." Accessed December 26, 2017. http://web.archive.org/web/20010519165033fw_/http://cybertext.net/pence /issues.html.

"The Unforgettable 107th Congress." United States Senate. Accessed January 28, 2018. https://www.senate.gov/artandhistory/history/minute/unforgettable _107th_congress.htm.

Thomas, Cal. "Gov. Mike Pence: National Government Is Not the Nation." *Washington Times*, December 15, 2014. http://www.chicagotribune.com/news /columnists/sns-201412151330--tms--cthomastq--b-a20141215-20141215 -column.html.

———. "Interview with Vice President-Elect Mike Pence." Townhall.com, December 10, 2016. https://calthomas.com/columns/full-transcript-mike-pence -interview.

———. "Pence Salt to Trump's Pepper." *Great Falls Tribune*, July 20, 2016, 6A.

Torres, Alec. "The Ten Dumbest Common Core Problems." *National Review*, March 20, 2014. https://www.nationalreview.com/2014/03/ten-dumbest -common-core-problems-alec-torres/.

Trares, Ryan. "Pence Used Radio Talk Show to Build Name, Reputation." *Daily Journal*, January 18, 2017, A1+.

Traub, Patrick J. "Coats Campaign Feels Vindicated by Probe." *Indianapolis Star*, December 22, 1990, C1+.

———. "Coats' Campaign Manager Resigns for Part in Criticized Election Tactics." *Indianapolis Star*, November 10, 1990, A1+.

———. "GOP's 1990 Election Roster Still Has a Lot of Holes." *Indianapolis Star*, October 8, 1989, F4.

Trump, Donald. "Donald Trump Introduces Running Mate Mike Pence." Recorded July 16, 2016, by Bloomberg Politics. https://www.youtube.com /watch?v=QZsjSQ4c62A.

Trump, Donald J. (@realDonaldTrump). "I am pleased to announce that I have chosen Governor Mike Pence as my Vice Presidential running mate. News conference tomorrow at 11:00 A.M." Twitter, July 15, 2016, 10:50 a.m.

Tully, Matt. "Mike Pence's Horrible Idea." *Indianapolis Star*, January 28, 2015, A3.

United Press International. "Palin Pick Called 'High Risk, High Reward.'" April 18, 2009. https://www.upi.com/Palin-pick-called-high-risk-high-reward /39391240071258/.

———. "3 Dartmouth Students Suspended." *Philadelphia Inquirer*, March 11, 1988, 13B.

United States Senate. "Tie Votes." Accessed March 8, 2018. https://www.senate .gov/pagelayout/reference/four_column_table/Tie_Votes.htm.

Valente, Judith. "Catholic Sister Recalls Her Pupil, Gov. Mike Pence." WGLT. org, August 1, 2016. http://wglt.org/post/catholic-sister-recalls-her-pupil-gov -mike-pence#stream/0.

Varvel, Gary. "What Motivated Pence to Run with Trump?" *Indianapolis Star*, September 3, 2017, A21–22.

"Vespers Looking Up." *Triangle* LXXIII, no. 1 (September 27, 1980).

"Vice President Mike Pence Speaks at Latino Coalition." Live Satellite News, March 9, 2017. https://www.youtube.com/watch?v=0fpzSHJhaWE.

"Vice President Pence Wreath Laying and Veteran's Day Service at Arlington Nat'l Cemetery." Recorded November 11, 2017, by Right Side Broadcasting Network. https://www.youtube.com/watch?v=a23ftWQ8HGA.

Wang, Stephanie. "Law's Roots Tied to Marriage Fight." *Indianapolis Star*, April 2, 2015, 1A+.

Ward, Ken. "A Columbus Connection in the 2nd District?" *Republic*, January 17, 1988, D6.

Weaver, Gregory. "Robert Rock to Face Mike Pence. *Indianapolis Star*, May 3, 2000, A6.

Webber, Mark. "Hometown Reaction: Pence Was Trump's Winning Ticket." *Republic*, November 10, 2016, A6.

"Whitaker-Batten." *Indianapolis News*, September 2, 1978, 5.

"Who Has Pulled Their Support?" *Indianapolis Star*, October 9, 2016, 4B.

Will, George F. "Pence May Be a Favorite for Conservatives in the 2010 Race." *Daily Spectrum*, December 10, 2010, A6.

———. "Pence the Pliable: Trump's VP Pick Playing Along." *Clarion Ledger*, July 24, 2016, 5C.

———. "Tea Party Would Back Pence for President." *Daily Times*, December 11, 2010, A10.

———. "The Mike Pence Conservative Paradox." *Palladium-Item*, February 12, 2015, B5.

Wines, Michael. "Indiana Hometown Molded Mike Pence Even as It Began to Change." *New York Times*, July 21, 2016.

Witcover, Jules. *The American Vice Presidency: From Irrelevance to Power*. Washington DC: Smithsonian Books, 2014.

Witt, Evans. "Young Hoosier Is an Appealing Choice." *Republic*, August 17, 1988, A2.

Yencer, Rick. "ECI Put in 6th District." *Star-Press*, May 11, 2001, 1B.

———. Family Remains at Core of Pence's Life." *Star Press*, October 3, 2004, A1+.

———. "Pence Convinced Iraq Poses Threat." *Star Press*, October 4, 2002, 8A.

———. "Pence Encouraged Bush to Veto Bill." *Star Press*, July 20, 2006, 2A.

———. "Pence Targeted by Democrats." *Star Press*, December 7, 2001, 1B.

———. "Pence-Welsh Campaign Not Seen as Competitive." *Star Press*, October 29, 2006, A1+.

———. "Pence, Wife, Staff Undergo Treatment." *Star Press*, October 28, 2001, 1A.

———. "Pence Wins Big, McIntosh Loses Home Precinct, 191–119." *Star Press*, November 9, 2000, 1A+.

Yepsen, David, and Holli Hartman. "Dole, Buchanan Finish 1–2." *Des Moines Register*, February 13, 1996, 1A+.

# INDEX

ANDREA NEAL is a journalist, American history teacher, and native Hoosier. A graduate of Brown University, she is author of *Road Trip: A Pocket History of Indiana*.

Congressman Pence was in the stands when the Butler University
Bulldogs defeated the Florida Gators in the 2011 NCAA
tournament. He joined Senator Dan Coats and Curt Smith,
a long-time Republican aide and father of Butler star Andrew
Smith. *(Photo courtesy of Curt Smith.)*